SOCIAL AND ECONOMIC HISTORY OF ASSAM (1853-1921)

This study unravels the under-researched aspects of social and economic history of Assam.

It analyses the erosion of the old ruling class and disappearance of the traditional and artisanal industries and examines the extent to which foreign rule and intrinsic limitation were both culpable for the eventual decline. The remarkable resilience of handloom weavers is another area of investigation.

Introduction of the ryotwari land system, increase in cultivated acreage, introduction of cash crops, commercialization of agriculture and how a large section of marginalized peasantry broke into the labour market have been studied in depth. The author gives an interesting interpretation of the peasant uprisings in Kamrup and Darrang in the early 1890s.

He plumbs the origin of the Assamese middle class and shows how its class personality crystallized in a process of cooperation and confrontation. He marks out the creative and constructive role of the middle class so characteristically trivialized by many.

The impact of tea industry has been studied from a new perspective. Exploration of coal, petroleum, exploitation of the forest resources, floral and faunal disturbances have also been discussed.

This is regional history, but it fully takes into account the all-India background.

Rajen Saikia taught History at Nowgong Girls' College. A recipient of the Sahitya Akademi translation award and Assam Publication Board award for historical research, Dr Saikia was the Chief Editor of the *Asamiya Viswakosh*, History volumes published by the Asam Sahitya Sabha.

Presently he is engaged in a Political History of Assam Project of the Government of Assam for the post-colonial era.

Social and Economic History of Assam
(1853-1921)

RAJEN SAIKIA

MANOHAR
2022

First published 2000
Reprinted 2022

ISBN 978-81-7304-344-4 (Hb)
ISBN 978-81-7304-431-1 (Pb)

Published by
Ajay Kumar Jain for
Manohar Publishers & Distributors
4753/23 Ansari Road, Daryaganj
New Delhi 110 002

Printed at
Replika Press Pvt. Ltd.

Contents

Preface

THE PRESENT work deals with the major aspects of the social and economic history of Assam in the Brahmaputra valley from 1853–1921 which then comprised six districts, namely Goalpara, Kamrup, Darrang, Nagaon, Sibsagar and Lakhimpur.

The year 1853 has been taken as a starting point, because (i) it marked the beginning of an indepth study of the province of Assam by an agent of the Company government and (ii) it saw the first constitutional mobilization of enlightened opinion and public protest.

As a result of the study undertaken by A.J.M. Mills in 1853 on behalf of the Government of Bengal, Assam decisively came under the economic orbit of British colonialism. They did not have to grope in the dark any more. In the wake of Mills' visit, a voice was heard for the first time, it was the voice of a new social force. The study has been rounded off with the culmination of a process signified by the merger of the Assam Association with the Indian National Congress. By 1921, the middle class acquired complete social and political leadership in the province. To my mind those were momentous decades. Researchers have yet to explore fully the social history of the period and appreciate its significance.

Recent studies have brought some aspects into focus and I have referred to them at appropriate places. This work is an attempt to give, as far as possible, a comprehensive picture of the situation. The importance of such study needs no explanation. Without the knowledge of social history, perfect social engineering is impossible. One cannot avoid the feeling that lack of proper understanding of the social history has led to multiple complications.

I propose to begin with an account of the poverty and increasing inability of the old ruling elite to cope with the changes wrought by the extension of British rule over Assam. Their failure has been juxtaposed by the gradual decline of the traditional crafts. I have also discussed the survival, though not on a very attractive and promising note, of the handloom products. I have tried to understand the problems and prospects of agriculture and the condition of the peasantry. The period saw the development in communication system where boat, elephant, steamer services and railways played a part. Discovery of coal, petroleum and development of tea plantation were the major events of this period.

The Assamese middle class grew out of this remarkable transformation of economy of Assam. The colonial experience shaped their ideas and world-view. The Assamese sense of belonging was based on a significant literary movement of the second half of the nineteenth century. I have noted that by 1921 the middle class established its social credibility in Assam.

Readers would find it useful to keep the demographic map of Assam in mind while going through the pages of the work. Though it could not be charted with accuracy, in 1853 Mills assessed the total population of Assam proper including the Goalpara district at above 12 lacs. It increased to about 15 lacs in 1872. In 1891 the population figure went above 24 lacs and 76 thousands; after a decade in 1901 it rose to 26 lacs and 20 thousands. It had since then a stable growth but the size of population in 1921 and even after was geared up by immigration.

In preparing for the work, I examined official records in various research institutions. I have also examined the old files of various Assamese, Bengali and English newspapers and journals, besides a whole corpus of contemporary memoirs, essays, fictions, etc., I have taken instructive hints from some works by competent authorities. I have referred to them in the text.

I wish to dedicate this book to my teacher Professor Baneswar Saikia as a small token of gratitude.

This book has grown out of my doctoral thesis submitted to the University of Delhi in 1993. It was prepared under the supervision of Professor Suhash Chakravarty. I have considered it a great privilege to get to know him and to work under him. He directed me to purposeful readings on the subject and his insightful comments have enriched the form and content of the work. I must place on record the hospitality and kindness of Dr (Mrs) Sachi Chakravarty at Delhi, during my long sessions of work there. I owe a great debt to them.

I am thankful to the UGC who awarded me a scholarship and to my college authorities for giving me lien to undertake the study. I am also thankful to the officers and staff of the National Archives of India,

Nehru Memorial Museum and Library, New Delhi, W.B. State Archives and the National Library, Calcutta, the Delhi University Library, the Nowgong Girls' College Library and the Assam State Archives for all their assistance.

Sri Prafullachandra Bezbaroa of Sibsagar and my former colleague Dr Jogendranarayan Bhuyan lent me many rare books and journals from their personal collection. Mrs Banti Bhuyan lent me a copy of late B. Chaudhury's Ph.D. thesis in the University of London. Sri Manashyam Barkakati supported my research in Calcutta. I am deeply beholden to all of them. I do wish to thank Mr Ramesh Jain and his son Ajay of Manohar for their encouragement and Mr B.N. Varma and Mr Bansi Ram for their neat and prompt work. To my wife Geetimallika I owe a special kind of debt.

In spite of proper guidance and help that came my way there may be omissions and or errors of judgement for which I am alone responsible.

Nagaon RAJEN SAIKIA
5 May 1999

CHAPTER 1

Erosion of the Ruling Elite

INTRODUCTION

VENTURESOME BRITISH traders established commercial contact with Assam even before the East India Company assumed power in Bengal in 1757. In the early years of the eighteenth century 'forty vessels from five to six hundred tons of burden each' came annually from Bengal to Assam chiefly with salt which gave the traders a record profit of 200 per cent. Business documents show that they also brought betel-nut and tobacco. They received, in exchange for their goods—silk, lac, *mugadhotis*, ivory and timber from Assam.[1]

The East India Company dithered and drifted for long enough. In 1786 it resolved to open trade with Assam. It was sort of a calculated march on the part of the Company, from commerce to political control of the situation, which passed off in a dramatic speed. The Ahom monarchy was tottering under the impact of a series of internecine power struggles from the last quarter of the eighteenth century. The crisis was all-embracing. Ultimately, it gave the Company an opportunity to interfere and project its image as the saviour. It seemed as though the force of events was irreversible and everything lay in the logic of history.

In 1792, the dispossessed Ahom King Gaurinath Singha sought succour from the Company. Lord Cornwallis, the Governor-General (1786–93), after a good deal of calculation decided to send an expedition under Captain Thomas Welsh to Assam.[2]

The Mayamoria rebels were mainly responsible for the ouster of the King Gaurinath Singha. Other opponents of the king, rising mainly from Kamrup, Darrang and Nagaon took full advantage of the chaotic situation created by them. We may note, in passing, that the Mayamoria rebels represented a socio-religious sect of the same name. It started off as a popular social movement but the arrogance of the ruling class gave it an odd twist. Things moved from bad to worse when the leading priests of the sect suffered humiliation at the instance of the king. It burnt deep into the hearts of their followers and they threw a challenge to the king. The monarchy was not equipped to face their desperate attack. A grim sequel followed; a social movement led to political consequence.

As a 'popular revolt' the Mayamoria uprising may be compared to the Pilgrimage of Grace (1536) in England. The suppression of the monasteries, use of religious imagery, use of banner of the Five Wounds, marching song, capture of the royal castle of Pontefract and the cruelty in putting down the revolt bear comparison with the course of the Mayamoria uprising.[3]

On his arrival, Captain Welsh correctly guessed that a carrot-and-stick approach would be more rewarding than a policy of hot war. The rebels and other opponents of the king were gradually brought under control and Gaurinath Singha's position was consolidated. A commercial treaty was prized out of the thankful king by Captain Welsh. He eventually became an adviser to the king.[4]

In October 1793, Lord Cornwallis was succeeded by Sir John Shore as Governor-General. Shore was loath to recognize any merit in the work of his predecessor and would have loved to upset everything done by Cornwallis. To fit in his policy of non-intervention, he recalled Captain Welsh. Gaurinath was restored to his throne beforehand. Welsh and his army left Assam in May 1794. With the departure of Welsh, confusion, anarchy and darkness sank upon the scene. There were claims and counter-claims of princes and pretenders, court intrigues, insurrections giving tempting calls to the adventurous neighbours and distant foes.[5]

To put it briefly, Badanchandra Barphukan, a villainous viceroy posted in Guwahati implored the East India Company to intervene in his favour which they refused. But a curious thoughtlessness possessed him, so he could not rest content. He next rushed to the king of Burma who agreed to send his troops in support of him. First they came and left. The political arrangements made by them were immediately unsettled. Their best man Badanchandra was assassinated and the protege was dethroned. On hearing this, the Burmese king hurriedly sent in his forces. Like a mighty rushing wind the Burmese troops reached Assam, took and occupied it with a vengeance. The marauding force stalked the land for several years.

Thus began what Edward Gait calls the 'Burmese rule' in Assam which lasted from 1819 to 1824.[6] It was cruel and ugly as sin. The Burmese were known as the Maans. They left behind a lore, *Manor Din*, the days of the Maans, a metaphor for any experience of organized violence. The inhabitants of Assam neither put up resistance against the Burmese nor accorded any welcome to them. They really found no cause to live and die for. They could act manfully only under an organized leadership. Such society can neither defend self-interest nor counteract self-destruction.

The easy success of the Burmese in the Brahmaputra valley inspired them to expand towards Cachar in the south. Cachar was also reeling under similar crisis. Politically, it was under the three Manipuri usurpers and the King Govindachandra sought shelter in Sylhet.[7] From there he asked for assistance from the East India Company to regain his throne. Geographically, the position of Cachar was important and the British thought that it could be used by their enemy as a base of operation against the Company's territory. The officers of the Assam-Bengal border kept themselves informed of the dramatic developments. Towards the end of 1823, when the Burmese force spread out in Cachar, the British struck hard at the root of their campaign. The battle at Badarpur on the bank of the Surma sealed the fate of the Burmese in Cachar.[8] The Company restored Raja Govindachandra to the throne and in March 1824 he entered into a treaty with the East India Company whereby the Raja put the 'territory of Cachar, or Herumba under their protection'; J.B. Bhattacharjee justifies British occupation of Cachar in these words:

> ...the internal condition of the country was so chaotic and the government so feeble that sovereignty had become a myth. May be it was fortunate for the people that they were subjected to the British, and not the Burmese.[9]

Sylhet was a district of many signs and wonders. In the fourteenth century it came under the Muslim rule. Under the Nawab of Dacca, Sylhet was governed by an officer called Amil.[10] With the grant of Dewani in 1765, Sylhet and Goalpara, the western 'frontier of the old Ahom kingdom' passed into the hands of the East India Company.

In 1874 Assam was made a Chief Commissioner's province. The districts of Sylhet, Cachar and Goalpara were brought under the administration of the Government of Assam. Eastern Duars formed a part of Goalpara district.[11]

After Cachar, the Company took up operation against the Maans in the Brahmaputra valley. The British troops had to advance haltingly for lack of information and adverse climatic conditions. The Maans in the meantime went on with their mad frolics. 'Some they flayed alive, others they burnt in oil, and others again drove in crowds into the village, *namghors*, or prayer houses, which they then set on fire.'[12]

Amid all the crying and chaos of those dark days, the British appeared on the scene as the 'deliverer' of the inhabitants of Assam.[13] They welcomed them and offered their cooperation. An Assamese folk song may suggest the eagerness of the people to know the news of the English victory over the Maans. One cannot overlook the strange admixture of curiosity, admiration and expectancy.

> Up the Brahmaputra comes the steamer of the
> English, it comes shaking the earth
> Moor, moor it, O steamer of the English
> Is there any news[14]

The Maans were completely routed. The Burmese king was forced to sue for peace and he signed the Treaty of Yandaboo with the English in February, 1826. According to the terms of the treaty, the Burmese king abandoned his claim upon 'the principality of Assam and its dependencies'.[15] Since then Assam formed a part of the Company's territory. Historically speaking, Assam became a part of political India by fluke. It helped to crystallize her emotional bond with Bharat. Geography shaped her sense of direction and culture confirmed her spiritual identity. Company's territory means company's administration. They had their own priorities. Life was tuned to the Anglo-Saxon view of things. Two major objects of social stability and augmentation of revenue were clearly perceptible in the extension of pax Britannica.

The Ahom kings, as a matter of policy, did not favour the growth of feudalism in Assam as a distinct social system. There was no landlord class who could exert political influence upon the king. The producers in the field were also the fighters in the battlefield. The saints and the lords of shrines, though powerful and complex in their respective social cause, were not strong enough to constitute a social class by themsleves.

David Scott, Agent to the Governor-General, North-East Frontier, at first tried to propitiate a section of the nobility through awards of office. He was not prepared to accomodate all of them since he had a very poor opinion about their administrative ability. As the sentinels of a poor and decadent state apparatus the old aristocracy could not equip themselves with the brasstacks of a circumspect colonial government. The communication gap between the ruler and the ruled straining under long years of political turmoil was deepening.[16] In spite of this, David Scott pleaded for some structural adjustment in the administration. He rightly thought that 'It would be unreasonable to expect that the Ahom nobility and the members of royal family whose predecessors ruled the country for several centuries would relinquish their ancient rights upon the appearance among them of a handful of strangers.'[17] He suggested different measures for improvement and the Governor-General, Lord William Bentinck, was far too willing to consider them. But before any decision was taken, David Scott passed away in August 1831. It deserves mention that David Scott is held in high esteem in Assam. H.K. Barpujari hailed him as 'the patriarch of the Assamese'.[18] S.K. Bhuyan contended that 'no Assamese could have more efficiently championed the cause of his country as did Scott'.[19] N.K. Barooah remarks, 'He ended, as many of the great administrators did, by identifying himself with the interests and the good of the people under him, by being truly paternalist.'[20]

Scott's successor T.C. Robertson was also an enterprising officer best suited to the need of a government with ever increasing responsibility. In accordance with the suggestion of Robertson, Lower Assam was organized into four districts—Goalpara, Kamrup, Darrang and Nagaon in March 1833 and in Upper Assam the Ahom monarchy was restored next month.[21] Purandar Singha donned the crown of a contractual monarchy in April 1833. The restored monarchy had a precarious existence from the very beginning. He did not receive any cooperation from the gentry and the experiment began to flounder. Robertson, who admired some qualities of Purandar, saw no reason why he should not be buttressed.

In 1834 Francis Jenkins succeeded Robertson as the Commissioner and Agent to the Governor-General. The new Commissioner soon received petitions complaining about the tyranny of Purandar. Jenkins formed an unfavourable opinion about the king and recommended 'immediate resumption of Upper Assam'. The Governor-General, Lord Auckland, approved of the resumption which was carried into effect in 1838. It is on record that the moment government resumed possession of the territory of Purandar Singha, the *pykes* universally 'deserted their masters'.[22]

The year 1838 saw the end of the experimental phase and it marked the beginning of a common system of administration. Officers of proven capacity were put in charge of the districts. But things were not smooth for them either. The former rulers and the nobility were unwilling to come to terms with the emerging situation. They resented the 'levelling tendency' of the British and Jorhat became a centre 'of innumerable do-nothing nobles'.[23] But Jenkins solved the problem with tact and imagination. The result was a gradual erosion of the ruling elite.

LISTENING TO THEIR TALE

Our account of the erosion of the ruling elite and the old aristocracy must begin with Kandarpeswar Singha, the Saring Raja. Kandarpeswar was the son of Kameswar Singha and grandson of Purandar Singha who was removed from the throne in October 1838. To soft-soap Purandar, the government offered him a monthly pension of Rs. 1,000 which he refused. Hurt and humiliated, Purandar was unable to challenge the authority of the British. A thoroughly disillusioned man, he died in October 1846. He was then barely 38. His son Kameswar flattered himself with the title of 'Maharaja' conferred on him by the Company Bahadur. He was also offered a monthly pension of Rs. 1,000, but having been impelled by Maniram Dewan, the former sheristadar of his father's government, Kameswar declined the pension as well. Far from organizing his own resources for a respectable living, Kameswar frittered away his money and energy. He died in 1852 leaving his son in the lurch.[24]

Kandarpeswar, then a boy of eleven, threw himself upon the mercy of Maniram Dewan. In his memorial[25] dated 27 February 1863 to the Lt. Governor of Bengal, Kandarpeswar recalled that he 'was a minor at the time of the demise of his father' and as such was under the control of his late father's Dewan, who led him to entertain the most sanguine hopes of getting the country restored to his management.... He also noted that earlier in 1853 he waited on A.J.M. Mills to urge his claim to the territories held by his grandfather.[26]

But Mills was forthright to tell him that the question of restoration of monarchy did not simply arise. When Kandarpeswar found his efforts 'unavailing' he privately intimated to Mills his willingness to accept the pension. The government, however, remained unmoved. Kandarpeswar repeated his requests for the pension in 1854 and in 1856. Everytime his request was turned down. In October 1856, Lord Canning observed that he saw no reason to give it as a favour.[27]

Kandarpeswar then engaged a solicitor, P.J. Paul, who memorialized on behalf of his client. P.J. Paul was categorically told that the government would not reopen the case.[28] Soon after, Kandarpeswar was arrested on an unverified charge of complicity with the rebels of the unaccentuated uprising of 1857 in Assam. He was sent to Calcutta and confined for a few months in the Alipore jail. The Government of Bengal recorded: 'In consideration of his youth and inexperience, and the fact that he appeared to have been rather a tool in the hands of others than a voluntary agent in the conspiracy, he was never put upon his trial for intrigues against the State, in which he was, however, to some extent, implicated.' Though released from jail, Kandarpeswar was kept under survelliance at Burdwan. He was given an allowance of Rs. 50 which he had never drawn.

In October 1858 the Government of Bengal directed that all his property be restored to him. For some unknown reasons a part of his property was sold by auction at Jorhat.[29] The sale proceeds of the property amounting to Rs. 5,331–9–4 was sent by draft in favour of the Raja after payment of his debts and deduction of commission, etc. In his petition dated 12 May 1859 addressed to H.B. Lawford, Magistrate of Burdwan, Kandarpeswar stated that he would 'incur great loss, as the articles sold will only realise about a quarter of their original value'. He then requested the government that 'such part of my property as can be removed to this place (i.e. Burdwan) at a moderate expense may be remitted to me here, and that such articles as cannot be removed from Sibsagar without great expense and risk in the transit, may be sold at Sibsagar, or at any other place at my mother's directions'.[30] Apparently, Kandarpeswar took assistance from some lawyer, so his petition could not be swept under the carpet. To reach at some compromise, the Commissioner of Burdwan, at the instance of the Commissioner of Assam, made some 'proposals' to Kandarpeswar Singha. The latter sent his reply to the Commissioner of Burdwarn through Lawford, the Magistrate of Burdwan. Lawford was peeved by the spirit of the letter. He remarked, 'the Raja's language, considering the position he is in, is very unbecoming and haughty'.[31]

In his reply Kandarpeswar reiterated his earlier stand that he never requested the government to dispose of his personal property by auction. He wanted 'those precious stones, gold and silver and utensils and boxes containing my clothes to be brought and delivered to me here'. He suggested that the elephants, cattle, etc., be disposed of at Guwahati at prices agreed to by his mother and the sale proceeds be sent to him. He alleged that his guns and swords were sold at one-fourth of the real price. He urged the government 'to nullify the sale' and wanted all his property 'to be disposed of by me in your presence to my best advantage'.[32] The Government of Bengal, upon that representation directed the Commissioner of Assam to 'send down the entire unsold property of the Raja to Burdwan and the proceeds of the goods already sold to the commissioner of Burdwan'. Our inquiries fail to reveal if Kandarpeswar came into contact with the Raja of Burdwan. There was hardly any such possibility, because the Raja, Mahtabchand Bahadur actively supported the government in suppressing the Sepoy Mutiny. He donated eight elephants and sixteen bullock carts to the government during the Mutiny.[33] He could have had no sympathy for the projected rebel.

In January 1860, Kandarpeswar represented through Baboo Aushootosh Chatterjee, Sudder Pleader to the Government of Bengal for his restoration to the original 'position'. He pleaded innocence and promised loyality towards the British Government. He pointed out that 'those who had taken an active part in the Mutiny were restored to favour, and were not only pardoned, but allowed to return to their homes'. Disposing of the petition, E.H. Lushington, officiating Secretary to the Government of Bengal, observed that Kandarpeswar's prayer for permission to return to Assam 'cannot be granted'.[34]

On a review petition by Kandarpeswar, the Government of Bengal revised its earlier decision and in December 1860, he was permitted to return and take up his residence at Guwahati. Obviously, government's attitude was influenced by the general amnesty declared by the Queen of England in November 1860. This time Kandarpeswar changed his mind and declined to go to Assam. Perhaps he wanted the restriction of the government to be removed and thereby keep his option open. Except as an object of historical interest, his life became heretofore socially insignificant. After obtaining permission to move house Kandarpeswar developed cold feet and frittered away the fortune he acquired from Assam. His inadequate education and poor upbringing could not afford him a respectable place in the babu society of Calcutta. An unknown driveller as he was, we have no means to see him in his groove as he lived. Even if he were looked upon as a rebel for his alleged role in the upheaval of 1857 he should have felt flattered. In the absence of any shred of evidence to the contrary, the conclusion is unavoidable that no man of consequence took any notice of Kandarpeswar either in Calcutta or in Burdwan. Such inattention could not inspire him to live to fight another day. Neither did his resource permit him to live the life of Riley. His resolution slackened and his character went soft. It came as no surprise, therefore, that he failed his wife and daughter too.

On 15 August 1862, Rani Kamalapriya Devi, wife of Kandarpeswar Singha, sent an application to the Government of Bengal. Kamalapriya thankfully recalled that Jenkins was pleased to shift her along with her mother-in-law Lakshmipriya Kunwari, on their request, from Jorhat to Guwahati in 1858. At the time of making the petition, Lakshmipriya went to Calcutta to meet her son Kandarpeswar and her stay there left Kamalapriya without any source of income at Guwahati. Since Kandarpeswar failed to keep up regular correspondence with the Rani, she developed a nagging fear about the real intentions of her young and inexperienced husband. About him she complained, 'He has stopped every correspondence and does not seem to think how I may be supported.' She, therefore, pleaded that her husband should be sent back to Assam 'by force'. Otherwise she felt he would never return unless the whole of his property was squandered.[35] Was she distressed by her husband's spending of his youth, energy and wealth in giving other women a good time?

Kamalapriya bewailed, 'I, with a little daughter, am lingering in poverty and distress...I have sold off whole of my personal ornaments in defraying the monthly charges and have nothing more in hand to go on any longer.' Earlier, Kandarpeswar sent her two iron chests said to have contained some valuables and her mother-in-law also left another at the Agency Treasury. But she had no authority to open them. She prayed that either she might be permitted to open one of the chests or the government allow her a monthly stipend.[36]

Major J.C. Haughton, Officiating Agent to the Governor-General, informed the Government of Bengal that the statement of her distress was heart-rending and that the Deputy Commissioner of Kamrup had already passed orders to give her Rs. 500 pending enquiry. Haughton further stated that the Raja Kandarpeswar Singha was asked to take up his residence at Guwahati in December 1860. But he was not willing to come and was 'leading a very dissolute life alternately in Calcutta and Burdwan'. Haughton observed, 'He is undoubtedly a very dissipated young man and until all his jewellery is disposed off, he will probably continue his present mode of life in Calcutta.'[37] With regard to Kamalapriya's request to send back Kandarpeswar to Guwahati 'by force' the government showed wistful impartiality. Haughton turned down her request by saying that he did not find 'any reason why the Raja should be compelled to return to Assam against his will'. He ordered that Rs. 25 per mensem, half of the allowance assigned to Kandarpeswar in Calcutta, be paid to her till her husband's return to Guwahati.[38]

When, after two years Kandarpeswar decided to shift to Assam, he was not sure if he could keep up his appearance before public 'as his fallen fortune, his degradation for alleged infidelity and disloyality, will hold him forth as an effigy towards which the finger of scorn will ever be pointed'.[39]

Having been in Calcutta, Kandarpeswar must have realized the growing utility of land as a source of capital. He must have seen the opulence of the Calcutta zamindars and dreamt of becoming one. He requested the government to permit him to enter into a (permanent) settlement to the estates of Rangpur and Gargaon in Upper Assam. Kandarpeswar laid his claim for a monthly pension of Rs. 1,000 as the same amount was offered to his father and grandfather. He further asked for an allowance of Rs. 5,000 to enable him to meet the liabilities in Calcutta and render him free to return to Assam.[40]

The Government of Bengal forwarded the petition of Kandarpeswar Singha to the Government of India for decision, saying that Kandarpeswar 'was reported to be leading an idle and useless life in Calcutta, and to have contracted debts...'. Inspite of his professed sympathy, the Lt. Governor was not in favour of entertaining all the claims of Kandarpeswar as laid down in his petition. The former recommended a monthly pension of Rs. 500 for life for his support and that of his family. The Governor-General in Council conceded that 'great allowances should be made for the conduct of a mere youth' and in their opinion Kandarpeswar's case was 'one of those which should be regarded by the British government very indulgently'. The 'indulgence' measured up to a monthly pension of Rs. 500 for Kandarpeswar Singha which was to commence from 27 February 1863, the date of his petition to the Bengal government.[41]

The petition of Lakshmipriya Kunwari dated 10 February 1864, to the Lt. Governor of Bengal throws some light on the penury of the royal family. She claimed that at the time of resumption of Upper Assam by the British in 1838, she, 'as the wife of the heir to the Raj, was in the enjoyment of a Gavroomel or a Jugir yielding an annual profit of Rs. 8000'. In the absence of any corroborative evidence the claim as to the profit from the Jagir seems exaggerated but there is no denying the fact that whatever little fortune she had, she forfeited it in 1838. She complained that the Ranis inferior to her in rank, the concubines of Raja Purandar, continued to receive pension. She justified her refusal of the pension of Rs. 100 offered to her by Major Jenkins, the Commissioner of Assam, following the death of her husband Kameswar Singha in 1852 by saying that 'her means were far more ample than they are at present...'. She stated that the jewellery she possessed might have been sufficient to support herself for life, but at the time of the Mutiny, they were seized and then confiscated.[42]

It will not be amiss here to record the amount of monthly pension paid to the daughter and the concubines of Purandar Singha out of the original aggregate pension of Rs. 1,500 offered to him. It will be seen in Table 1.1 that out of the original pension granted, Rs. 1,233 remained undistributed.[43]

All the ladies used to live at Sibsagar. Lakshmipriya's petition was also favourably disposed of by the Governor-General; a pension of Rs. 100 per month was sanctioned to her for life with effect from May 1864. The Secretary of State for India confirmed the grant in November of the same year.[44]

At the time of resumption of Upper Assam, Rupahi Aidew, daughter of Purandar, was awarded a monthly pension of Rs. 50 out of the sum allotted for the maintenance of her father. Rupahi Aidew was married to Trinayan. She submitted a petition to the Lt. Governor of Bengal on 21 January 1862 for renewal of her pension. She stated that she and her husband Trinayan were thrown into jail 'on charges of the nature of which she was not aware', and the latter was ultimately sentenced to transportation, where he soon died broken-hearted. After Trinayan's death Rupahi Aidew was released. During the trial they forfeited their property and the pension enjoyed by Rupahi Aidew was also stopped. Although she complained of her distress, the fate of her petition could not be ascertained.[45] The statement given by Lakshmipriya two years later claimed that Rupahi Aidew received a pension of Rs. 37 (see Table 1.1).

Balochandra Gohain wrote to the Agent to the Governor-General on 10 *Phalgun* 1261 B.S. (February 1855) praying for a monthly pension. He was the grandson of the late Raja Chandrakanta Singha. His early youth was supported by Lakshmipriya, the widow of Raja Kameswar Singha. At the time of applying for the pension Balochandra Gohain had been living with Ghanakanta Singha Joobraj. Though F. Jenkins recommended a monthly pension of Rs. 16 for

TABLE 1.1

	Rs.	*Anna*	*Paisa*
Chandrakantee Kuwari	80	0	0
Parbati Kuwari	80	0	0
Rupahi Aidew (daughter)	37	0	0
Madhabi Kuwari	50	0	0
Rupati Khatonier	20	0	0
Total	267	0	0

Balochandra, the Lt. Governor refused to consider the petition for a monthly pension 'from a youngman of twenty five years of age'.[46]

Joobraj Ghanakanta Singha had a *khat* or estate at Kandoolemaree *chaparee* in the district of Nagaon. In 1852, he resigned his *khat* and tried to take up land in the Kamrup district 'equivalent to the land resigned' in a locality near his residence at Guwahati. Having failed in his attempt to aquire the land, he wanted to resume his old *khat*. Though Jenkins recommended the resumption with exemption of half of the rents, the Government of Bengal did not accept the recommendations of the Commissioner in toto. They allowed the resumption of the *khat* but turned down the proposal for any exemption of revenue.[47] When Ghanakanta Singha died in 1858, his wife Padmarekha had to borrow an amount of Rs. 400 to meet the expenses of the *sradhha* ceremony. Their only son Keshabkanta was then a minor. The provincial government, as a gesture of sympathy towards them granted an annual pension of Rs. 500 to Padmarekha and permitted Keshabkanta to use the honorific title Joobraj.[48]

One Barpatra made an application to Capt. C. Holroyd, Collector of Sibsagar seeking financial support to meet the funeral expenses of his father. Holroyd might have been amused by the request, yet he 'made an advance of Rs. 300' for the purpose.[49]

Giridhar Gohain Namrupia Raja was in receipt of a monthly pension of Rs. 30 since 1839. Giridhar was a cousin of Raja Purandar. Giridhar's son Lambodar Gohain prayed for an increase of his father's pension and a separate stipend for himself. Lambodar pleaded on the ground that the two uncles of Purandar, Indunath Sarumelia Raja and Bhubaneswar Tipam Raja each received a monthly pension of Rs. 50 and, besides them, their two sons Srimanta Gohain and Manjur Gohain, enjoyed a monthly pension of Rs. 30 and Rs. 40, respectively and that Giridhar held an equal rank with Indunath and Bhubaneswar. On the recommendation of the Government of Bengal, the Government of India took a favourable view of Lambodar's plea. They increased the pension of Giridhar from Rs. 30 to Rs. 50 per month and sanctioned a separate pension of Rs. 30 per month for life for his son Lambodar.[50]

Another petition for continuance of pension and grant of rent-free lands from the descendants of the Raja Jogeswar Singha should merit our attention. Jogeswar Singha was a puppet king installed by the Burmese in 1821 and he was a silent spectator to all the misdeeds of the Burmese troops in Assam. Jogeswar met with an accidental death in 1825 at Jogighopa, Goalpara. As his son, Dambarudhar, was very young, the government allowed personal pensions to several members of the family of Jogeswar besides 80 *pooras* of rent-free land in Parbatia *mauza*. The rate of pension granted to the descendants of Jogeswar was as follows:

To the Queen Mother	Rs. 25
To the 3 widows of Jogeswar (Rs. 10 each)	Rs. 30
To his brother Dhaniram Gohain	Rs. 50
To his son Dambarudhar	Rs. 50
To the 2 daughters, each a dower of Rs. 200 on their marriage.	

We gather from a report of W.S. Clarke, the Deputy Commissioner of Sibsagar that the Queen Mother went to Burma and died there. So, the pension had ceased. Of the three queens, one was alive, two were dead, their pensions too had ceased. Dhaniram went to Burma with his mother. The pension assigned to him was equally divided and paid to his two wives who were still living in Assam. Dambarudhar died in August 1863 and his pension ceased from the date of his death.[51]

On 2 October 1867, Padmarekha Gabhooroo, the widow of Dambarudhar and her two sons Krishnaram Gohain and Tilak Singha Gohain made a petition to the Lt. Governor of Lower Provinces. They brought to his notice their 'deplorable circumstances' and sought relief. They stated that the rent-free land owned by the late Dambarudhar continued in their possession for three successive years since his death in 1863. In 1866, the mauzadar brought action against them under Act X of 1859 for arrears of revenue estimated at Rs. 111–14–3.

Padmarekha and her sons prayed for continuance of the original grant of land free of rent as well as the pension enjoyed by Dambarudhar. The Commissioner of Assam, upon enquiry, reported that Padmarekha was 'a respectable old lady' and was really in 'impoverished circumstances' and that 'all three are apparently dependent for support on the charity of a relative, the mauzadar of Holongassar'. The Lt. Governor recommended life pension of Rs. 12 per month to each of the petitioners, totalling an amount of Rs. 36 which was less than the pension drawn by Dambarudhar. With regard to the plea for continuation of the rent-free grant, he concurred with the opinion of the Commissioner and turned down their request.[52]

Padma Konwar was a scion of the old aristocracy. He was in the receipt of a pension from the government at the rate of Rs. 50 per month. During his lifetime he got his pension transferred to his adopted son

Biswanath Konwar but the latter having died some time after his marriage with Surya Prabha Kunwari, the pension was reassigned to his father Padma Konwar and held by him during the remainder of his life.

After the death of his adopted son Biswanath, Padma Konwar married Tara by whom he begot three children, Raj Bahadur and two daughters. On Padma Konwar's death, the pension was assigned to Raj Bahadur and it was paid on his account to Rani Tara as the head of the family. Biswanath's widow Surya Prabha was also provided for out of the same pension. Rani Tara and Surya Prabha soon fell out and could not live together. The matter having been brought to the notice of the government, a monthly pension of Rs. 10 was settled upon Surya Prabha separately out of the family pension. But a tragedy upset the arrangement. Raj Bahadur, the only male member of the family met with a sudden death. Surya Prabha then raised her claim to half of the pension amount. On her representation, the Agent to the Governor-General proposed that the pension should be divided between Rani Tara and Surya Prabha in the proportion of Rs. 35 and Rs. 15 respectively. The Governor-General in Council rejected the proposal. They observed that the widow of the adopted son was not entitled to any portion of the grant, but as she had already been allowed a sum of Rs. 10 the Council consented to the continuance of the stipend to her for life. Rani Tara was allowed a life pension of Rs. 25 on the understanding that it would lapse after her death. By this decision the government saved Rs. 15 per month to the exchequer.[53]

Maju Aidew was the elder sister of Raja Chandrakanta Singha. She received a monthly pension of Rs. 40 which lapsed after her death. Her only daughter Kindumati Aidew applied for the same sum of pension granted to her mother. Upon enquiry, H. Sconce, the Deputy Commissioner of Sibsagar reported to the government in December 1864 that Kindumati, then aged 23 was married and that she had no private means of subsistence, 'she is at any rate poor'. The Governor-General in Council approved a monthly pension of Rs. 20 which was confirmed by the Secretary of State for India.[54]

The descendants of Matibar Barsenapati, the Muttock chief, also complained of destitution. Matibar's fourth son, Soorath Kaptan Gohain, like all other members of the family of the late Barsenapati, was in the enjoyment of a monthly pension of Rs. 50 and *lakhiraj* rent-free grant of land measuring more than 84 *pooras* for more than twenty years until his death in January 1862. As the provision was only for his life time, the pension and the land grant lapsed on his death. Soorath Kaptan Gohain left behind a large family of three widows—Pepeli, Sehani and Suwagi; eleven sons—Priyabar, Tambar, Sundar, Monodhar, Joydhor, Haladhar, Sukura, Ratnadhar, Rubbebar, Sarudhar and Kedai and one daughter—Merani. All of them appeared before Major H.S. Bivar, the Deputy Commissioner of Lakhimpur during his tour in Muttock division and submitted a petition praying for the renewal of the privileges granted to Kaptan Gohain.[55]

Major Bivar was quick to point out that it was the responsibility of the head of the family to bring up his children in such a manner as to enable them to maintain themselves by their own exertions. They should not, on any account, expect to live solely on the liberality of the government. Bivar further reminded that even in the event of the government making some provision to the family of the deceased pensioner, it could not be claimed by any single member of the family, rather it will have to be portioned out to all the heirs and therefore, the amount of pension will dwindle away.

However, Bivar brooded over the problem of the widows and the orphans of the family of the Muttock chief who was always 'friendly' towards the British. He rationalized that the late Soorath Kaptan Gohain also behaved quietly, he gave no trouble, his conduct was such as to merit a recognition, and finally recommended their case to the government. The Governor-General in Council sanctioned a pension of Rs. 10 per month to each of the three widows for their lives and the continuance to the sons of the rent-free estate held by their late father with the condition that the tenure would expire on the death of the last survivor.[56]

Rubbebar Gohain, the ninth son of Soorath Kaptan Gohain received a yearly pension of Rs. 180. After his death his sons, the number of whom we have no means to ascertain, applied for the continuance of the pension. The Governor-General in Council sanctioned the pension of Rs. 15 per month drawn by Rubbebar 'to his sons jointly, the share of any son dying to lapse to the survivors'.[57]

Bhogbar Gohain was the eldest son of Matibar and was in receipt of a yearly pension of Rs. 1,800. Bhogbar died in December 1866 and his pension lapsed with effect from the date of his death. All his five sons, Joybar, Joysing, Horoocato (Sarukato?), Bethabar and Horoojeet (Surajit?) prayed to the government through their petition dated 21 December 1868, for renewal and continuance of the pension granted to their father. They also requested that the 60 *pooras* of land held by their father under a rent paying *patta* might be given to them rent-free. Without the grant of pension from the government, they said, 'it will be impossible for us to maintain ourselves'. They cited the instance of Bhagirath Maju Gohain, the second son of the late Barsenapati who was also drawing a pension of Rs. 1,800 and after his death, which was continued to his children. Similarly, Rubbebar's pension was also continued to his sons. But the Foreign Department of the Government of India opined that the case was not 'politically important'. The quiet disposition and helpful conduct of the applicants, instead of earning praise and promotion only devalued their political significance. The Governor-General in Council reduced the amount of monthly pension from Rs. 150 to Rs. 100 and stipulated that all the five sons of Bhogbar should share it in equal proportion and the share of each son would lapse on his death.[58]

A glaring instance of penury of the old aristocracy was the Buragohain family of Sibsagar which threw up four prime ministers—Ghanashyam, Purnananda, Ruchinath and Mahidhar.[59] Mahidhar was one of those who lost office during the resumption of Upper Assam. From 1840 he used to receive a monthly pension of Rs. 100 besides rent-free grant of 100 *pooras* of land. Likewise his brother Bengalee Gohain received 20 *pooras* of rent-free land but no pension. Bengalee Gohain died in 1841. In spite of owning land sufficient to support a big undivided family, the descendants of Mahidhar and Bengalee applied for financial assistance from the government.

From a statement on record showing the land held by Durgeswar, son of Mahidhar Buragohain and Nilkanta son of Bengalee Gohain under the collectorship of Sibsagar, it appears that Durgeswar owned more than 143 *pooras* and Nilkanta owned 160 *pooras* of land and after deduction of the remission from the total Jumah, the amount of arear revenue payable by Durgeswar stood at Rs. 21, annas 12, and paise 7 and by Nilkanta at Rs. 41 and annas 3. Captain T. Brodie, the Principal Assistant of the district, took a sympathetic view of the plight of the two families who had suffered a great deal from the desertion of their slaves since the passing of Act. 5 of 1843. It was quite likely, he reminded the government, that if the families received no support from them larger part of their cultivable land would run waste which was not the desire of the government. 'The want of means has made their dependants forsake them and reduced them to beggary at once,' he noted. F. Jenkins, Agent to the Governor-General also recommended pension for Durgeswar and Nilkanta. But the Governor-General in Council sanctioned the continuance to the family of late Mahidhar, i.e. Durgeswar, but they refused to sanction any pension to the family of late Bengalee Gohain. The families were, of course, allowed to hold the rent-free land.[60]

Some priests and pundits professionally associated with the old ruling families suffered as a result of the fall of their patrons. Many of them were rehabilitated by the government with pension and revenue free land.[61] But their professional competence did not go begging and they made themselves useful. Kamoda Devi's husband was in the enjoyment of an annual pension of Rs. 60 and 10 *pooras* of land at half-revenue rates. On the death of her husband, the pension was stopped. Kamoda Devi failed to continue with the cultivation in her land for want of labour. Caste restriction prevented her from going to the field to work. In a petition to the Commissioner, she complained of her distress as a widow with three children. She claimed her family association as pundits, with the Ahom royal house for generations. She offered to resign her entire cultivable land and prayed that in lieu of it the family pension should be revived and raised to Rs. 120.[62] The fate of her petition could not be ascertained.

In 1867, one Ghewmati Barua applied for pension. The provincial government could not trace her identity in the official records. Nor could the government ascertain who her late husband Ramakrishna was. The Commissioner, therefore, concluded that the applicant's husband could be at least a Ghew Barua who used to supply *ghee* to the former Ahom king and had no claim to pension.[63]

Modumbika, known to be the wife of Raja Chandrakanta Singha was granted a monthly pension of Rs. 40. Chandrakanta's surviving son Ghanakanta brought an allegation before Jenkins that Modumbika was a concubine and not the wife of Chandrakanta and that 'she was not living respectably'. Ghanakanta's statement could be factually correct but he had a motive—he wrongly expected that the pension so discontinued would revert to him. After several years Modumbika renewed her request for pension when Henry Hopkinson was the Commissioner. Hopkinson was moved by the reduced circumstances of Modumbika. He observed, 'her age may now probably be accepted as a guarantee for her respectability' and favoured her petition. But the same Commissioner turned down the petition of Kumudini Gabharu, the grand-daughter of Tipam Raja who applied for a monetary pension on grounds of poverty.[64]

Hemkanta Gohain, the second son of Raja Chandrakanta Singha was a pensioner. When he came of age he applied to the government for a grant of Rs. 1,000 to meet the expenses of his proposed wedding 'together with a new dwelling house' befitting what he thought to be his 'rank and respectability'. Jenkins, Agent to the Governor-General of India recommended a sum of Rs. 500 for Hemkanta's marriage and a further sum of Rs. 500 to be placed at the disposal of Jenkins himself for the construction of a house. Jenkins assured the government that with the amount so reserved, 'I will endeavour to make the best arrangement in my power for his permanent and comfortable accomodation.' Though we do not come by any further record on the matter, the proposal of Jenkins was likely to be accepted by the Government of Bengal. After a few years Hemkanta sent another petition wherein he stated that during his marriage he incurred debts 'at exorbitant rate of interest' and asked for an advance to enable him to pay off the loan to the merchants. Accordingly, Jenkins paid an advance amount of Rs. 400 which was to be liquidated by instalment of Rs. 50 per month from his pension. Jenkins' action was immediately approved by the Lt. Governor.[65]

After a few years, another petition seeking financial assistance to meet marriage expenses came up for decision of the government. By a policy instruction, the Government of India had asked the officers to discontinue receiving such applications as early as 1846. But exigencies compelled the officers to ignore such an instruction. The instant case shows with what rapidity poverty gained upon the falling stars of the old nobility.

Narain Gohain, the Majoo Raja was a nephew of the late Raja Purandar Singha and received a monthly pension of Rs. 30 since March 1839. In early 1863, Narain Gohain applied for financial assistance from the government to enable him to meet the expenses of his daughter's marriage. Major W. Agnew, the then (officiating) Commissioner of Assam wrote to the Lt. Governor of Bengal that in view of the Government of India's policy instruction he ought to have hesitated to endorse the petition had he not 'on my late tour happened to see real indications of his poverty'.[66]

We are reproducing Major Agnew's note to show the wretched condition of a man who was nothing short of a true representative of his class.

Agnew wrote,

> (as) I passed his *Barri* at Jorehaut, I turned off the road to see him, and my visit being wholly unexpected, I saw the place quite in its everyday garb.... The homestead consisted of some four or five wretched hovels, without even an apology for a *tatti* round them, nor was there any other indications to show that the place belonged to a man of even ordinary respectability.

Narain Gohain 'complained of his scanty means, and that the demand now a days for labour at the tea factories was so great, he could get no one to work for him at wages he could afford to pay'. The Commissioner then observed that 'the general increasing prosperity of the country was not only not shared in certain sections of the community, but they actually suffered by it. In other words, the government servant, on fixed salaries, and pensioners found the expense of living doubled and their incomes reduced by four per cent...'. He also pointed out that a similar grant was sanctioned to Giridhar Gohain Namrupia Raja in 1846 on the occasion of his grand-daughter's marriage. The Lt. Governor too, having concurred with the views of the Commissioner, the Governor-General in Council felt obliged to grant Rs. 300 for the purpose but on the distinct understanding that no future application of the same kind would be considered admissible.[67]

The Dimasa chief Tularam Senapati's territory covered an area of about 2,160 sq. miles which he ruled with the help of his two warring sons, Nakulram and Brajanath.[68] Tularam received a monthly pension of Rs. 50 from the government but paid an annual tribute of Rs. 490 to them.[69] He died in October 1850. His territory became a victim of frequent raids from the Angami Nagas. As a remedy, Jenkins suggested resumption of the territory. Jenkin's proposition was strengthened by A.J.M. Mills. The resumption of the territory of Tularam was accomplished by Lt. H.S. Bivar in early 1854.[70] Tularam's territory included a large tract covering the present North Cachar Hills, Karbi Anglong and parts of Golaghat and Nagaon districts. Like other ruling families of the province, the descendants of Tularam were also reduced to poverty. The rut had begun during Tularam's life. The pauperized chieftain helplessly looked on his own decline.

The fate of Tularam was like that of a roving bird put into a cage. His condition was pitiable. He had a territory but no title. John Butler, a military officer in civil employ at Nagaon in the forties of the nineteenth century gives us a grim description of Tularam—

> After wading through a very high reed jungle, we at last came to his dwelling—a wretched grass hut situated on the edge of a tank choked with rank weeds.... A few straggling huts, inhabited by Cacharees and dependents of Senaputtee formed all that could be called a village, a few pigs, fowl, and ducks, were wandering about, but there were no signs of comfort around any of the huts, or gardens or enclosures, all appeared poverty stricken, as well as sickly.... Tularam Senaputtee, an infirm old man, was clothed in the meanest cotton garb, and looked more like a skeleton than a living being.[71]

Bivar's resumption of Tularam's territory in 1854 did not meet with any resistance from the heirs of the former ruler. Rather, on his visit to the main residence of the family at Moho Dungah, several members of the family assembled and laid their claims to certain lands on rent-free basis. In all, there were twenty claimants—the younger son of the Senapati, Brajanath Barman, his three sons and three daughters, widow of Nakulram, the elder son of the Senapati and their three children, younger widow of Nakulram and her daughter, the son-in-law of the Senapati and his son and two daughters, a minor daughter of the Senapati, a daughter of the Senapati's younger brother, late Madhooram and a grandson of Madhooram. Their total claim amounted to 1,50,450 *pooras* of cultivable and jungle land.[72] The abstract of revenue and taxes reported to have been collected annually by Tularam and his sons from the country under their rule was presented before Bivar. He accepted them as a mere 'guess work' and 'a gross misrepresentation'. The sources of taxation included house tax, duty on elephant hunting, elephant catching, rhinoceros hunting and customs on traders' boats at the three *ghats* of the river Jamuna, viz., Augooree, Bakoleah and Potimaree. They claimed that the total annual income from these sources was Rs. 3,624. But they could not explain their inability to pay the tribute at the rate of Rs. 490 annually, the payment of which would have guaranteed the continuance of their rule as per the provisions of the treaty of 1834. Already they fell in arrears of tribute for the three preceeding years. The ryots too had little or no sympathy with their rulers. They complained that whenever they grew a flourishing crop, the rulers did not fail to help themselves to the best portion of it.

By incompetence and rapacious behaviour, the rulers distanced themselves from the ryots and could no longer seek and rely on their support to resist the intrusion of the British into their territory. On their part, the British fully realized the political significance of that part of Assam as an effective buffer zone against the Naga raids besides its economic potential.

H.S. Bivar listed the natural products of the country—timber, coal, lime, stone, iron, salt, ivory, lac, bees wax and *manjeet*. There were also a few salt wells at Samkur. The salt which was prepared by boiling down the water appeared to Bivar 'much purer than sea salt'. It was sold for Rs. 7 a *maund*. Bivar was struck by the indigence of the ruling family. He scrutinised the merit of the various claims, prepared a list and recommended that the Moho Dungah village and some adjoining cultivated and waste jungle land be given to them rent-free. He also proposed annual money pensions to them. The Lt. Governor of Bengal approved and confirmed the recommendations of Bivar. There were seven receipients (see Table 1.2).

TABLE 1.2

Name	Amout of pension	Cultivated land			Jungle land		
		B	K	L	B	K	L
1. Brajanath	600	119	0	0	1,001	0	0
2. Kanooram	120	66	0	0	400	0	0
3. Juggernath	138	86	0	0	516	0	0
4. Bunessure	72	46	0	0	200	0	0
5. Myadee	72	46	0	0	200	0	0
6. Indraprava	72	13	0	0	100	0	0
7. Atuka	72	13	0	0	100	0	0

Note: B.K.L. means, in land measurement, *bigha*, *katha* and *lecha* respecitively. In Assam, *lecha* is the smallest unit of 144 sq. ft.; 20 *lechas* make 1 *katha* and 5 *kathas* make one *bigha*; 4 *bigahs* of land make 1 *poora*.

It was also made clear that the land was exempted from taxation only during the lives of the respective holders and was therefore liable to resumption upon his or her death. The pension was to commence from 1 January 1854. The Lt. Governor agreed with Bivar that the government must not attempt to collect the arrears which were due from Brajanath on account of revenue or tribute and from the ryots, on account of revenue. These concessions were necessary, they felt, 'to keep all the members of the Senapati family quiet and peacable'.[73]

Bivar next completed the settlement of the Jamunamukh Mahal which comprised 4 *mauzas*, viz., Noamatty, Dubokamukh, Hozaee and Thercho Purbat and appointed Bodram Laskar, Dyaram Laskar, Bidoor Barman and Jinlur mauzadars of those *mauzas* respectively. The Thercho Purbat was inhabited solely by Karbi people.[74]

Desh Dimoria in the district of Kamrup did not present any better picture.[75] Shortly before the acquisition of that tiny tract by the British, the three sons and successors of Gopal Singha—Komul Singha, Harry Singha and Outum Singha held the '*pergunnah*' in succession. At the time of British occupation Outum Singha was the Raja of Desh Dimoria. He died in 1833 leaving his only son Dodhee Singha who was then a minor. Robertson, the then Commissioner appointed Bhakat Singha, the son of Komul Singha to act as Surbarkar until Dodhee Singha came of age. But Bhakat Singha died shortly after his appointment.[76] There being none in the family of Dodhee Singha capable of administration, 'an Assamese gentleman', Dhurmessur, was placed in charge of Desh Dimoria.

Dhurmessur was hardly placed in charge of Desh Dimoria when he too died. The government then decided to put two 'konwars', Man Singha and Mil Singha jointly in charge of the *pergunnah.* They were distantly connected with the family of Dodhee Singha. Man Singha and Mil Singha botched up their job and engrossed themselves in a ruinous quarrel. After enquiry government dismissed Mil Singha and the charge of the *pergunnah* was allotted to Konwar Mohendra and Man Singha. This agreement also did not last long. For better management, the *pergunnah* Desh Dimoria was divided into three *mahals*, one *mahal* was given to the Khasia king Burmanick of Khyrum and the other two were given to Sazwal Koosram Barua Mauzadar and Man Singha. The Khyrum Raja was given 6 *mauzas* besides a tract with defined boundaries through which the Khasias had to pass their way to Sonapore Hat. The ink of this mandate was barely dry when there were allegations of mismanagement. Koosram mauzádar and Man Singha were both dismissed. The portion held by Man Singha was finally given to Dodhee Singha, though still a minor, and the other portion was given to Seekaram, a friend of the boy king. Within two years Seekaram's portion was taken over by Dodhee Singha.

In early 1853, Mil Singha, the one time ruler of the *pergunnah* died leaving his three widows and a minor son 'totally destitute'. Within a few month the boy King Dodhee Singha also passed away leaving his mother and two widows. Man Singha was again asked by the government to take charge of the Desh as Surbarkar which he did in 1854. It was finally settled that Man Singha would manage the *pergunnah* and receive the usual commission of a choudhury. After a series of experiments warranted by the changing situations some answer to the administrative question was found at last. The government was hard put to it and no ill feeling or prejudice dictated its course of action. But the single common problem of the vanishing regalia still remained. The widows of Outum Singha, Mil Singha and Dodhee Singha petitioned the government seeking 'some consideration and support'. Col. F. Jenkins reported to the Government of Bengal that the petetioners were 'perfectly destitute' and that they deserved extreme compassion. He also proposed some grants of land to them.

In May 1856 the Government of Bengal approved the continuance of the grants of 20 *pooras* of land to the family of Mil Singha until his son attained majority. To the mother and two widows of Dodhee Singha the government sanctioned the remission equal to the rent of 50 *pooras* of *roopeet* land to be continued to them as long as the three survived but liable to revision on the demise of any one of them.[77]

But the irony was that before the above orders reached the District Collectorate the ladies had lost possession of the land. They had in fact resigned it, being unable to pay the revenue. The local authorities then recommended an annual allowance of Rs. 75 to the ladies in lieu of granting rent-free land. But the Lt. Governor turned down the recommendation and refused to sanction money allowance in lieu of the land resigned by them. The matter was closed, and understandably, the distress of the widows continued unabated.

The British were impelled to act in a friendly manner towards the Rajas of Darrang with their headquarters at Mangaldoi in view of their lineage, their relationship with the ruling families of Bijni and Koch Behar. In 1839, after the resumption of Upper Assam, the Rajas of Darrang were allowed to continue in their possession of half *jummah* terms for a period of 20 years. But the feudal gentry of Assam received the first mortal shock in 1843 when slavery was abolished.

The fleeing away of men and women engaged by the ruling families for cultivating their land and doing other ancillary works created a situation for which they were never prepared. They were used to seeing other people doing manual labour for them one generation after another as an ordinary fact of life and came to believe that physical labour was a natural incident of destiny of those people. It was unlikely that the same generation of people who grew up in such an ambience would change their attitude overnight and take to work so long done by others. Their inability to adapt themselves to the new situation was the root cause of their sharp decadence.[78]

All members of the family of the Darrang Raja failed to pay the revenue even at half rates as fixed earlier and sought permission from the government to resign part of their estates. They tried to impress upon the government what may be termed as their burden of bigness. Hundreds of *bighas* of cultivable land were lying useless and they found it difficult to pay revenue for land not really covered by cultivation. Moreover, agricultural produce in their area, they said, did hardly bring them any cash. Bolindranarayan Konwar was in arrear of revenue for the years 1260 and 1261 B.S. (A.D. 1853–4 and 1854–5) to the extent of Rs. 2,451 and declaring himself unable to pay the dues he offered to transfer to the government more than 5,392 *pooras* of land in liquidation of the revenue amount. The 5,392 *pooras* of land were lying in 27 *mauzas* and of which only 624 *pooras* were under cultivation.

The Commissioner of Assam accepted the offer of Bolindranarayan in March 1855. It was, as if an act of particular favour was shown to the petitioner. Similarly, Suryyanarayan Konwar had 434 *pooras* of land, out of which he resigned 411 and retained only 23 *pooras* paying a *sudder jummah* of Rs. 10–1–9. Amritnarayan Bahadoor, Rajooram Konwar and Rajnarayan Konwar were also in arrear. They too offered to surrender some portions of their cultivable land.

The large scale surrender of land by the members of this family created a flutter in the administrative circles. The Lt. Governor of Bengal asked the Board of Revenue to make a thorough inquiry into the problem. The Board of Revenue asked itself, 'what were the defects of the revenue system which appeared to be reducing the old families of the province to poverty?[79] Shortage of labour and low money income from land were the major causes of such a situation.

In the meantime a serious problem was brewing up in the tea gardens—the problem of contract workers running away from their employers. The Act XIII of 1859 was passed to provide punishment for breach of contract by artificers, workmen and labourers excluding domestic servants. The Government of Bengal extended the jurisdiction of the law to the districts of Cachar, Lakhimpur and Sibsagar in 1863. The Commissioner of Assam solicited the opinions of the other district officers and some leading men on the advisability of extension of the law to other areas.[80] The Assamese gentry, whenever their opinion was called for, tried to impress upon the government that the difficulties faced by the planters arising out of shortage and shuttling labour was identical with the problem faced by the landed gentry following the release of the men and women from their control. They supported the demand of the anxious planters and thereby tried to regain, if possible, their lost world. The grievance of the old ruling class found a representative echo in Lalitram Singha, the Raja of Desh Rani. He posited his strong views before the government in these words, 'Since the introduction of Act V of 1843 the people of Assam have suffered greatly for want of a proper control over their servants....' He said that some code had become 'indispensably necessary' for the interest of both the employers and those employed by them.[81]

Lakshmi Singha Chowdry, Hony. Magistrate in Kamrup observed that there were no provisions in the said Act XIII of 1859 for punishment of breach of contract by domestic servants, or persons who might voluntarily engage themselves to serve as workmen at any description for a stipulated term. He felt that some law on the matter had become absolutely necessary.

Captain E.P. Lloyd, Deputy Commissioner of Kamrup, fully concurred with the opinion of Lakshmi Singha Chowdry. Such a measure, he thought, 'will offer an easy and effectual remedy of those who suffer from breaches of contract, or from servants willfully and without warning quitting the service of their employers'.[82] The descendants of the ruling families of Upper Assam, including the Muttock territory never lost an opportunity to complain against the abolition of slavery. The Government of Bengal consistently refused to reopen the matter. It was prepared to flatter the vanity of the gentry to a limited extent only. To hope to regain their pelf and power under the new dispensation was a day-dreaming on their part. The government fended off every sting of their hunger with an iron fist under a velvet glove.

Declaration of general amnesty by the Queen and the softening of attitude of the Government of India towards the people variously penalized for their role in the Mutiny of 1857 prompted four associates of Maniram Dewan to send petitions to the government praying for release and permission to return to Assam. Some select portions of those petitions can be discussed here. From a social point of view they did not belong to the ruling class. But when the question of a choice arose they stood for revival of the Ahom monarchy and threw in their lot with the revivalists. Evidently they were not happy and contented with the new rulers and had an axe to grind against them. They entertained hopes of gain from the revival of the monarchy and therefore, made a common cause with Kandarpeswar Singha. They were internalized and relied upon by the gentry.

With Maniram Dewan and others, Dooteram Burooah, Sheikh Bahadoor Goan Boora, Sheikh Fermoodh and Mayaram Nazir were also arrested in the wake of the revolt of 1857 in Assam. They faced trial as accomplices of Maniram and were punished with various terms of imprisonment. Of all the four persons, Dooteram and Mayaram had some education, Dooteram was a Sheristadar of the Fauzdari court at Sibsagar when he was arrested. As a convict at Port Blair, he came to know of the general amnesty declared by the Queen of England. In December 1861, Dooteram sent up a petition to the Government of India praying for pardon.[83] His prayer was at first rejected on the ground that 'he was in the employ of the government when he committed treason'. In July 1862, the Lt. Governor of Bengal, Sir Cecil Beadon paid his first visit to Assam. Dooteram's second son Lakshmilal Burooah was then serving as the Head Writer in the Deputy Commissioner's office at Guwahati. He waited upon Sir Beadon and submitted a petition on behalf of his father, renewing prayer for pardon on the ground that the trial of Dooteram was 'partial' and that he was an old man of seventy and had already suffered imprisonment for four years. The Lt. Governor sought the opinion of the Commissioner on whether the prayer could be entertained. Major J.C. Haughton, the officiating Commissioner, reported on 1 August 1862 that they had no objection to pardon 'either as regards his case, or as regards the state of the province'. The Lt. Governor, on board the Yacht *Rohtas*, on 19 August 1862 remitted the remainder of the sentence and directed his release on condition that he did not return to Assam. But soon after, he wrote to the Government of India to remove the condition and allow Dooteram to return to Assam.[84] We do not find any basis of the story that Dooteram's son Priyalal pleaded with the Governor-General in Calcutta in the guise of the Mahanta of Dihing *satra* or that Priyalal appealed to the Privy council and secured the release of his father.[85]

Sheikh Bahadoor Gaon Boora moved his petition for release on 26 April 1862 from the island of Andaman. His long petition,[86] of which we have on record an authenticated English translation, shed light upon his earlier life and times. He narrated that when in 1838 'the people of Assam' had suffered under the aggressions of the Raja Purandar Singha and his family, they asked for British protection. The Gaon Boora reminded that he 'was also one among the number of applicants' who had applied to Col. F. Jenkins, then Agent to the Governor-General, to protect them against the tyranny of the king. So how could he, in 1857, repose faith on Kandarpeswar Singha who was 'too young, inexperienced and void of any knowledge whatever' he asked. He pleaded not guilty before the tribunal but then his plea was not accepted.

He stated that he was an ordinary man living on a small shop of what he called 'national profession of sewing'. He noted that as a Muslim it was unusual and beyond his power to have an access to the Raja's durbars. Next he referred to one petition of the Upper Assam Mussulmans submitted to Major J. Butler, the Deputy Commissioner of Assam, to admit them to government employ, which 'can be well proved from the report of Captain C. Holroyd of 1856 or 1857'. On these grounds, the Gaon Boora said, 'it was quite impossible to believe that the people of Assam, especially such a low race as Mussulmans, could ever join in, or seduce the Raja to convene a council to make conspiracies against the government'.[87]

Sheikh Bahadoor Gaon Boora, towards the end of his petition, referred to the Queen's general amnesty. He pointed out that Mudoosoodun Mullick who also faced trial with Maniram and was deported for life had already secured his release. The Gaon Boora's plea was strengthened by another petition from his son Sheikh Muneeroodin. The Agent to the Governor-General observed in his report that the petitioner was entitled to his release. Accordingly, the Lt. Governor passed orders on 27 July 1862 for release of Bahadoor Gaon Boora from his imprisonment at Port Blair.[88]

Sheikh Fermoodh was sentenced to imprisonment for fourteen years. After the release of Sheikh Bahadoor Gaon Boora, Fermoodh sent up his petition from Port Blair asking for the 'same lenity' and pardon shown to Bahadoor Gaon Boora. Thereupon the Lt. Governor ordered immediate and unconditional release of Sheikh Fermoodh.[89]

Mayaram Nazir of Golaghat was sentenced to fourteen years of imprisonment in the Alipore jail, Calcutta. In his case, the petition for release under the amnesty was submitted by his son Gopal Das, an inhabitant of Nangaltoop *mauza* under the Golaghat sub-division. Following a report from the provincial government the Lt. Governor of Bengal remitted the remainder of the sentence and directed immediate and unconditional release of Mayaram.[90]

There are also some other incomplete accounts in record to suggest that the petitions received from the near and distant relatives of the former rulers, were numerous and that not all of them evoked sympathy. As we have seen, the British provided relief in terms of exemption of land revenue and money pension to the direct descendants of the Ahom kings. But they were scrupulously selective with regard to the claims of the scions of the old nobility Bargohain, Buragohain, etc. As Captain T. Brodie, Principal Asstt. Sibsagar wrote to Jenkins, 'I need hardly mention to you how numerous are the applications made to me from the ancient nobles of the country for pensionary support'.[91]

Jenkins, in a report to the Government of Bengal on 21 June 1855, described the situation with frankness. He informed that the Assamese of rank were provided for as far as possible with offices and the charge of *mauzas*, but as none of them had trade or business talents, nor ideas to make good use of landed property, there were 20 applicants for every single situation. He noted, 'the members of the late ruling class, the Ahoms,..., have hitherto shown with few exceptions, little aptitude for learning or qualification for our offices, which consequently have generally fallen to the lot of the Brahmins and the Kagotees'.[92]

The commissioner stated what appeared to him a startling reality. The decline of the old ruling class was socially very significant. It was not only the poverty of the old ruling class in abstract economic terms, but it also signalled a drain on their moral reserve. By 1853 it was clear that the former Ahom kings or their sons who petitioned Moffat Mills had no authority to speak on behalf of the people of the province. Of the two important claimants, Ghanâkanta and Kandarpeswar, none came within an ace of the monarchy, yet, neither of them was prepared to stand down for the sake of the other.[93] There was no trace of the collective wisdom of the elders of the royal court around, which sustained the monarchy through thick and thin. Even as a class they could not unite themselves and create pressure upon the government for a fairer deal. There were examples of such form of agitation elsewhere before them. As we have already noted, they had to struggle hard for a mere existence and their pursuit of happiness was bewildering. They used to represent the case of their own families only and at times step brothers or sisters did not hesitate to jeopardize the interests of each other. Selfishness pursued collectively could earn a modicum of respectability as in the case of the landholders of Bengal. But the selfishness of the old nobility of Assam drove them into insignificance and isolation. It was a pathetic drift from the monarchy to the laity. But such a situation cannot occur abruptly. There were instances which showed that in the last decade of the eighteenth century itself, the ruling class set its life on chance. It lost much of its social weight during the days of the Burmese rule. Nirode Kumar Barooah has remarked,

> At the time of the British take-over of the administration, the influence of the nobility was so reduced that in Assam, unlike other newly conquered territories in India, there was no immediate political need to conciliate or destroy them, for the safety of the British power.[94]

As a class it had no financial standing worth the name. So it became toothless after the resumption of Upper Assam and the abolition of slavery; it soon began to disintegrate.

Lack of enlightened statecraft, education and all forms of economic virtue led to a deepening despair and shipwreck of the old ruling class in Assam. Since this class was at the top of the community in every respect, its fall had a demoralizing effect on the latter. Padmanath Gohain Barua, the founder of the Ahom Sabha observed that the period from 1838 to 1893, was a season of dead march for the Ahom community. Within these years, he said, they became 'insignificant and neglected'.[95] The situation demanded quick responses which they were unable to make. The more it called for circumspection, the more they became insular.

The importance of the dates lay in the fact that in 1838 Purandar Singha was removed from the throne and the administration of Upper Assam was taken over by the British; in 1893 the Ahom Sabha was founded at Sibsagar. It was the Ahom Sabha which blazed the trail of modern organized politics among the Ahoms. Padmanath felt distressed at the plight of the Ahom community and the Ahom Sabha was his brainchild. In fact, Padmanath was the godfather of invidious Ahom politics in the state.[96]

Slavery was the lamentable symbol of power and privilege of the old aristocracy in Assam. The slave owning people, as appeared from their subsequent fulminations, looked upon their privilege as a matter of right. The act abolishing slavery, therefore suddenly immobilized them because the slaves were the appendant productive force even under the *khel* system. The *khel* system based on an exploitative scheme of governance with the king as the centre of gravity went out of gear.[97] Socio-political turmoils, frequent raids by the hill tribes and demographic reverses due to other causes disturbed the ratio of slave population and their masters. Nonetheless the slaves could ensure some surplus product for the comfort of their owners. The village pundits, handicraftsmen, carpenters, fishermen, farriers, boatmen, tailors, washermen, etc., who lived by doing their professional work made up the intermediate strata. There is no reason to believe that antagonism between the slaves and the slave owners did not exist. But it was never raised to the level of an uprising. Protests against the government decision were made by the members of the ruling class everywhere. They were joined by the Brahmins and Mahantas of Kamrup. Moffatt Mills, while visiting the province after ten years from the abolition of slavery found that their misery was too circumstantial to be ignored. He was moved by the 'extreme distress which the Ahom gentry have been subjected to by the sudden emancipation of their slaves'. He held no brief for the slavophiles, yet he did not fail to see that the 'measure only reduced the men of substance in Assam to absolute poverty'.[98]

So far as the Ahom nobility and the writer-priest class combine were concerned, the results of the abolition of slavery were dissimilar to each other. The former had little or no education while the latter had. Without a second string to their bow the Ahom nobility was doomed to perdition. They were pushed out of the centre to the periphery despite themselves. Not a single man or woman did emerge from this class either to hold fast to what was best in them or to fight for a place in the sun. Those who had education had better future. Haliram Dhekial Phukan in his *History of Assam* written in 1829 observed that even by the standard of its own age the Ahoms were educationally the most backward.[99] The more fortunate of them was not necessarily distinguished by intelligence. Like a great tree uprooted by a storm, the old aristocracy lay sick unto death unnoticed and uncared-for.

A question naturally arises, how did the people react to the sudden miseries of the ruling class with no hope of recovery? Their attitude was marked by indifference not unmixed with irreverence. It was true that in Assam, as in other parts of India, 'the general life of the people, and the lives of the rulers had run along parallel lines.... The only relationship between a ruler and his subjects which was permanent and unbreakable was monetary.'[100] In Assam, though money was not the main form of revenue, the same 'unbreakable' link was maintained through other methods. Compulsion and state coercion were necessary to keep it going. As soon as it was exposed to outer challenges the system became unworkable. Over the years it was rusting away; the state functioned but symbolically. No writer had ever taken any notice of the plight of the ruling elite. The contemporary writers seem to have made unwelcome of the setting sun with the certitude of a new dawn. The vast corpus of Assamese literature on nationalism bears out the fact that the impoverishment of the old ruling class did not stir the imagination of the writers.

Lakshminath Bezbaroa particularized their moral bankruptcy in his play *Belimar* (Sunset, 1915). Indications were clear that their eclipse was awaited, not mourned.[101]

Fernand Braudel observed that the sixteenth century which saw the growth of the modern state in the Mediterranean world 'reduced the aristocracy to poverty'. He agreed with the general view 'that the modern state was the enemy of the nobility and of feudal powers'.[102] Though Assam did not fit into the classification of a modern state in the second half of the nineteenth century, thirty years of political interaction with an advanced European power since 1826 brought in some structural changes which marked a departure from the traditional moorings and gave the uncertain promise of a dawn of modernity.

Within the lifetime of a single generation the old ruling class including the vassal chiefs of Beltola, Rani, Luki, Dimaria, Gobha, Neli, etc., ceased to exist in their own consciousness. They could neither trust their strength nor their instinct. Their benign world of shared understanding vanished without a trace.

THE ZAMINDARS OF GOALPARA

The zamindars of Goalpara were the 'rulers' of permanently settled estates. They have not received much attention from the historians. Nonetheless we have dependable accounts of all the zamindars of Bijni,

Gauripur, Karaibari, Mechpara, Chapar, Parbatjoar and Sidli.[103] The first two of them were addressed as 'Rajas', but they were no more than glorified zamindars. There were nineteen permanently settled estates in the district of Goalpara. They covered a total area of 15,30,100 acres; of them the zamindar of Bijni owned the largest area of 6,03,283 acres and that of Gauripur owned 3,16,447 acres.[104] Their ancestors were the rent collectors of the Mughal emperor. They were happy with their lacklustre existence. Swashbuckling provided occasional excitement to their drab life.

Until the (Permanent Settlement) Regulation of 1793 came into force, the zamindars of Karaibari, Mechpara, Habraghat (under Bijni) and Kalumalupara (under Gauripur) carried on their exploitation of the Garos freely in the name of trade. (The Garos are now a dominant tribe of Meghalaya.) The Garos complained that they were forced to supply cotton at about one-sixth of its actual price and also subjected to other form of atrocities. Agents and sub-agents of the Raja of Bijni who kept stock of salt for the border *hats* were notorious dealers. Clay and water were mixed with salt to increase its weight by one-eighth part and then put up for exchange with the Garos at one *man* (or *maund*) of salt for 3 *mans* of cotton. What it meant in real terms?

> The Garo therefore, for a eight rupees worth of salt, which, were there no monopoly or duties except the Company's would cost about 5½ rupees, gives 3 *mans* 15 *sers* of cotton in the seed, which at Gowalpara is usually worth 5 rupees of the *man*. He besides pays a share of the cotton to the Raja, for permission to trade in his market.[105]

The Regulation of 1793 reduced the police and military powers of the zamindars. It was then the turn of the Garos to stage retaliatory attacks on the zamindars, N.K. Barooah finds some element of social banditry, a universal case made out by E.J. Hobsbawm in the retaliatory raids of the Garos.[106] This is how the zamindars lost their power and prestige among the Garos. Left to themselves, the zamindars did not show any sense of discretion. S.K. Bhuyan calls Ranaram Chaudhury, the zamindar of Mechpara, 'unruly and turbulent'. There were charges of 'depredations and robberies both in the river and his neighourhood' against Ranaram.[107] David Scott applied his mind to the question of the zamindars' authority *vis-a-vis* the complex reaction of the Garo chiefs and came to the conclusion that the zamindars had no scruple for principle and more truly, no zeal and capacity for work.[108] As old dogs refuse to learn new tricks, they also refused to learn. They would have loved to see the clock put back. The dark deeds of their past haunted their descendants and the ryots as well.

There was crisis in every zamindar family. Bijni would be the perfect index to the entire situation. By the mid-eighteenth century the Bijni-raj began to show signs of crack. It became a house of conspiracies, ignominious litigation and self-destructing laxities. When the British acquired the Dewani of Bengal, Bijay Narayan was the ruler of Bijni. Soon he got on bad terms with them and eventually became a victim of conspiracy. The British put him under house arrest and later took him away to Calcutta for trial. Bijay Narayan was shocked by the turn of events and took his own life by jumping into the Ganga.[109] What followed immediately after is not well-documented.

In 1793, Balit Narayan was the ruler of Bijni. Because of the Regulation the rule had to be refashioned from a chieftainship into a zamindari. Though reduced to the status of a revenue paying zamindar, the family kept up the law of primogeniture. Goalpara was organized into a district in 1822 and David Scott was appointed the First Collector. At Bijni, Balit Narayan was succeeded by Indra Narayan, Indra Narayan by Amrit Narayan. Anandaram Dhekial Phukan served as the Dewan of Amrit Narayan. With extraordinary skill and dramatic swiftness Anandaram gave shape to a set of reforms which could have benefitted both the zamindar and his ryots, but those who enjoyed themselves in disorder and chaos, falsehood and chicanery swept them under the carpet.[110] Binji knew no good governance or peace. The zamindar or his wife or the Court of Wards fulfilled the requirement of a mere form.

When Kumud Narayan, the prospective head of the family came of age, the Court of Wards handed over the charge to him in 1874. Ere long he came through some education at Benares. As an enlightened zamindar he initiated some reforms for the development of his estates. Kumud Narayan was conferred the title of Raja Bahadur in 1878 by the Government of India for his public spirit and liberality.[111] But constant clatter of his quarrelsome wives, Siddheswari and Abhayeswari made his life a misery. A frustrated man, he died an unnatural death in Calcutta in 1883. The quarrel between his wives fuelled ribald jests among the ryots. The *Sarurani Barranir Dhuma* as they called it, took a turn for the worse. Schemers of all hues had their field day. Finally, the court stepped in and allowed them joint estate for life. The elder Rani died in 1891. Abhayeswari endeared herself to her people through some public work. The present town of Abhayapuri owes its name to her. There was another spell of administration of the Court of Wards from 1918 following a serious dispute which defied solution for about twenty years.[112]

The zamindar family of Gauripur owes its origin to a *sanad* of 1606 given to Kabindra Patra. He was assigned the thana Rangamati and sarkar Dhekeri. The residence of the family was shifted to Gauripur by Pratap Chandra only in 1850. In recognition of his services during the Bhutan war (1864–6), the government honoured Pratap Chandra with the title of Rai Bahadur in 1867. Pratap Chandra died in 1880 without any issue. His wife, Rani Bhabanipriya Baruani adopted Prabhat Chandra Barua. Eventually the latter established himself as the most prominent of all the zamindars and became their leader.[113] He made himself thoroughly unpopular in 1920 by making a plea to the visiting Viceroy, Lord Chelmsford for transfer of all the zamindari estates of Goalpara to Bengal. He argued:

> It is admitted that historically and ethnologically we differ considerably from the rest of Assam and it is but too true that we get little charity from them. Goalpara proper was transferred against the wishes of its people in 1874 and the prayer for transfer had been repeated from time to time whenever occasion had arisen.[114]

Though there is nothing to write home about their estate-management, Raja Prabhat Chandra Barua and his immediate descendants patronized historical research, journalism, and animal study; some excelled in the field of art and culture. Mechpara found a redeemer in Prithiram Chaudhury. But immediately after his death in 1874, his sons fell out over the question of succession and everything went haywire. The estates of Karaibari, Parbatjoar and Sidli were plagued by endless quarrels and litigation giving little opportunity for the zamindars to work. Lack of competence made matters worse.[115]

The Garos continued with their periodic killing spree in the zamindari estates of Karaibari, Kalumalupara and Mechpara. In 1902 about seven hundred Garos ran over the Habraghat paragana and set up a Garo Raj at Dalgomaghat on the Brahmaputra. Subsequently they relented and withdrew. The Bhutan Duars were a source of irritation for the zamindars of Sidli and Bijni. The Bhutias, an unpredictable and haughty lot, very often swooped down upon the settlements and ravaged them. Once they killed Lakshmi Narayan, the zamindar of Sidli. The Bijni ruler was the target of another attack, arson and plunder of a Bhutia chief called Jaulia Bhutia. It survives in folk memory as *Jauliar Dhuma*. The sulky morale of the zamindars was no match for the tempestuous conduct of the Garos and the Bhutias.[116]

The zamindars, as a rule, also maintained houses within what was then known as the Company territory. In case of alarm they shifted their families there. The ryots also came to realize that the grass is greener on the other side and whenever they got a chance they fled away and took shelter in British territory. The condition of the under-tenants in the estates beggared description. The only property they possessed were the dingy mud hovels. Their misery knew no bounds; they paid rent and the worst of it, *abwab* or illegal cess above the rent. Right from 1793 the British Government tried to impress upon the zamindars that *abwabs* by whatever name it was called, was 'the source of oppression to the ryots' and urged them to limit themselves to one specific sum of rent. But the practice was so endemic that good souls simply despaired of it and threw up their hands.

Santo Barman who has made an indepth study of the system has recorded about thirty-three varieties of *abwab* collected by the zamindars of Goalpara. Some of them are: *dhap salami*—a complimentary fee of one rupee realized from leading tenants soliciting an interview with the Raja or the Rani; *darkhast salami*—a sort of court fee at the rate of Rs. 2 for each petition; *pan-bata*—a marriage tax varied from Rs. 2 to Rs. 15; *mankuji*—penalty for cultivation without the knowledge of zamindar; *britti*—a subscription for upkeep of idols, fees for festivals, etc.[117] The zamindars' men of action sniffed out the erring tenants and gave them hell. This gave rise to the *dewaniya*. Francis Hamilton Buchanan drew a penpicture of the system thus:

> The small farmers are in this district the most timid creatures imaginable. Being totally illiterate, and afraid to speak even to a common clerk, 5 or 6 families usually unite under a chief man, who manages what they called Dewanya, that is, settles the whole of their transactions with the agents of the landlord; and they are entirely guided by his opinion. These poor farmers are called Chenggoras and go nearly naked; the men merely wrap a towel (Gammochcha) round their middle, or pass it between their legs, pulling each end through a chord, that encircles their haunches.... The Dewanya wraps round his waist a cloth worth 8 annas, throws round his shoulders a sheet worth a rupee, and encircles his head with a turban worth 10 annas. He seldom does any work, and on all occasions is helped first to tobacco and betel.[118]

The ryots could seldom resist the tyranny, but there were occasional outbursts and localized agitations. The zamindars had more and the ryots less freedom than either of them deserved. So there was no scope for meaningful compatibility. In such a situation, no peasant society can produce what David Ludden calls the 'rhythms of inner motion that render societies dynamic'. (Until of course, he says, they were 'relegated to obscurity and robbed of history by cosmopolitan intellectuals, working in metropolitan centers that dominated the world by nineteenth century's end'.)[119] So there was immobility *ad infinitum*. That is one reason why the district of Goalpara lagged behind others. The zamindars were unable to create an environment for opportunity and talents.

Though there were a few high spots, the institution failed both the zamindars and their ryots. The zamindars never learnt the art of delegating authority and were either unreceptive to new ideas or slow on the uptake. At the best of times they did not shine at statecraft. They were unable to cross the bridge every time they came to it.

Every member of the old gentry exuded the pathos of the setting sun but every zamindar imbibed the spirit of the morning star. The former learnt to distrust British rule, their destroyer, the latter learnt to worship it as their creator. But history kept their exit route ready, one was followed by the other.

NOTES

1. *Fort William—India House Correspondence*, Delhi, 1958, Vol. I, pp. xxxviii–xxxix.
2. S.K. Bhuyan, *Anglo-Assamese Relations*, Guwahati, 1974, pp. 302–8.
3. See, C.S.L. Davies, 'Popular Religion and the Pilgrimage of Grace', in A. Fletcher et al. (eds.), *Order and Disorder in Early Modern England*, London, 1985, pp. 58–88.
4. Ibid., pp. 340–2.
5. See S.K. Bhuyan, op. cit., Ch. VII, Parts I & II, pp. 300–97 and Ch. VIII, Part I, pp. 424–58.
6. Edward Gait, *A History of Assam*, Guwahati, 1967, pp. 233–8.
7. J.B. Bhattacharjee, *Cachar under British Rule in North-east India*, Delhi, 1977, p. 28.
8. Ibid., p. 37.
9. Ibid., p. 39.
10. Gait, op. cit., pp. 329–30.
11. See W.W. Hunter, Preface to *A Statistical Account of Assam*, Delhi, 1982, Vol. I.
12. Gait, op. cit., p. 335.
13. H.K. Barpujari, *Assam in the Days of the Company*, Guwahati, 1980, p. 12.
14. P. Goswami, *Bihu Songs of Assam*, Guwahati, 1957, p. 77.
15. Barpujari, op. cit., p. 16.

16. See N.K. Barooah, *David Scott in North-East India*, Delhi, 1970, pp. 136–9.
17. H.K. Barpujari et al. (eds.), *Political History of Assam*, Guwahati, 1977, Vol. I, p. 27.
18. Barpujari, op. cit. (note 13), p. 66.
19. S.K. Bhuyan, op. cit., p. 574.
20. N.K. Barooah, op. cit., p. 245.
21. H.K. Burpujari et al. (eds), Guwahati, *Political History of Assam*, Vol. I, p. 29.
22. Barpujari, op. cit. (note 13), pp. 135–41, 169.
23. Barpujari, op. cit. (note 13), pp. 167–8.
24. Fort William Foreign Dept. Progs., March 1863.
25. It was a long memorial of about two thousand words where Kandarpeswar Singha related the entire story. Foreign Dept. Progs. (NAI), April 1863, Nos. 46–8.
26. Ibid., para 15.
27. Ibid., Introductory note on the enquiry.
28. Foreign Dept. Progs. (NAI), 22 May 1856, No. 10.
29. Fort William Judl. Progs., 29 July 1859, No. 238.
30. Fort William Judl. Progs., 14 July 1859, Nos. 24–8.
31. Ibid., Letter from the commissioner of Burdwan to Kandarpeswar Singha dt. 26 May 1859.
32. Ibid., Reply of Kandarpeswar to the commissioner dt. 4 June 1859.
33. Ibid., Letter of Govt. of Bengal to the commissioner dt. 9 July 1859 and S.C. Dan, *Bardhaman Parikrama*, Calcutta, 1992, pp. 118–23.
34. Fort William Judl. Progs., 23 February 1860, Nos. 88–9.
35. Fort William Judl. Progs., December 1862, Nos. 342, 343.
36. Ibid.
37. Ibid., letter of Haughton to the Govt. of Bengal dt. 11 September 1862.
38. Fort William Judl. Progs., December 1862, Nos. 344–6.
39. Petition of Kandarpeswar Singha, op. cit., para 20.
40. Ibid.
41. Letter of Govt. of India to the Govt. of Bengal, No. 391, dt. 4 September 1863.
42. Foreign Consultation, Pol. A (NAI), August 1864, Nos. 5-7.
43. Ibid., Letter of John Gregory, deputy commissioner (offg.), No. 952, dt. 15 April 1864.
44. Foreign Dept. Progs. Pol. A (NAI), July 1864, No. 308.
45. Fort William Judl. Progs., June 1862, Nos. 121–5.
46. Fort William Revenue Progs., June 1855, Nos. 41–3.
47. Fort William Revenue Progs., August 1855, No. 2.
48. *Sadaraminar Atmajivani*, Guwahati, 1991, pp. 114–20. Also Assam State Archives Record, Letters issued to the Govt. of Fort William, Vol. 35, No. 368, dt. 19 November 1867.
49. Assam State Archives Record, Vol. 19, No. 77.
50. Fort William Revenue Progs., August 1855, No. 2.
51. Foreign Consultation, Pol. A (NAI), July 1868, Nos. 321–5.
52. Ibid.

53. Foreign Consultation, Pol. A (NAI), September 1862, No. 33.
54. Foreign Consultation, Pol. A (NAI), November 1864, Nos. 59–60, February 1865, Nos. 32-3.
55. Foreign Consultation, Pol. B (NAI), July 1862, Nos. 21–3.
56. Ibid.
57. Foreign Dept. Progs. (NAI), July 1868, Nos. 367–9.
58. Foreign Dept. Progs. (NAI), October 1869, Nos. 104–10.
59. See, Hiteswar Barbarua, *Ahomar Din*, Guwahati, 1981, pp. 264, 301 and 341.
60. Foreign Dept. Progs. (NAI), May 1860, Nos. 58–60.
61. We find a list of such beneficiaries in Barbarua, op. cit., pp. 350–3.
62. Fort William Judicial Progs., April 1864, Nos. 404–5.
63. Assam State Archives Record, Vol. 35, Letters Issued to the Govt. of Fort William, No. 364.
64. Assam State Archives Record, Vol. 35, Letters Issued to the Govt. of Fort William, 1867, Nos. 369–70.
65. Fort William Revenue Progs., July 1855, No. 29.
66. Foreign Dept. Progs. (NAI), November 1863, Nos. 70–2.
67. Ibid.
68. John Butler, *Travels in Assam*, Delhi, 1978, p. 17.
69. Ibid., p. 20.
70. The resumption was done under instruction from Lord Dalhousie, See, Barpujari, op. cit. (note 13), p. 163.
71. John Butler, op. cit., p. 16.
72. The entire account of Lt. H.S. Bivar's visit and settlement has been summarised from Fort William Revenue Progs., August 1856, Nos. 13–18.
73. Ibid., letter of W. Grey, Secy. to Govt. of Bengal to Agent, Governor-General, N.-E. Frontier, dt. 20 July 1854.
74. Forth William Revenue Progs., December 1856, No. 16.
75. The entire account of the ruling family of Desh Dimoria has been summarised from Fort William Revenue Progs., May 1856, Nos. 25–7.
76. His wife Soneswari Kuwori received 20 *pooras* of rent-free land from the government. Barbarua, op. cit., p. 351.
77. Ibid., Letter of Govt. of Bengal, Fort William, 28 May 1856.
78. Cf. Barpujari, op. cit. (note 13), 'Higher Orders: Their Miseries', pp. 168–70.
79. Fort William Revenue Progs., July 1856, Nos. 8–10.
80. Fort William Revenue Progs., January 1863, No. 72.
81. Fort William Judl. Progs., January 1863, No. 74.
82. Ibid.
83. Fort William Judl. Progs., September 1862, No. 164.
84. Fort William Judl. Progs., September 1862, Nos. 161–4. Petition of Lakshmilal Burooah, No 160.
85. N. Talukdar (ed.), *Kanaklal Barua-Rachanawali*, Guwahati, 1973, p. 23.
86. Fort William Judl. Progs., September 1862, No. 157. Earlier, Bahadur Gaonbura's son Sheikh Muneeroodin also prayed for the release of his father under the Amnesty.

87. Ibid.
88. Fort William Judl. Progs., September 1862, Nos. 157– 9.
89. Fort William Judl. Progs., January 1863, Nos. 2–4.
90. Fort William Judl. Progs., June 1863, Nos. 68–70.
91. Foreign Consultation (NAI), 17 May 1850.
92. Fort William Revenue Progs., July 1855, Nos. 27–8.
93. We get a first-hand account of the heart burn of Ghanakanta Singha at the spread of a rumour in Guwahati that through the effort of Maniram Dewan, upper Assam was restored to Kandarpeswar Singha. See, *Sadaraminar Atmajivani*, op. cit., p. 91.
94. N.K. Barooah, op. cit., p. 136.
95. P. Gohain Barua, *Rachanawali*, Guwahati, 1971 p. 934.
96. For his role, see *Rachanawali*, op. cit., pp. 935–45.
97. See, Barpujari, op. cit. (note 13), pp. 50–1. S.K. Bhuyan, op. cit., pp. 251–2, 564 and 567.
98. Mills' *Report on the Province of Assam*, Guwahati, 1984, p. 17.
99. H. Dhekial Phukan, *Assam Buranji*, Guwahati, 1962, p. 101.
100. Nirad C. Chaudhuri, *Clive of India*, Bombay, 1977, p. 38.
101. S.N. Sarma remarks, '*Belimar* portrays the tragic fall of the Ahom power owing to the weakness of kings and petty jealousy, and selfishness of the nobles', p. 146, *Lakshminath Bezbaroa: The Sahityarathi of Assam*, edited by M. Neog, Guwahati, 1972
102. Fernand Braudel, *The Mediterranean World*, London, 1981, Vol. II, pp. 706 and 709.
103. The well-researched book on the subject is S. Barman's *Zamindari System in Assam during British Rule*, Guwahati, 1994. Also useful are: A. Guha, *Jamidarkalin Goalpara Jilar Arthasamajik Awastha: Eti Aitihasik Dristipat*, Dhubri, 1984 and A.C. Chaudhury, *Koch Rajbonshi Jatir Itihas Aru Sanskriti*, Bangaigaon, 1993.
104. S. Barman, op. cit., pp. 10–11.
105. N.K. Barooah, op. cit., pp. 41–6. The quote is from Montgomery Martin (1838) by Barooah, p. 44.
106. N.K. Barooah, op. cit., p. 45
107. S.K. Bhuyan, op. cit., pp. 170–1.
108. N.K. Barooah, op. cit., pp. 55–7.
109. A.C. Chaudhury, op. cit., pp 283–4.
110. G. Barua, *Anandaram Dhekial Phukanar Jivan Charitra*, Guwahati, 1971, pp. 78–80.
111. L.N. Ghose, *The Modern History of the Indian Chiefs, Rajas, Zamindars*, Part II, Calcutta, 1881, p. 577.
112. A.C. Chaudhury, op. cit., pp. 289–90 and S. Barman, op. cit., pp. 23–4.
113. S. Barman, op. cit., pp. 27–37.
114. S. Barman, op. cit., see Raja P.C. Barua's memorial, Appendix I, pp. 233–9.
115. S. Barman, op. cit., pp. 45, 61, 71–2.
116. S. Barman, op. cit., pp. 84–6.

117. S. Barman, op. cit., see the Glossary.
118. Quoted in A. Guha, op. cit., p. 50.
119. David Ludden, *Peasant History in South India*, Delhi, 1993. Ludden studied the agrarian history of Tirunelveli, Tamilnadu, of the millennium before 1900 and came to some challenging conclusions, see pp. 200–20.

CHAPTER 2

Decline of Handicrafts and Survival of Handloom

THE STABILITY of the colonial administration contributed to a gradual growth of monetized economy. The various domestic products which so long satisfied the need of the people came to be replaced by imported wares. The impact of the import was felt at various levels with varying intensity, but there was nothing the hard hit people could do about it. They could neither obstruct the traders to expand market of imported wares, nor expect people to keep away from the habit of using those ready-made goods. As for instance, towards the end of the nineteenth century a lac dye-factory was established at Guwahati fully considering the demand in the market. But following the discovery and availability of cheaper substances for the same purpose, there was a sharp fall in demand of the home products. Ultimately, the dye-factory had to be closed down.[1]

DYES

The first victim of import trade was the age-old practice of preparation of various dyes in the province. It was not a cottage industry in the ordinary sense of the term. It was typical of the rural economy catering to the needs of individual family or at best a group of families in a locality. It was produced for domestic use. Before we relate the story of dyes dying out, we should enlist the names of a few favourite dyes, and note their description, availability and use for its obvious historic importance. The well-known botanist Albert Hill tells us that the use of natural dyestuffs and stains, obtained from the roots, barks, leaves, fruit or wood of plants is known since long among all nations.[2] Dyes were introduced in Europe by the Arabs which they brought from the Buddhists of India for trade.[3]

In other parts of India indigo seemed to be the important dyestuff. 'In Mughal India', we are told, 'there was compulsion to grow crops like cotton or indigo almost everywhere....' Agra area was known for indigo production. Likewise, a particular red dye of high demand was produced in the Coromondal coast. Dyestuff fetched money to the peasants of Gujarat who had either produced the dye themselves or sold the leaves to buyers who knew the art of production.[4]

The largest variety of dyestaff was perhaps produced in Assam. We have not come across any contemporary account of other province which might stand comparison with it. The list of dyes available to us is, in fact, a very long one.[5] Different items were used in different districts of the province for producing the same colour. There was also preference of colour among the people in every district. It is, however, doubtful if double-dyed technique was known to the people.

Achhugachh was the most common dye agent in use all over the province. *Leteku* was used to produce a red dye in Kamrup, Goalpara and Golaghat. *Bharathi* which produced a yellowish colour was used as a mordant in Darrang district. *Palash* mixed with the roots of *Achhu* produced a mauve colour which was a popular dye in Nagaon district. The dried leaves of *Kujithekera* and *Dhopabar* were used in the Mangaldoi sub-division of Darrang district. For black dye the people of Nagaon, Darrang and Lakhimpur used mainly the bark of *Jamu*, sometimes they mixed *Silikha*, *Amlakhi* and *Madhuriam*, etc., with it. But in Sibsagar, people produced black dye from the bark of lemon and pomegranate trees boiled with iron filings. In Jorhat black dye was produced from the bark of *Amlakhi* mixed with those of *Silikha*, *Jammu*, and *Madhuriam*. *Rum* or Assam indigo found a place in the *Dictionary of the Economic Products of India*.[6] The widely used common dye extracted from *Rum* was blue, but when mixed with other ingredients, it gave black, purple or green dye. Likewise, use of lac was common all over the province. The lac insect was reared on some select group of trees which varied from place to place. The mode of preparation of dye from lac which could be used alone or mixed with other substance was different in every district. Like lac, *Kendu* fruit was widely used for several purposes. The juice of *Kendu* fruit was used for colouring fishing nets. Besides taking off the white colour of the thread used for making the net, the mixture ensured the durability of the nets, the practice still survives. Those who made boats had a different use of *Kendu*. They pounded the half ripe fruit and got a brownish dye which they used like varnish on boats to prevent the damaging action of water.

Majathi was an important item of dyeing throughout the province. It is a creeper found only in the hills. For the hill tribes it was a profitable commodity. Demand for *Majathi* was statewide. They either sold it for cash or bartered for other goods. The people of Kamrup collected *Majathi* from the Bhutias in the north bank and from the Khasis in the south. When not mixed with any other thing *Majathi* produced a reddish yellow colour. People of Kamrup used it with lac, pounded leaves of *Bhoira*, *Barthekera* and *Leteku* trees which together could produce scarlet red. People of Darrang got *Majathi* from the Daflas which they used with *Bhomrati* to get reddish colour. The same combination was used in Lakhimpur district also. Some people there mixed other things like *Achhu*, mustard oil and ash water to extract red. In Nagaon, it was mixed with *Achhu*. Use of *Majathi* was very rare in the district of Sibsagar because of its non-availability. Another substance called *Jarath* was used throughout the Brahmaputra valley. An excellent green dye was produced from *Urahimah*, also known by its Bengali name *Shim*. The practice was common all over the districts.

Besides these, some ingredients were used in particular districts only. For example, a very common product *Nil* or indigo according to our information was grown in Mangaldoi area by the Muslims and they used it as a dye. It was also popular among the Meches of Goalpara. Another aniline dye, magenta was mainly used in Goalpara. *Sewali* yielded a deep yellow colour which was a favourite dye with the people of Darrang. The Boros of Kamrup district produced dyes from a plant called *Kulikatagachh*. *Changeritengaa* was used as a mordant almost for all dyes in Nagaon.

The Meches of Goalpara extracted a mordant from the bark of a tree they called *Tepar Tenga*. It was used with indigo, madder and turmeric. *Raspat* was utilized for dyeing yarn in Sibsagar only. In Nagaon and Darrang split bamboo and cane painted with *Raspat* were used for making hand-fans and *Jhapis*. Boats were also decked up by imaginative use of colour. A mixed colour of *Hengul* and *Haital* was used for the purpose. The black acrid juice of *Bholaguti* was used only in Nagaon by the Dhobis to mark clothes for washing. Some people of Darrang extracted a dye from *Teteli*. *Keharaj* juice was widely used as ink and only in Darrang it was used to make grey hair black. Red dye extracted from *Chandan* was a much sought after thing in Nagaon, particularly in the north-eastern part. *Kusum* was used for dyeing only in Goalpara. A strong dye yielding plant called *Kalapat* was grown in the Boro villages of Kamrup and Goalpara. Among the non-Boros it was used at Barpeta.[7]

Though the various tribal communities excelled in the preparation of various dyes and weaving of cloths for their own use they were unable to produce attractive works of art like the Gonds, the Konds and the Bhills.

Three tribes of Arunachal Pradesh, namely the Sherdukpan, the Khamba and the Monpas who are still famous for their artistic talents used to import colouring stuff from Assam.[8] Their migratory habits, close outlook and self-satisfying mentality debarred them from interaction and inspiration to draw out their talents for marketable arts.

As a product of ordinary domestic skill, the people could not think of its commercial value, or at least they never tried it. The production was need-based and within the domestic scale. Traditionally, the Boros wore coloured clothes. As soon as the coloured yarns of Britain became available with the Marwaris and the Dacca merchants in the towns, the people gradually began to avoid the trouble of preparing the dyes. The shining and showy yarns and their products dyed in aniline dyes had a particular appeal.

The suffering of the professional Tanties of Bengal in the face of Manchester market mechinations is well-known. An extract of the report of the Governor-General (1834–5) bears testimony to it. 'The misery hardly finds a parallel in the history of commerce. The bones of the cotton—weavers are bleaching the plains of India.'[9] But such a class of professional Tanties did not exist in Assam. Cloth-making was a domestic accomplishment in every house. Yet, there was a small number of professional Tanties in the northern part of Kamrup district. With more and more dyed yarns and piece-goods coming in from Manchester, the Tanties found their profession unremunerative and their children instead of carrying on their family profession preferred to take to agriculture.[10]

By the end of the nineteenth century, the number of people engaged in domestic preparation of dyes and dyeing was few and far between. Within the next twenty years it became a thing of the past. Of more than three hundred known varieties of plants in the valley, of which we have mentioned a few, the use of only three or four varieties has survived to the present. Secondly, it came out in course of our queries that at present not even 10 per cent people could identify the local plants having dyeing properties.

The dyer's broom had thus worn off, but cotton, *Eri*, *Muga* and silk cloths of Assam did not fail. They are perpetual charmers.

WOODCARVING AND IVORY CARVING

Woodcarving and ivory carving were two well-known crafts.[11] But the number of people engaged in the works was so small and the use of their products was so limited that the crafts had no chance of becoming an industry. The superior skill which was required for each work was not common to every family or every place. It was confined to select families where the male members developed the art, trained up the junior members of the family and handed down the expertise from one generation to the other. But there was no lack of persons in the villages who were capable of doing small bits of woodcarving. Woodcarving was a popular art among some tribes of the north-east. The Wanchoo, the Konyak and the Phom tribes deserve mention.[12]

A government official noted that skill and ingenuity employed in woodcarving in the Brahmaputra valley was 'for the most part bestowed on places of worship'. Generally, the *satras* were the centres of beautiful woodwork collection and decoration. The Kamalabari *satra* of Majuli was well-known for its decorated carvings. The carvings of such situations usually represented some well-known episodes of Hindu mythology.[13]

In a recent study, it has come to light that at Bardowa, the birth place of the Vaishnava saint Sankardeva, the woodcarvers depicted secular art objects, besides the religious ones. Popular pastimes like buffalo-fight, horse-fight, elephant-fight, etc., were neatly represented in the carvings preserved in the *satra*.[14]

The *singhasana* or the multi-tiered raised platform on lions, from which the name *singhasana* is derived, in a village *namghar* or a *satra* was the first object that attracted the visitor. Varied in size and degree of sophistication, they were made of good and durable timber. Available local skill was called into play to make them attractive and meaningful.

The *singhasanas* in the Auniati and Dakhinpat *satras* were inlaid with gold and silver. The Kamalabari *satra* possessed the most beautiful and the largest *singhasana*. The seven-tiered throne of God was 10 ft. square supported by four sculptured lions in the four corners. Thrones were also made with peacocks, geese and elephants as supporters, they were called *mayurasana* when made with peacocks, *hangasasana* when made with geese and *gajasana* when made with elephants. Mythical characters like Garud, Mayur, Hanuman and Ananta also used to find expression in the woodcarvings of the *satras* and the *namghars*.[15]

The representation of *magar*, an imaginary animal resembling fish with a trunk at both ends of boats and rafters of a house was common in the valley. Those who could afford to pay the labour cost got their doors and doorframes decorated in carvings. But the appreciation was not confined to the rich alone nor was the object of decoration a thing connected with religion only. There were many things of daily use which were decorated with carvings, and equally appreciated and possessed by both Hindus and Muslims. Carvings were done in furniture like *paleng*, *salpira* (both bedsteads), *barpira*, *karani*, *barpera* (wardrobe), *kharam* (wooden sandal), *thaga* (bookstand) and *gasa* (lampstands). Ornamentation of loom accessories including the *jatar* (spinning wheel), was common throughout the province. A kind of small *palki* called *dola* was decorated with figures of parrots, peacocks, horses or lions. Bits of beautiful carving could be seen in the handles of knife, spear, umbrella, stick, comb, etc.[16]

Kalyankumar Dasgupta has noticed an indigenous idiom in the traditional work of the Assamese woodcarvers. He further remarks, 'Viewed as a whole, Assamese woodcarvings belong to the mainstream of Indian art, contemporary as well as ancient, and draw inspiration therefrom, yet it has its own distinctiveness.'[17]

There was no scope of any export trade of these articles. The artifacts, big or small had their own admirers but demand for them in the every day market was not regular or consistent enough to ensure financial support to the producers. As the need for ready cash was growing fast such producers could no longer rest content with chance sale of their goods. So they took to other professions, mainly agriculture. The Assam Census returns (1901) showed that there were only four 'wood and ebony carvers'. According to the census reports there was none in any part of the province whose sole occupation was carving. Khanikargaon of Sibsagar was famous for woodcarving. By the end of the last century the craft became a secondary occupation. The four well-known carvers of that period were Adiram Mistri of Daikalangiagaon, Sibsagar; Lerela Sarmah of Puranigudam, Nagaon; Bholaram Bayan of Kamalbari Satra and Giri Kanta Adhikar of Nij Chutia.[18]

The abandonment of profession by the traditional families and the attitude of looking down upon such labour resulted in the importation of carpenters from Punjab and other provinces. Not even the assisting hands were locally available. A British engineer, J.K. Kipling observed, 'It is a curious fact that in scarcely one of the buildings erected by the Public Works Department has any use been made of native skill in carving.'[19] Some people did care about *Vaastuvidya*, but generally speaking, there was no remarkable advance from the traditional devices. Construction of palatial buildings for residential purpose was not in vogue in Assam. Even the well-to-do people used to have a huddle of huts of different names for different purposes instead of large compact houses serving all purpose. A fixed code of do's and don'ts guided the people with regard to timing, layout and other details of construction. There were also restrictions on planting of trees in residential compound.[20]

The first ever concrete construction of a private residential building was started in 1874 by Haribilash Agarwala (1842-1916), a tea planter and a merchant. The construction was completed within two years. Built in the town of Tezpur, on Rajasthan model, it was known as 'Tezpur Paki'. Masons and carpenters were brought from Rajasthan. The great earthquake of 1897 could do no harm to the building.[21] Many celebrities visited the house as guests during the freedom movement.

Like woodcarving, ivory carving was once a thriving profession. The ivory carvers were known as Baktars or Baktar-Khanikars. Records have it that all the Baktars of that period were Muslims. During the Ahom rule, work on ivory was not altogether an optional business. There was a method of selective compulsion. Ivory articles constituted a major portion of royal gifts to visiting grandees as well as distant dignitaries. Side by side with ivory carving the Baktars worked on deer horns. Deer horn artefacts were meant for decoration only.[22]

It was officially ascertained that in the closing years of the nineteenth century there were men who were skilled in the art of ivory carving, about forty of them lived in Goalpara, two in Kamrup and two in Dibrugarh but none depended on it for livelihood. They took to agriculture which required less labour and ensured a no less comfortable life than that of an ivory carver.[23]

The 1891 census reports showed that there were only four ivory carvers in Assam, three in Kamrup and one in Sibsagar. It became a languishing craft. In 1898-9 there was but one man in the whole of Assam whose occupation could be described as ivory carver. He was Fiznur of Jorhat. The civilian monographer James Donald lamented, that from an important flourishing and honourable industry, it had, within a period of 70 to 80 years, been reduced to the work of individual initiative.[24] But it was not totally dead and gone. When ivory carving was languishing in Upper Assam, flag for that craft was flown at Barpeta town, home of many a native skill and excellence in Assam. Atmaram Mistry took the lead in this field. His example was followed by Radhanath Das, Bhagawan Das, Jagannath Das and others. They held fast to it and quite a few firms that dealt in ivory and ivory works came up there in course of time.[25] Decline of ivory was said to be a 'cause' of disappearance of the art. To us it appears that more than shortage of ivory, the prospect of a better external market of ivory was at the root of the collapse of the craft.

The effect of the Elephant Preservation Act which prohibited the random killing of elephants was marginal.

The Marwari dealers found that the simple mechanism of buying tusks in Assam and selling them in Calcutta fetched them much profit. Tribal hunters beyond the Inner Line sold out tusks to the traders who in turn sold them in Calcutta with a good margin. Dibrugarh was an important centre of the tusk trade.[26] The government had no policy to protect the craftsmen against the trickery of the traders. In the absence of an organized market they could neither sniff out the real demand for their products nor hold out for a better price.

Sabyasachi Bhattacharya spoke about three levels of development in production organization in artisanal industry. Wood and ivory carving, according to his classification, belonged to the primary level of organization where 'production was dispersed, each artisan working in his residence, often with the aid of family members, the products in final demand was as a rule made in one domestic unit, involving minimal diversion of a labour, marketing...unmediated by any trader...'.[27] The second level of development is characterized by the middlemen's involvement for purchase and resale of products leading to advance of cash (*dadan*) to the artisan. The important features of the third level are: expansion of the work group beyond the families of the artisans, differentiation in functions and wages of labour, advanced integration with the market through middlemen's assistance and thus facilitating the emergence of an entrepreneur-proprietory.[28] When Barpeta revitalized the craft and took over the trade, the features of the second and third level of development became clearly discernible.

The decline of the old aristocracy in Assam deprived the artisans of their nearest class patrons. We have no precise idea as to the nature and level of demand from the Zamindars outside the state but it could not have been negligible in any case. With the introduction and easy availability of Western fashion wares, a change of taste came over the rich. Haribilash Agarwala's residential building about which we have already stated, was decorated with imported articles only. The professional class which was gradually emerging was disdainful towards the products of the local artisans. Generally speaking, love for anything foreign was their guiding principle. Foreign rule patronized alien tastes and artistic sensibilities. There was a race for imitation and no articulation of traditional artform in a thoughtful world of creativity.

For common men ivory articles were luxury items. A look at the price of different articles will show that they were beyond the means of average household. The well-known ivory articles and their price as in the years 1898-1900 are: (1) Comb from Rs. 5 to Rs. 20, (2) Back-Scratcher Rs. 20 to Rs. 50, (3) Spoon and Fork Rs. 30 to Rs. 50, (4) Toys: (a) Elephant from Rs. 30 to Rs. 35, (b) Horse Rs. 8 to Rs. 10, (c) Fish Rs. 1.8 to Rs. 5, (d) Cart Rs. 50 to Rs. 60, (5) Bracelet Rs. 8 to Rs. 10, (6) Knife Handle Rs. 3 to Rs. 8, (7) Ring Rs. 4 to Rs. 6, (8) *Tema* (Small Box) Rs. 4 to Rs. 6. The problem of lack of popular demand was perhaps complicated by an unhealing rarity of the select clientele which infused a spasmodic habit into the artisans. Their children, under such circumstances, could not look up to the profession with confidence. 'Their inclinations, if of good family, tended, as in the case of the son of Fiznoor, the well-known carver in Jorhat, towards an office stool.'[29]

GOLD WASHING

Over and above the artisanal industries already stated, there were other smaller crafts which too started declining with the opening of free trade with Bengal and within a short time all of them disappeared. Once the British decided to hold on firmly, enterprising officers started smelling around its potentialities. The Court of Directors of the East India Company began to take notice of the mineral resources. The Government of Bengal, accordingly, asked Jenkins to obtain reports from select areas. Major I.F. Hannay supplied information to Captain Edward F. Dalton, Collector of Lakhimpur for carrying out research on quality and deposit value of the gold fields of Assam.[30] Hannay reported that the sources of the metal were contained in rubble dufts from which a considerable quantity of gold dust was obtained yearly by the gold washers on the different gold bearing streams. Hilly rivers with strong currents always had good quantity of gold deposits. It was further stated that almost all the rivers in Upper Assam were gold-bearing and big rivers, namely the Subansiri, the Dihing, the Na Dihing and the Brahmaputra were the 'most prolific'.[31] People used to dredge out gold even from the smaller rivers like Tengapani, Parua, Dehong, Dibong, Digaru, Disang, Dhal, Diburu, Kakoi, Kadam, Somdiri, Kharai, Boroi, Borgang, Bordikhari, Mansiri, Kalijuri, Dekajuri, Pama, Garua, Disoi, etc.[32] It was substantiated by Pemberton's report, 'Almost all the streams which flow into the Burhampooter are in a greater or less degree auriferous, the gold obtained at the junction of the Burhampooter and Dhanseeree river alone, was estimated by Buchanan, in 1809, at 1,80,000 rupees per annum.'[33] But Buchanan's estimates are not always reliable.

Captain Dalton's 'Account of a visit to Jugloo and Seesee rivers in Upper Assam' is an interesting first hand report of his adventurous journey to the Jugloo river far above the Burhi Dihing and the Seesee river, another small river to the north of the Brahmaputra. In his expedition undertaken in 1852, Dalton was accompanied by a large number of labourers and gold washers. By engaging his people in his presence he found that by washing about a ton of gold dust and sand his men could derive about 18 grains of gold. In this process one person could extract about 8 grains of gold in a day. In the Seesee river fifteen days' hard labour of one person could produce enough gold to meet the revenue demands of the government.[34]

The gold washing process did not involve any expensive input. One basket called *leheti*, one big wooden dish (4½' x 1½') with a high edge called *durum* and a bamboo net were all that was necessary for the work. Four persons known as *pali* constituted one group, the fifth person who supervised the work of the *palis* was called the *pati*. Gold particles were collected with the help of mercury which was produced locally by the gold washers themselves. In the second stage tests were conducted to ascertain whether the gold collected was genuine or adulterated. On the whole, gold washing was a highly strenuous job.[35] In the absence of any element of compulsion and agriculture and tea gardens providing alternative occupations to fall back upon, there was no reason for the people to stick to the toilsome pursuit.

Captain Dalton suggested that only specific expedition would fetch positive results. The Lt. Governor of Bengal was pleased with the reports from the gold field areas and encouraged expedition to the gold bearing deposits.[36]

In October 1855, Dalton reported Jenkins about the existence of a gold washing site at Goroomarachapari situated 18 miles below the Brahmakunda. Each gold washer could wash about 25 *maunds* of rubble in a day and on the average each obtaining rather more than one anna weight or about 15 annas worth of gold. The gold washers of Sadiya always displayed superior ability in gold collection. Choonpora and Parghat were two important gold collection centres.[37]

Reports of Major Campbell, Major Hannay and Captain Dalton conclusively proved that gold washing was not the general profession of the people living by the side of the rivers carrying gold deposits. During the Ahom rule, the people who were engaged in the work were called the Sonowals. They were drawn from four communities: the Kacharis, the Bihias, the Koches and the Keots. Of them, the Kacharis and the Bihias excelled in the work. One particular river was assigned to one particular community to work out gold. Silver was found only in the Dhansiri river, the silver washers were called the Thengals. Every year they used to start the work after harvesting the winter crop, from late January and continued it for three months. The major part of their collection went to the royal treasury. Obviously, gold washing as a profession did neither ensure a stable income nor hold out any promise of economic prosperity. It could not be an absorbing and profitable occupation.[38]

The government at first adopted the policy of leasing out the river *mehals* of Chari Duar, Naduar and Lakhimpur for gold collection. But the auction price of the *mehals* was falling every year, so much so that by 1865-6 no bidder came forward to take them. Campbell explained it away by saying that the *amlahs* of the court used to purchase the *mehals* in the auction and realised revenues from the actual gold washers at an oppressive rate. Besides, the mehaldars gave advance of cash to the goldwashers on condition that they would sell their product at the rate of Rs. 8 to Rs. 10 per *tola*, whereas the market price of gold was Rs. 16 to Rs. 17. The producers had no option but to sell their product to their creditors. As a result, the gold washers found their work wholly unremunerative. The system of leasing out some rivers of north Lakhimpur at a nominal price continued till 1874–5.[39]

Colonel Keating, the first Chief Commissioner of Assam tried to revive gold washing in Assam in 1876. But his efforts did not succeed.[40] In 1884, the government under Charles Elliot renewed its efforts. With the help of some hired people the government could procure only 52 ounces of gold by washing exactly 52 tons of sand in the Subansiri. The whole exercise proved so expensive that the government washed its hands off it. A final attempt by a group of tea planters also met with the same fate. In 1899 some British tea planters had formed into a company with a capital of Rs. 1 lac and started their gold hunt in the Subansiri. In three years they spent about Rs. 70,000 and found that they still needed much of a muchness. So, they turned away from the daunting venture.[41] One particular reason of the government's repeated efforts to revive the gold washing trade and thereby augment its production if possible, was that gold was still the most important mineral product of India. It was only after 1902 that coal replaced its importance as a mineral product.[42]

The expansion of the tea gardens led to the increase of labour rates. Working in the gardens guaranteed a stable income round the year. So more and more people gave up gold washing and they either took to agriculture or enrolled themselves as labourers in the tea gardens. The Sonowals thus let go their hereditary profession down the wind for ever.

We would like to turn to the other aspect of this industry where only a handful of artisans were able to hold out against an unfavourable situation. Though gold washing fell into disuse there was no question of any fall in demand of gold and silver wares. Calcutta was the source of import as it was for any other valuable item. The monograph prepared by the British civilian F.C. Henniker is the only exhaustive and dependable source of information for us in this regard.[43]

JEWELLERS' CRAFTS

Goldsmiths were there in Assam even in the old days. The King Rudra Singha (1696-1714) of Assam is said to have imported goldsmiths from Benares to train local hands.[44] Jewellery with or without stone was valued for its ceremonial, astrological or ritualistic utility.

The Census Report of 1881 shows that the total number of goldsmiths, silversmiths and jewellers in Assam, including Sylhet and Cachar, was 2,102, the number of dependents on them is not known. But the total number of population supported by these professions in 1891 was 18,651, in the next ten years their number decreased by about 22 per cent, i.e. to 14,560.[45] During these years there was noticeable increase in the number of population directly or indirectly connected with agriculture. As in case of other indigenous craft more and more people gave up the old craft and took to cultivation. Secondly, the new commercial channels of trade in these luxury items of gold, silver and precious stones, etc., were not within the reach of the average workers. The trend of decline which started in the closing years of the nineteenth century was never reversed.

The reputation of the Assamese goldsmith is now a thing of the past. His works were 'distinctly pleasing even to the critical eye and would attract notice in the midst of quite a good collection of Indian wares'. A few of them who still survived had to train themselves to satisfy the changing tastes of their customers. The distinctiveness of the Assamese ornaments was gradually lost. It is a matter of some interest to find that though every district of Assam had artisans that lived on this branch of manufacture, yet the items were not common. Barpeta and Jorhat were the two important centres of this trade. The gold ornaments made at Barpeta were (1) *Sitipati*, (2) *Jankar Chakeli*, (3) *Hajeri*, (4) *Kanor*

Sona, (5) *Nakphul*, (6) *Galkanthi*, (7) *Jon Madli*, (8) *Keselura Har*, (9) *Cheek Har*, (10) *Baju* and (11) *Muthi*. Silver ornaments included (1) Silver *Muthi*, (2) *Bala*, (3) *Chandrahar*, (4) *Mal Kharu* and (5) *Beki Kharu*.[46]

Madhabchandra Bardaloi studied the peculiarities of Barpeta jewellery. He noticed that the Barpeta jewellers did not enamel, and did not usually, produce work where stones were set. Some ornaments produced by them had stones. They excelled in filigree, which distinguished the Barpeta wares, just as enamel and set stones were specifically located in the Jorhat productions.[47] The price of a filigree necklace which weighed 14 *tolas* of gold was Rs. 378 about the year 1905. Jorhat was the centre of production of delicate Assamese jewellery. A British officer Mr. Darrah had studied the problem of some local industries of Assam. In his 'Notes on some Industries of Assam', 1896, Mr. Darrah said, 'Enamelling on gold is done mainly at Jorhat in the Sibsagar district, the artificers are Sonars, and possess a fair amount of skill. As they work almost entirely for the native trade, the articles produced lack the finish to be seen in ornaments manufactured for European customers....'[48] The number of families engaged in the enamelling trade at that time was 38. The enamel was usually of three kinds, a dark blue, dark green and white, but red and yellow were also used. All these had to be bought from the Marwari merchants who imported them from Calcutta. Enamel was the decorative feature of the ornaments called *Gejera*, *Thuria*, *Keru*, *Biri* and *Dugdugi*. Jorhat was famous for seven varieties of *Thuria* or earpiece, namely, *Minakara*, *Karsipi Minakara*, *Nejpata*, *Talpata*, *Sach*, *Jangphai* and *Langkeru*; seven varieties of necklace, namely, *Kotmani*, *Bena*, *Gejera*, *Dhariabiri*, *Oloma*, *Lep biri* and *Chaki* or *Galpata*; five varieties of rings, namely, *Chamchow*, *Sen*, *Pohari*, *Tarjani* (a rosette with stones) and *Pani Parua*; four varieties of bracelets, namely, *Son Khatoa Kharu*, *Patia Kharu*, *Bala* and *Baju* besides *Kardhani* and *Chandrahar* for wearing round the waist, *Kapali* for the forehead and *Makara Kundala* worn by a bridegroom in the ear.[49] The Jorhat jewellers attained a high degree of excellence. Their fame lingers on.

The general tendency of the Assamese goldsmith was to give up his craft and engage himself in some easier mode of living. But there was no shortage of men to carry on that profession. Even before 1905, greater number of up-country Sonaris began to settle down in the growing urban centres. Many of them seem to have preferred the neighbourhood of the tea gardens, especially, to cater to the sprawling settlements of the labourers. Chasing the Bengali babus came the Bengali jewellers.[50] Though the use of delicately worked jewellery was the rule, imitation jewellery, or cheap and gaudy brummagem, trinkets, etc., had their customers. Crown and temple jewellery was not popular in Assam.

IRONMAKING

Ironmaking was not extensive but it was an important industry in Assam under the Ahom rule. The northern *talus* of the Naga Hills was rich in iron deposits. As the Sibsagar district shared, in the south, a common boundary with the Naga Hills, ironmaking was organized and developed in the screeline. Tiru Lohakhat was the main centre of iron production.[51] Like gold washing, ironmaking was also a seasonal occupation. Colonel S.F. Hannay estimated that the number of ironmakers 'in the zenith of the Ahom power at 3,000, but they did not exceed 100 after the Burmese invasion'.[52] Relying upon Hannay's Notes (1857) it has been observed by S. Bhattacharya, that as in Bihar and Orissa indigenous iron of Assam was replaced by imported iron in the eighteenth century. The substitution, according to him 'threw back the industry to the primary level of tribal household organization in Bihar, Orissa and Assam'.[53] But such a thing did not really happen in Assam. It had a different story. It is true that the people engaged by the kings of Assam to work on the ores and produce rough iron were the Boros, then called the Tiruwals. Their production did not belong to any particular domestic unit. Having been given settlements near the iron ores they were collectively responsible to the king for some fixed quantity of iron from their site. Their smelting process was primitive and labour intensive. Even by contemporary standard, they lived in a wretched condition and were therefore ridiculed by others.

> What does the Tiruwal eat?
> Life passes him by
> Offering a strip of fell as his waist band.[54]

The total output of the Tiruwals could not meet the consumption demand, so iron and iron products were imported from the Khasi Hills. The Garos used to hawk about iron in the *hats* and annual fairs of Kamrup and Goalpara. Many people from Upper Assam went there and bartered paddy, rice, mustard, etc., for iron.[55] With the import of pig iron and steel bars from Calcutta which began in the second half of the nineteenth

TABLE 2.1

Name of the District	*Numbers of forges*	*Number of persons*
Goalpara	166	400
Kamrup	227	918
Darrang	110	–
Nagaon	98	300
Lakhimpur	145	455

century, smelting, including digging out clay iron gradually disappeared. Mallet in his note on Records of the Geological Survey of India wrote that iron smelting was once an important art in Upper Assam. But even when he was writing his notes in 1877, it had been extinct for many years.[56] It was, in fact the victory of the new industry system. Marx correctly observed that wherever the factory system extended itself at the cost of the old handicrafts the result was 'as sure as the result of an encounter between an army furnished with breach loaders, and one armed with bows and arrows'.[57]

The steady growth of agricultural population and availability of imported iron gave rise to the number of forges in the province. Implements of agriculture, domestic use, carpentry and other crafts were manufactured in the forges. The articles included hoe, ploughshare, cart axle, cart wheel ring, various types of *dao*, sickle, scythe, folding knife, sacrificial knife, adze, curved adze, large spear, barbed spear, fishing spear, fish knife, fish hooks, axe, spade, hammer, anvil, chisel, nail, iron-ring, tongs, pincer and razor.

We have an incomplete account of the number or forges and persons engaged in them at the turn of the century[58] (see Table 2.1).

The demand for the various implements was met locally within the district. The Kamrup district being the largest producer with some fine articles not easily available in the other districts, particularly carpentry and craft tools, inter district trade of those products cannot be ruled out. People of Sibsagar were particularly fond of some implements of daily use produced in the Naga Hills. In the period under review there was none who could manufacture iron trunk and lock and key.[59] Similarly, golden vessel, gold casket and silver patera produced elsewhere and discussed by G.C.M. Birdwood in his book, the *Industrial Arts of India*, were not manufactured in Assam.[60] Damasceened work was also unknown.

SALT, PAPER AND BELL METAL WORKS

Salt production was carried on in the brine springs of Borhat and Sadiya. The production operation was fraught with uncertainities. The Borhat and Sadiya springs were virtually under the control of the Naga and the Adi tribes respectively and their consent and cooperation could not always be taken for granted.[61] The Ahom kings did not seem to have insisted on their right to obtain salt from the springs and towards the end of their rule, they rather preferred to depend solely on salt imported from Bengal. Local salt involved high risk and high cost of production. An old adage, gift of salt is equal to gift of gold, reminds us that salt was a rare commodity in Assam. It is a striking case of increasing dependence on adjacent colonial economy on the part of a frozen society in decline.

The Buddhist Shyams of Dibrugarh in Upper Assam were manufacturers of a fine quality of paper. Unlike people from other parts of the province they did not use bark of *Sanchi* tree to write on. They developed and brought to perfection their own technique of paper production from fibres of *Jari* and *Sanchi* trees. The paper was of fine and durable quality but the quantity of production was so small that they had no chance of entering market. There is proof of use and availability of handmade paper in Assam down to 1879. Manuscripts on such paper prepared in 1846, 1867, 1869 and 1879 and in good condition have been preserved at Srimanta Sankardeva Research Institute, Batadrava, Nagaon.[62]

Though the statement of import for the period did not include paper in the list, yet there is enough evidence to believe that use of imported paper among the later Ahom kings was extensive. The abolition of Hadira Choki opened the floodgate of imported goods into Assam.

The decline and disappearance of the artisanal industries cannot be explained in terms of the 'domination effect'. Because the East India Company (i) did not dominate the market as the sole buyer, (ii) did not impose restrictions on the producers, and (iii) did not oust local capital from its own area of operation. Assam never passed through such experience.[63] There was not even the distant possibility of its coming into conflict with any external capital.[64] The absence of local trading capital was a constraint which the producers could not overcome. That they could not raise their production even to the subsistance level was largely due to this inhibiting economic factor. But perseverance of artisans and patronage of the people in general kept the flags of two traditional industries flying all through these years. Within our period, Sualkuchi and Sarthebari in the district of Kamrup developed as important centres respectively, of silk and bell metal products and trade. These products acquired a distinctive grandeur of their own and though there were seasonal fluctuations, the demand level did not go down so much as to drive away the producers to greener pastures. Next to Sarthebari, Titabar developed as a centre of bell metal works. The Mariyas who specialized in bell metal works, were itinerant craftsmen. As demand for their service was not high they took to small-size agricultural holdings.[65]

POTTERY

Survival of pottery is yet another notable event. The local vends faced competition with imported wares but the handicraft survived primarily as a caste occupation. A sheer force of habit and a value system of their own made the potters go further and fare worse. They carried on their traditional craft unmindful of the economic shift around them. There was no evidence of their endeavour to improve the quality of their products. They had to blame none but themselves for their impassivity to the changes beyond their social contours. As a class, therefore, the potters remained socially and economically backward.[66]

The use of earthenware for a variety of purposes was common to the rich and the poor alike. We may list here the names of some earthenwares of popular use with their variant names, viz., *kalah* (pitcher), *ad kalahi, keri, hari* (for preservation of wine), *tekeli* or *madi, thuku* or *bhuruka, dohati, chupi* or *tari, kata charu, phelai, patcharu, ga-khera, kumaricharu, chakalicharu, mola, sanjmola, dhunadiya mola, chaki, ghot* for marriage, *pot* for worship, *gacha, dunari, shiker*, for eating, *gura* for fishing net, *junuka, sarai, pat or chuk* (earthen rings for well) and a variety of toys.[67]

In Assam, earthen rings were in great demand and the Barpeta potters were famous for their make. They were called to other stations for their service. Construction of a well with earthen ring cost Rs. 40 in 1873 at Nagaon.[68] Judged by the money value of that time the cost was fairly high.

It may be noted that barnished or coloured pottery was not made in Assam. The ware lacked sophistication of design and finish. Making of *kagzi* or paper-thin pottery of north India fame was an impossibility.[69]

DOMESTIC CRAFTS

In the period of our study there was nothing like drugs and pharmaceutical industry. Use of herbal medicine was common. The use of the Ayurvedic system of medicine was limited. The royal house engaged an Ayurvedic physician with the designation of Bezbaroa. Dinanath Bezbaroa (1813-95) was perhaps the last of such physician engaged by the Ahom king. The system survived as a family tradition in some towns supplying the need of a fewer people.

Other domestic crafts which survived were basketry and making of various implements of daily use like box, container, comb, hand-fan, umbrella, mats, agricultural, gardening, marking and measuring tools, writing and painting tools, some musical instruments, fish-catching equipments, cooking implements, etc.[70] Mute artistic appreciation from the user was the only reward for the unsung heroes who made them with care and commitment just for the love of keeping up their art. Lacquer, leather, papier-mache and gesso work, mother-of-pearl and shell work and work on precious stones were not known in Assam.

SURVIVAL OF HANDLOOM

We now pass on to the meaningful story of survival of handloom. The large scale cultivation of all the three varieties of worms, namely, the *Eri* (*attacus Ricini*), *Muga* (*antheroea Assamoea*) and the *Pat* (*bombyx textor*) and the huge output therefrom brought into existence one of the prospering cottage industries of Assam.[71] These handloom products lent grace and respectability to the user and not quite a few of them had a touch of class. The Manchester products could not easily hold them down. We have to appreciate that notwithstanding certain deprivation of life, the poor also tried their best to keep up their appearance through selective use of their own products.

The varieties in quality, colour and texture offered some advantage as people of varying incomes could choose things within their means. Wearing a particular cloth for a particular occasion had a force of convention and inability to do so carried with it the stigma of indigence.[72] We have already noted that the use of silk was a mark of social differentiation to the discerning eye. The *Eri* cloth could be used by the poor without any difficulty.

Of all the three varieties, *Eri* was the cheapest and the most common thing of daily use in winter. Kamrup was the largest producer of *Eri*.

Since the domestic and local needs could be satisfied in every district, demand for *Eri* in the local market was not high.

This, perhaps, was also due to its limited and seasonal use. Some Marwari traders of Palasbari, Rangia, Tamulpur and Baroma in the Kamrup district made attempts to develop trade in *Eri* textile. But *Eri*, as a commercial product, had little future. The hill tribes were the only consistent customers of *Eri* which they procured from the annual fairs or weekly *hats*. For the Boros, Meches and Rabhas, *Eri* was an easy means of quick cash. They met revenue demands from its income.[73] A.C. Campbell, Deputy Commissioner of Kamrup with backing of the provincial government, once made an effort to rear it on a commercial scale, but his experience was not encouraging. So long as he had a limited number of worms he could manage things without loss. But when he raised them to over one lakh worms, almost the entire crop was carried off by disease. Another Englishman, Crowe raised a big farm of castor plants to feed his stock of *Eri* worms at Pathalipam, north Lakhimpur. But the flood waters of the Subansiri swept off everything. In 1889 a third attempt was made by Mackenzie, a tea planter in Cachar. Half the cost of his experiment was borne by the government, but he met with the same fate as Campbell.[74]

Muga and *Pat* are finer products. They were mostly used by women. Except men of social status, others could not afford to use them as their daily wear. Jorhat earned a good name in the quality production and extensive use of *Muga*. *Pat* or silk was the finest and costliest of all. *Pat* cloth was an essential part of marriage, ceremonies at the *satras* and other similar festivities. *Eri*, *Muga* and *Pat* have their own natural colour and the general practice was not to dye them. But a red variety of *Eri* called *Bhumoko* was produced in and around Mangaldoi in order to alluring customers from Bhutan. Even *Pat*, which is whiter and brighter than the other two with a smooth lustre was dyed in the sub-division.[75]

A brief account of the different uses of all the three varieties of handloom products would reveal why the best of Manchester products could not hold down the native industry. That it was a local make was no reason for its success because there were instances of local produce being replaced by imported goods. There were no matching substitutes for these products and there was no necessity of engaging extra labour for payment. Generally, the ladies of one family used to help their neighbours out in the first phase of the work, as it was a long haul and they got their neighbours' assistance in turn. The weavers could, in a single process of the loom, produce diverse wears, like, *chadar*, *mekhela*, *dhoti*, shirt piece, etc. This advantage of diverse production kept a balance between demand and supply and satisfied the needs of the male as well as the female members of the family.[76] Lastly, the people held them in high esteem for the traditional reputation of its fine texture and distinctiveness.

Let us note the different kinds of silk wear: *Borkapor*, as the name suggests, was a big piece of cloth traditionally presented at the time of marriage of either side by the bride and the groom as a mark of respect and gratitude. In Goalpara it was called *Gilap*. *Borkapor* or *Gilap* was not meant for daily use. A cloth called *Patar Cheleng*, smaller in size and more convenient, was used by the rich and the respectable people. In Mangaldoi a similar cloth called *Bachal* was made for daily use, in Kamrup it was called *Sal kapor*. There were three varieties of *Patar Cheleng*: (i) *Uka Patar Cheleng* was *uka* or plain, (ii) *Guna kata patar Cheleng* was a kind of cloth with a decorated border; (iii) *Mugaphulia Patar Cheleng*, had a Muga silk border and very often with some picture sketch. There were some mixed varieties like (*i*) *Mugahonia Cheleng* made of mixed fabric of *Muga* and cotton. It was longer in size and so worn in double exclusively by men. Its price was higher than *Mugabania*, but much lower than *Mugaphulia* (ii) *Muga bonia Cheleng* made of mixed fabric of *Muga* and cotton and was meant for everyday use, and (iii) *Garidia Patar Cheleng* in which there was straight and bright lines of cotton, *Muga* or dyed *Pat* running both horizontally and vertically on either side. Kanaklal Barua, the later-day historian, noted in 1890–1 that their use was shrinking and lamented over the disappearance of those objects of art.[77]

The number of wears woven in *Muga* or silk for men was smaller than those for women. *Borchuria* which we now call *dhoti* was an important item of luxury. They were available in various sizes made of *Muga*: of *Muga* and *Pat* mixed, of *Muga* and cotton mixed, the former for the weft and the latter for the warp, etc. *Saru churia* used by ordinary men was made of cotton only. A smaller variety was called *dhuti churia* which was almost compulsorily used by every male member of the house at meal times. Here the word *dhuti* means pure. H.K. Barpujari says, 'The texture, size and price of silk *churias* or *dhuties* used by males varied according to the rank of the buyer; *pat*, *majankari*, *titakaria muga*, *bar churia*, *Kapahi tiyani*.' He gives an estimate that the yearly value of the clothing of a poor man was between Rs. 1.75 to Rs. 2.[78]

Women garments were as numerous as they were colourful. Take for example *Mekhela*. There were at least nine varieties and we will discuss each of them.[79] *Dharidia mekhela*, 'the finest example of the art of weaving as known amongst the Assamese'; it was made of the best quality of *Pat* with regular diamond and gold coloured twists extending from the decorated border lines at the bottom. More than half portion of the *Mekhela* was so decorated. It gave a gorgeous look and attracted even a casual viewer. In the year 1890 a single piece of such *Mekhela* cost Rs. 80 to Rs. 100. Next to *Dharidia mekhela* was *Patat phulbacha* or *Bonkara mekhela.* Here decoration was not continuous but scattered to form a symmetry. It was expensive and no woman from a family of moderate means could ever hope to wear it. *Patar mekhela* was made exclusively of *Pat.* To lessen the trouble of manufacturing *Pat* at home, the tendency of mixing indigenous with foreign *Pat* or silk was growing fast. *Mugabania mekhela* was a mixed product of *Pat* and *Muga* thread. *Muga* yarn was used as warp and *Pat* as weft. *Pat* and *mugabania mekhelas* were very common, almost every housewife wove and wore them lavishly. There were three varieties of *Muga mekhela*: *Titakaria, Sukaṇkaria* and *Mahura lerelai bowa.* With some variation in the making process depending on the weaver's own skill, advantage and habit, all these products were durable, though not within the reach of common people. The unmarried girls preferred *Muga mekhela* to any other variety particularly on formal occasions. *Eri mekhela* was also in use. In Lower Assam a mixed product of *Eri* and *Muga* yarn was available. Its price was slightly higher than *Eri mekhela. Riha* is yet another garment worn by married women in the upper part of the body. Like *Mekhela, Riha* was also made of *Eri, Muga, Pat* or mixed yarns. In Goalpara they were coloured and were called *Panchrangi* or five coloured. There were six varieties of *Riha,* namely *Dharidia, Bonkara, Karsipi, Garidia, Paridia and Uka. Dharidia* was made of *Pat* with decorated borders and one-fourth portion from one end was covered with regular diamond and gold coloured twists. This portion hung in the wearer's front side. This was an expensive variety and not meant for common use. *Bonkara riha* was much like *Dhardia* without the coloured portion. *Karsipi riha* had borders of coloured thread and a portion at one end was embroidered. *Garidia* had bright strips running lengthways and crossways. *Paridia* had a mild border line and *Uka* or plain was the simplest of all.[80]

Haliram Dhekial Phukan wrote (1829) that three varieties of silk *dhotis* were woven for use by the well-to-do people. They were known as *Barabhuni, Majubhuni* and *Mahilabhuni.* Very often those were dyed in single or multi colour.[81]

The commercial importance of *Eri, Muga* and *Pat* was well-known to some British traders long before their rule in Assam. Later, some official and non-official Englishmen became interested to learn the craft of rearing but they did not succeed. Within a period of less than two decades from the battle of Plassey, the East India Company looked for expansion of market beyond the borders of Bengal.[82] Broadcloth was an important item of their trade. But unlike other places they found that the demand for broadcloth was low in Assam as a variety of local manufacture existed to resist its sale. They could appreciate the essential value of *Muga* and *Pat* and adopted a policy to encourage production. They visualized a good future for the industry, because Assamese silk cloth had reputation for consistent quality and competitive price.

In 1831, David Scott, Agent to the Governor-General of Fort William, established a factory at Darrang. He introduced reels, reelers and plants of 'morus alba' from Rangpur to expand cultivation and production. But his experiment was not wholly successful.[83] A private company called Lister and Co. made some effort in that direction and engaged an enterprising person named Lepper for the purpose. Lepper took up his residence at north Lakhimpur and developed a farm with the aim of manufacturing *Pat* on a large scale. But shortage of farmhands became an unsurmountable problem and with no alternative before him he was compelled to abandon the enterprise. After giving up the Lakhimpur project, Lister entered into an agreement with a tea planter in Nagaon and made a second attempt. But all their sincerity, drive and care notwithstanding the venture fell through.[84]

Muga did not attract any Englishman. An Assamese entrepreneur of Jorhat, Krishnakanta Gogoi Hatibarua drew up a plan for cultivation of *Muga* on a large scale. He particularly wanted to revive the *Chapa* and *Mezankari* varieties. Accordingly, some villagers of Holongapar *mauza* planted *Chapa* crops and reared worms. But Hatibarua's efforts did not produce the desired results. The cultivation of *Mezankari* had almost entirely fallen into disuse.[85] The disappearence of *Mezankari* silk which caught the fancy of every user was a big loss to the art of weaving in Assam. Some genius might revive it and it would be profitable to do so.

Towards the end of the nineteenth century demand for Assam silk was growing outside and the domestic use of silk became restricted. The external demand increased the price of silk goods. People took to imported cotton goods. They found them cheaper and easily obtainable. Moreover, as export trade brought in quick cash, the businessmen ignored the local demand which was unsteady and conditioned by many factors. The same set of people who collected the silk or silk cloths directly from the producers, and controlled the local market were also making money as exporters. For internal market they were the merchants, for external market they were middlemen. The value of export of silk cloth had gone up to Rs. 3,66,310 in 1897–8.[86]

It is worthwhile to remember that Radhakishore Saraswati, a Bengali businessman of Guwahati took great interest for promotion of silk and *Eri* cloths outside the province. He owned a firm under the style 'M/s R.K. Saraswati & Co.' which sold silk piece good and *Eri.* He not only sold them to traders but also displayed those products in exhibitions outside Assam. He won medals for them. Three such beautiful medals are still in possession of the grandson of R.K. Saraswati. The first medal was awarded to his company in the United Provinces exhibition held in Allahabad in 1910, the second was awarded in the Coronation exhibition at Malda in 1911 and the third, Sivachandra Padak for industrial excellence at Mymensing in 1912.[87]

Yet, successive attempts made by British officers and private entrepreneurs to put Assam silk on the commercial map of the country failed. It failed not because of shortage of labour as it was widely believed. As in the case of tea in Assam and other plantation work elsewhere they could have overcome this problem.

The peasantry in Assam took little interest in raising non-food crop in an organized way. Sericulture was known to them since long but no particular attempt was ever directed to develop it into a distinct branch of cultivation. The people remained similarly indifferent to horticulture. Traditionally silk was a product of leisure of the womenfolk. Though we cannot prove it by empirical data, there can be little doubt that in the 'men induced social conditioning' the womenfolk had but little leisure. They, side by side with the male members of the family, used to participate fully in cultivation. At home, husking of paddy for rice and other quick food was their routine work. The common husking implement was the *dhenki*; hand pounding was also done by the women. Creative leisure for them, therefore, was very limited. The male members of the family were generally callous if not positively hostile to silk-rearing. Their active participation could have ensured the success of silk in Assam.

There was no lack of commercial stimulus for production of silk, but it did not receive much attention from the people. They were unable to stand the occasional uncertainities that silk, a commodity of international market was bound to face. Appearance of sari as substitute wear was not looked upon favourably; yet it set the fashion for some families.[88]

Silk production involved certain risk and larger the production effort bigger was the risk. As it is well-known, the crop either comes forth fully on time or it goes to seed, there is not middle way. So, it could not supersede any other existing crop. Finally, silk rearing required peculiar skill and every hand just could not be good enough. Traditions have it and our personal enquiries have revealed that personal cleanliness of the men or women who are supposed to rear *Eri*, *Muga* or *Pat* worms is the secret of success. Such absolute cleanliness and perfect handling could not be expected from hired hands, more so when their number became numerous. Rearers believe that a single touch of impure body is enough to finish off the whole crop in a week. There is superstitious belief about women rearers who practise some secret crafts to ward off danger to their stock. Very often one could see them talking sweet nothings to the worms. Another striking similarity among them is their form of address; every single worm is addressed as 'rani' or 'queen' though they are supposed to have one 'queen' in a lot. Besides the superstitious crafts, there was a practice of applying a *mantra* for rearing *Muga* worms. The *mantra* is devoid of any esoteric substance; it contains only a story involving the Lord Siva, his consort Parvati and an old man of the Kachari tribe.[89]

Worship of a protector goddess called Kamikshya Devi was practised in the Midnapore district of West Bengal which was an important centre of silk production and silk trade. A poet Sankar by name, composed *Kamikshyar Bondana* in 1737. An edited version of the work shows that the characters of the theme belonged to both the Hindu and the Muslim communities.[90] Absence of scientific knowledge about the cause of recurring diseases of the worms and systematic cultivation of proper food for them made the rearers believe one or the other form of secret art.

Commonality of avocation was an important aspect of weaving in Assam. People belonging to every caste or faith living in Assam were engaged in weaving. The loomshed was as common to every family as the kitchen. The historian Suryya Kumar Bhuyan remarks that it was due mainly to the efforts of the enterprising Ahom official Momaitamuli Barbarua, during the reign of Pratap Singha, that weaving became a household craft. Queen Sarveswari Devi, the consort of Siva Singha is known to have 'admitted the girls of the neighbourhood within the palace enclosures and taught them to spin'.[91]

Weaving talents of the Assamese women received due recognition. Gandhiji's comment on them in *Young India* in 1921, after his first visit to Assam may be repeated. He said, 'Every woman of Assam is a born weaver. No Assamese girl who does not weave can expect to become a wife. And she weaves fairy tales in cloth.' Having seen some patterns in the residence of his host Tarun Ram Phukan, Gandhiji admired their 'matchless beauty' and said, 'as I saw these beautiful patterns, I could not help shedding a silent tear over Indian's past glory and her lost art'.[92]

The Brahmo scholar Sivanath Sastri is said to have remarked during his visit to Assam in the nineteenth century, that it was there in Assam only he found a justification for the alleged derivation of the word 'wife' from 'weave'.[93] The appreciation of the national leaders scores of years ago continues to inspire the weaving industry of Assam.

When everything seemed to have gone out of hand, the *Asom Dipak*, a monthly journal published from Majuli, pleaded with the public, in November 1876, to patronize native manufacture and suggested remedies against the crippling effect of the imported commodities. It called for formation of trading companies by Assamese people, patronization of Assamese shops and use of articles against the foreign ones.[94] But it was no more than a cry in the wilderness.

Lack of enough security of livelihood in the pursuit of the old crafts was the single common factor of decline of the artisanal industries of Assam. Tapan Raychaudhury in his survey of the pre-British non-agricultural production of India has pointed out that 'the Indian artisan lived a life of utter misery, underpaid, flagged and kicked by the minions of nobles and traders alike'.[95] The situation in Assam would not perhaps justify every word of the remark but that there was always a 'downward pressure' on him, as elsewhere, cannot be denied. There is no evidence of any period of buoyancy for any artisanal industry in Assam. Technological innovation could not take place in a politically morbid state. Poverty of the people exercised a brake on demand and poverty of the artisans 'reinforced a culture of hopelessness hardly conducive to innovative efforts'. This dual poverty sucked up the vitality of the industries. The appropriate 'label' for the regressive account of manufacture, according to Raychaudhury is 'industrial involution'.[96] Assam cannot claim any exception. Agriculture involved minimum or no risk for those artisans who were not averse to a new type of physical toil which promised them a sure living. Absence of compulsion to keep up the old crafts facilitated cooperation between crafts and agriculture from the beginning of the British rule. We do not come across any evidence of conversion of artisans into wage labourers. As there was no pressure on land, the causation of this remarkable development could be traced in this specificity.

At this moment one should see if the decline and disappearance of some valuable crafts or fortuitous survival of a few others can be interpreted as incidence of 'deindustrialization'. Under the Ahom rule, there were only a few *khels* (production guild) which were attached to some particular craft or artisanal industry. When the *khel* system broke down, the members were no more under compulsion to stick to it. The new situation gave them freedom of choice. They were not rendered jobless by the decomposition of the system; they took to agriculture, which for many of them was already a subsidiary occupation.

Historically speaking, there was no exclusively industrial population in Assam; it is impossible, therefore, to secure precise information about the size of the workforce, output and market to which any particular craft was related. The workforce involved in crafts like woodcarving and ivory carving was small and crafts like paper making, iron making, gold washing and dyeing, so far as they went, never made vibrant manufacturing. As they belonged to the low productivity area, increase or decrease in output of all these crafts had marginal effect on the economy.

The survival of handloom was significant. There was no noticeable rise or fall in the number of persons engaged in handloom and rearing of *Eri*, *Muga* and *Pat* worms, nor did a fall in output ever led to economic imbalance. There is no evidence, general or particular, to say that people gave up the traditional activity of weaving and worm rearing under some stress and over-crowded in agriculture.

Having been kept, wisely, out of the *khel* system spinning, weaving and worm-rearing became a common household activity. The quantity and quality of the handloom product—whether of cotton, *Eri*, *Muga* or *Pat* depended on the family who owned it. With the progress of monetization, every now and then the primary producers were in for a disappointment when middlemen squeezed the larger part of profit and destroyed their incentive. In spite of such negative pulls, the very nature of its location and operation was a guarantee against fall in employment or in output.

Even though Alexander Tchitcherov has discovered a process of proto-capitalist formation in Bengal, Gujarat, Tamilnadu and Mysore during the eighteenth century, in regions like Assam, Orissa and Rajasthan, he admits, the process was 'slower'. One would better say, it was non-existent in Assam. Out of fifty-one 'large industrial and commercial centres' identified by Tchitcherov, besides 'a multitude of smaller towns', there was not even one to the east of Malda.[97] As there was hardly any scope of money flowing into the world of craft there was no social division of labour and no separation of craft from agriculture in Assam. Where was, then, the locus of deindustrialization?

Nor do we see in Assam any class of merchants, moneylenders and service gentry—the tireless townbuilders of the Ganga Valley fame whose significant role in socio-political transformation throughout a long period of time has been brought to focus by C.A. Bayly.[98] In the absence of these classes Assam was not commercially integrated with the rest of India. Assam experienced the fringe benefits of commercialization only after she came into contact with the British. This might have been preceded by a very low level of border trade with her more backward neighbours.

Tirthankar Roy, in his study of the traditional industry in colonial India—of handloom and weaving, golden thread (*jari*), brassware, leather and carpets, has, on hard evidence, shown the rare adaptability of these carfts to changing situation. Breathing down the neck of advanced technology, the ubiquitous unsettler, market organization and production of these goods are today more secured exactly in those centres where they prospered in pre-colonial days. This implies, paradoxically, that change in productive technology was necessarry for their survival.[99]

Roy argues elsewhere, '. . . a decline in industry due to technological obsolescence always has a beneficial side. When more efficient and productive suppliers drive out the less productive ones, one outcome is a fall in price of the good or service in question. Such a change benefits consumers and raises total demand, even if it hurts the less productive suppliers.'[100]

J. Krishnamurty who studied occupational structure of India of the late nineteenth and early twentieth centuries, is of the view that 'even for the period 1881–1911, the term deindustrialization cannot be applied, for the decline in manufacturing's share in employment occured alongside a rise, relative and absolute, in manufacturing output'.[101]

He also makes use of A. Heston's estimates which shows that 'between 1868–9 to 1872–3 and 1908–9 to 1912–13 real net domestic product (NDP) rose by 53 per cent, while population increased by only 18 per cent'.[102]

Even without colonial hegemony, let us not ignore the fact, the artisanal industry could not hope for better days. The major impediment was, as pointed out by Marx, with some exaggeration, the 'unchanging market'. To generalize his hypothesis Marx went a step farther and invented a stereotype 'the unchangeableness of Asiatic Societies'[103] There lay the necessity of force as an engine of change and Marx had not any doubt that social dialectics itself would produce it. He postulated, 'Force is the midwife of every old society pregnant with a new one. It is itself an economic power'.[104]

NOTES

1. *Monograph on Dyes and Dyeing in Assam*, p. 7. Author, place and year of publication not known (NAI, New Delhi).
2. Albert F. Hill, *Economic Botany*, Delhi, 1983, p. 126
3. M.S. Randhawa, *A History of Agriculture in India*, Delhi, 1982, Vol. II, p. 5.
4. Ibid., p. 273.
5. For information on dyes and dyestuff I had to draw heavily on the *Monograph on Dyes and Dyeing in Assam*. I have also used Pradip Chaliha's monograph *Purani Asamar Karikari Silpa*, Guwahati, 1998, pp. 113–22. For scientific names or other equivalents of words used in this section see P. Chaliha, loc. cit.
6. *Monograph on Dyes and Dyeing in Assam*, op. cit., pp. 48–9.
7. The above account is a brief summary of the preparation method and the description of their use as discussed in the *Monograph on Dyes and Dyeing in Assam*, pp. 9–53.
8. L.P. Vidyarthi, *Art and Culture of North-East India*, Delhi, 1986, pp. 100–1.
9. Quoted in Karl Marx, *Capital*, Moscow (n.d.), Vol. I, p. 406.
10. The situation was discussed by Samman in his *Monograph on Cotton Farbrics in Assam*, Shillong, 1897. Anguish against the lack of popular interest was at first expressed by Kanaklal Barua in an article 'Amar Silpa' in 1890, see *Kanaklal Barua Rachnawali*, Guwahati, 1973, pp. 37–9.
11. For this part I have drawn on
    (i) *Monograph on Wood-Carving in Assam*, Shillong, 1903, by A. Majid.
    (ii) *Monograph on Ivory-Carving in Assam*, Shillong, 1900, by J. Donald.
12. L.P. Vidyarthi, op. cit., p. 101.
13. Report of Annadachuran Bhattarcharji, SDC, Jorhat, quoted in A. Majid, op. cit., p. 12.
14. Naren Kalita, *Bardowar Silpavastu*, Nagaon, 1985, p. 14.
15. In almost all the old *satras* and *namghars* these art objects still survive. See, Birinchi Kumar Barua, *Asamar Loksanskriti*, Guwahati, 1961, pp. 211–12, and K.K. Dasgupta, *Wood-Carving of Eastern India*, Calcutta, 1990, pp. 31–3.
16. A. Majid, op. cit., pp. 3–5.
17. K.K. Dasgupta, op. cit., p. 48.
18. A. Majid, op. cit., pp. 8–9.
19. Fort William (consolidated) Judl. Progs., January 1871, No. 160.
20. For details see B.K. Barua, *Asamar Loksanskriti*, op. cit., pp. 127–40.
21. The building was handed over to the Govt. of Assam on 17 January 1977. Report in *Ajir Asom*, 12 February 1989.
22. H. Barbarua, *Ahomar Din*, Guwahati, 1981, p. 470.
23. J. Donald, op. cit., p. 3.
24. J. Donald, op. cit., p. 1.
25. Ratan Saud, 'Vanishing Craft', *The North East Times*, 24 March 1991.
26. J. Donald, op. cit., p. 2.
27. S. Bhattacharya, 'Eastern India', in *The Cambridge Economic History of India*, Delhi, 1984, Vol. II, Ch. III, pp. 283–4. I find this classification more useful than

the eight-fold classification of R.K. Mukherjee. See, *Economic History of India*, edited by V.B. Singh, Delhi, 1981, pp. 292–6.

28. S. Bhattacharya, op. cit., p. 284.
29. J. Donald, op. cit., p. 2. Also, H. Barbarua, op. cit., p. 471
30. Fort William Revenue Progs., 17 August 1854, No. 15.
31. Ibid., Letter of Major Hannay from Dibrugarh, 7 July 1854.
32. H. Barbarua, op. cit., p. 458.
33. R.B. Pemberton, *Report on the Eastern Frontier of British India*, Guwahati, 1966, p. 84.
34. *Journal of the Asiatic Society of Bengal*, Vol. XXII, 1853 and Kshetradhar Bargohain, 'Asamat Son', in *Awahan*, Vol. 4, 1855 *Saka* (1933).
35. H Barbarua, op. cit., pp. 455–7.
36. Fort William Revenue Progs., August 1854, Nos. 15 and 16.
37. Fort William Revenue Progs., 31 July 1856, Nos. 22 and 23.
38. H. Barbarua, op. cit., pp. 454–5.
39. Kshetradhar Bargohain, op. cit.
40. Ibid.
41. Jagatchandra Dev Goswami, 'Asamat Son', in *Awahan*, Vol. 2, No. 3, 1852 *Saka* (1930).
42. D.R. Gadgil, *The Industrial Evolution of India*, Delhi, 1982, p. 114.
43. See, *The Gold and Silver Wares of Assam: A Monograph* by F.C. Henniker, Shillong, 1905.
44. Ibid., p. 7.
45. *Report on the Census of Assam*, Delhi, 1984, 1901. Subsidary Table VIII, p. 175.
46. Henniker, op. cit., pp. xvi–xvii.
47. Ibid., p. 8.
48. Quoted in Henniker, op. cit., p. 2.
49. Henniker, op. cit., see index pp. xxii–xxiv. I find photographs of some of these ornaments in Birinchi Kumar Barua's, op. cit., pp. 321–3.
50. For the story of decline of the local craft, see, Kanaklal Barua's *Amar Silpa*, in *Rachanawali*, pp. 37–9. H. Barbaruah, op. cit., pp. 460–1.
51. H. Barbarua, op. cit., p. 464.
52. *Monograph on Iron and Steelwork*, Shillong, 1907, p. 1.
53. S Bhattacharya, op. cit., p. 285.
54. Kshetradhar Bargohain, 'Asamar Lorkhani', in *Awahan*,Vol. 4, No. 9, 1855 *Saka* (1933).
55. H. Barbarua, op. cit., p. 466.
56. *Monograph on Iron and Steelwork*, p. 1.
57. Karl Marx, *Capital*, Vol. I, p. 424.
58. *Monograph on Iron and Steelwork*, pp. 3–4.
59. Ibid., p. 5.
60. G.C.M. Birdwood, *The Industrial Arts of India*, London, 1971, pp. 144–53.
61. John M'Cosh, *Topography of Assam*, Delhi, 1986, pp. 61–2; R.B. Pemberton, op. cit. pp. 84-5 and H. Barbarua, op. cit., pp. 471–2.
62. Kshetradhar Bargohain, 'Asamat Baudhadharma Abalambi Shyamjati', in

Chetana, Vol. 1, No. 2, 1841 *Saka* (1919) and Naren Kalita (ed.), *A Descriptive Catalogue of Manuscripts*, Nagaon, 1990, pp. 26–7, 60–1, 68, 69, 92 and 93.

63. Origninally developed by Francois Perroux, S. Bhattacharya makes use of this concept. See, *The Cambridge Economic History of India*, Vol. II, pp. 287–9.
64. Cf. 'Subordination of Native Capital' by S. Bhattacharya, op. cit., pp. 289–95.
65. P.C. Goswami, *The Economic Development of Assam*, Bombay, 1963, pp. 167–8 and *Assam Administration Report 1880–1*, p. 14.
66. For my views on pottery I am indebted to G.C.M. Birdwood's essay on Indian pottery in his *Industrial Arts*, pp. 301–24, Sonaram Chaudhury, 'Matir Saj', in *Awahan*, Vol. 1, No. 9, 1855 *Saka* (1933).
67. Ibid.
68. J.N. Bhuyan, *Uwali Joa Nathir Para*, Nagaon, 1991, pp. 74–5.
69. *Assam Bandhu*, Guwahati, 1984, p. 177.
70. Cf. *Assam Bandhu*, op. cit., p. 186.
71. The production method of each variety was discussed in detail by W. Robinson in his *Descriptive Account of Assam*, Delhi, 1975, pp. 227–34.
72. B.K. Barua, op. cit., pp. 146–53.
73. *Monograph on the Silk Cloths of Assam*, p. 9.
74. Ibid., p. 2.
75. Ibid., p. 18.
76. P.C. Goswami, op. cit., p. 166.
77. *Kanaklal Barua Rachanawali*, op. cit., pp. 37–9.
78. H.K. Barpujari, *Assam in the days of the Company*, Guwahati, 1980, pp. 258, 283.
79. The entire account has been summarised from the *Monograph on the Silk Cloths of Assam*, op. cit.
80. Readers may find some photographs of the products of unforgettable quality in B.K. Barua, op. cit., pp. 299–318.
81. Haliram Dhekilal Phukan, *Asam Buranji*, Guwahati, 1962, p. 106.
82. *Fort William India House Correspondence*, Vol. VI, p. 80.
83. *Monograph on the Silk Cloths of Assam*, p. 1.
84. Ibid., pp. 1–2.
85. Kanaklal Barua, 'Amar Silpa', in his *Rachanawali*, pp. 37–9.
86. *Monograph on the Silk Cloths of Assam*, op. cit., p. 4.
87. I visited the Saraswati family on 16 September 1992. Mr. Tarakishore Saraswati, grand-son of Radhakishore, showed me some papers and all the three medals mentioned.
88. *Kanaklal Barua Rachanawali*, pp. 38–9.
89. Lila Gogoi, *Asamiya Loksahityar Ruprekha*, Golaghat, 1968, p. 14.
90. Tripura Basu, 'Dakhinbange Resamsilpa O Ekti Puthi', in *Akademi Patrika*, Calcutta, 1990, pp. 68–84.
91. S.K. Bhuyan, 'Weaving in Assam', in *Silent Revolution*, Guwahati, 1991, p. 153.
92. Quoted by S.K. Bhuyan, op. cit., p. 152.
93. Ibid.
94. Based on a report prepared by the Deputy Commissioner of Sibsagar (1877) in J. Barua (ed.) *Jorhat 200*, Jorhat, 1997, pp. 392–3.

95. Tapan Raychaudhury, 'Non-Agricultural Production', in *The Cambridge Economic History of India*, Delhi, 1984, Vol. I, p. 297.
96. Raychaudhury, op. cit., p. 307.
97. Alexander I. Tchitcherov, *India: Changing Economic Structure in the Sixteenth-Eighteenth Centuries: Outline History of Crafts and Trade*, 3rd revd. edn., New Delhi, 1998, pp. 142 and 259.
98. See C.A. Bayly, *Rulers, Townsmen and Bazaars: North Indian Society in the Age of British Expansion 1770–1870*, Indian Edition, New Delhi, 1998.
99. See Tirthankar Roy, *Traditional Industry in the Economy of Colonial India*, Cambridge, 1999.
100. Tirthankar Roy, *The Economic History of India 1857–1947*, New Delhi, 2000, pp. 124–5.
101. *The Cambridge Economic History of India*, Delhi, 1984, Vol. II, pp. 540–1.
102. Ibid, pp. 396–401, p. 534.
103. Karl Marx, *Capital*, Vol. I, p. 338.
104. Karl Marx, op. cit., p. 703.

CHAPTER 3

Agriculture and Peasantry

ANANDARAM ON AGRICULTURE: 1853

IN ASSAM, modern 'agrarian thinking' is older than modern agriculture itself. Anandaram Dhekial Phukan (1829–59), as we will see in the course of our study, was a champion of new ideas. He made his mark as a planner and an advanced theorist of agrarian relations. In Bengal, Rammohun Roy 'set a trend of thinking by 1830, which broadly continued till the eighties of the century'.[1] After Rammohun, we are not aware of any Indian, other than Anandaram, in the history of Indian agriculture, who went trumps on the contemporary ideas. He was not an agricultural scientist by training yet he imbibed the true spirit of a scientist and his commitment to the development of agriculture was total. But he did not live long enough to set the stage for improvement.

Among other Indians, Sir Gangaram, Sir M. Visvesvaraya, Maharaja Ganga Sing revolutionized agriculture in India. They were all born in the later half of the nineteenth century.[2]

Anandaram Dhekial Phukan submitted before Moffatt Mills in 1853 that until then 'not the slightest exertions have been made by government to improve the agricultural prospects of the country'.[3] He explained that in Assam the rich and the poor alike were dependent on agriculture. As a down-to-earth realist and an ardent advocate of change, he had almost dogmatized that improvement of agriculture was a sine qua non for a better condition of life of the people of the province. He closely observed and detailed the drawbacks of the prevailing system of agriculture. Anandaram noted, among other things, that the implements of agriculture were 'the rudest', the animals used in the plough were 'the feeblest' and the conditioning and manuring of fields for better harvest were ill understood. He pointed out the ignorance of the peasantry about the good chance 'of the most valuable articles of commerce' which could be grown in Assam with little effort. He also criticized their non-reliance on the methods of irrigation, drainage and embankments. The cultivators rest content with raising a single crop throughout the year. The availability of food-stock was, therefore, necessarily so scanty that the slight vagaries of weather led to famine conditions.[4]

For the improvement of agriculture Anandaram suggested that: (i) the government ought to bring from Europe and upper India a sufficient number of men well versed in the art of agriculture, (ii) every village be furnished from Europe with a supply of the most useful and important agricultural implements and machines, ploughs, harrows, hoes, spades, etc., and (iii) improved breed of cattle, viz., bullocks, etc., from Bengal and upper India. He further solicited government favours for 'a sufficient stocks of seeds, plants and every other species of produce both Indian and European' for distribution in every village.[5]

The zamindari system in the other parts of the country did not meet with his approval; he assumed that the zamindars had not done enough to effect improvement in agriculture.[6] It was possible that as an admirer of the Young Bengal movement, Anandaram was familiar with the views of its journal *Bengal Spectators* which highlighted the misery of the Bengal ryots under the zamindars.[7] Early in 1849, he had an opportunity to observe the zamindari system closely when he was deputed by the government to settle some long pending disputes between the Raja of Bijni and his ryots. He had also seen the resistance of the ryots of the pargana Ghulla against the settlement proposals of the zamindar. By settling the land permanently with zamindars, he held, the government had 'lost all interest in the improvement'.[8] In Assam, the government being in the place of the landholders, any improvement in agriculture would result in a proportionate increase in the government revenue.

Anandaram spelled out that a single year's land revenue would 'enable the government to procure the requisite supply of implements and seeds, etc., and to secure the services of an establishment of agriculturists from Europe and upper India for a period of two years. Should the government be incapable of bearing the entire cost of the project', he declared that the people will gladly share a part of the investment.[9]

We will discuss in Chapter 5 how the progress of England captured Anandaram's imagination. His 'Account of England' published in *Orunodoi* confirms that he was fairly acquainted with the agricultural revolution in England in the eighteenth century.[10] He could not but be aware of the efforts of Marquis of Hastings, Governor-General of Fort William, to protect and improve two important gardens of Saharanpur (U.P.) and Lalbagh (Bangalore). They were later converted into botanical gardens. The Saharanpur garden naturalized many plants from America. 'Some of them were potato, tobacco, pineapple, guava, chillies, papaya, sapota, logwood, mahogany, etc.'[11] They were subsequently introduced in other parts of the country including Assam.

The first government cattle farm of India was established in 1809 at Hissar (Haryana). The breeding of healthy cattle was started there from the year 1815. 'In 1853 it was restricted to the breeding of bullocks for artillery.... The farm also produced siege-trained bullocks and bull for the districts.'[12] With the patronage of Hastings, the Royal Agri-Horticultural Society was founded in 1820. William Carey (1761–1834), the well known name in the missionary history of India, was the founder secretary of the society[13]. Anandaram might have had much admiration for the society which together with its many branches worked for the extension of improved agriculture 'by distributing better seeds, plants, implements and livestock and dissemination of useful information in various parts of India'.[14]

The society imported various types of vegetable seeds from Europe and took steps to popularize them. In 1824 the society imported seeds of spinach, artichoke, asparagus, lettuce, sugar, loaf, parsnip, cabbage, cauliflower, squash, vegetable marrow, brussels sprouts, celery, white beet and garden cress. The seeds were distributed to the branch societies and private growers. The society also introduced improved implements of agriculture. When Anandaram pleaded for European implements, foreign needs, etc., he must have had the activities of the society in mind.

Positive and encouraging results from the improved west Jamuna canal (1820) and opening of eastern Jamuna could not have remained unknown to Anandaram. The Grand Upper Anicut (1844) under the Cauvery Delta Scheme, the Dowleshwaran and the Madduru Anicuts (1848) under the Godavari Delta Scheme were already completed by that time and the construction of the Ganga canal and the Krishna Delta Irrigation Project Works were then in progress.[15] Anandaram naturally thought that similar projects for irrigation and embankments were of equal necessity for Assam. But his suggestions in this regard did not evoke any response. Undaunted, Anandaram carried on, how so ever in a small measure, works for diversion and control of water streams at various places of Nagaon. His determination to go under his own steam emanated from his clear-headed perception. A miss was as good as a mile as we find that no such project was ever undertaken by the British in Assam.

The problem and prospects of agriculture highlighted by Anandaram dominated the agricultural scene of the province during the period of our study. Mills was unable or unwilling to take serious note of the thoughtful suggestions made by a native officer who was less than twenty-five years of age. In such matters Mills appeared to have relied much on his own experience in Orissa and on the opinions of the British officers in charge of the districts. Subsequent experience, however, proved to the hilt that alround development of agriculture in Assam was possible only through endeavours of the government in the direction proposed by Anandaram. Bit by bit his suggestions were carried into effect by the government over a long period of time. Yet for about a century from then, till the end of the alien rule, the impediments identified by him were not fully removed.

THE DISTRICTS

Goalpara was organized into a district as early as 1822 comprising the three thana areas of Goalpara, Dhubri and Karaibari which, until then, formed a part of the district Rangpur. In revenue matters, therefore, the Permanent Settlement Regulation of Bengal was allowed to continue in the newly formed district. The Eastern Duars, comprising Bijni, Chirang, Sidli, Ripu and Guma were attached with Goalpara district in 1864–5. In this part, except Guma, the ryotwari settlement was given to the tenants; in Guma, settlement was given to the jotedars, a section of priviledged tenants. Thus, the temporarily-settled estates in the district included the Eastern Duars and some other smaller estates and the Chars. Rice was the major crop of the district. *Ahu* or *aus* or *bitari*, sown and reaped without transplantation, *bao*, a kind of long stemmed rice, sown and reaped without transplantation but grown only in marshy land and *sali*, or *haimantik* or *aman*, the well-known transplanted crop, all the three varieties of rice cultivation were widely prevalent. Though the actual figures for area and production of different crops are not available, yet it was officially held that in terms of quantity or quality rice cultivation did not signalize progress. Other crops grown in the district were wheat, barley, *sarisa* (mustard), *but* (gram), *kaon*, china, *mug*, *matar*, *til*, *musuri*, *arhar*, *matikalai*, *khesari kalai*, jute, *san* (hemp) and sugarcane.[16]

In Kamrup, all the three varieties of rice noted above were cultivated.

Other crops included Indian corn, mustard seed, *til*, *matikalai*, *mug*, *masuri*, hemp, jute and sugarcane. Cultivation of rice was common to every family engaged in agriculture and between 1850 and 1875 the area of rice cultivation was stated to have increased by 27 per cent. The 'exact return for 1875–6 showed that out of 4,50,792 acres under cultivation, 3,42,481 acres or more than 76 per cent was covered by rice, 24,363 acres by other foodgrain, 55,335 by oil seeds, 3,391 by sugarcane, 2,351 by cotton, 4,515 by tea and 19,352 by other crops'.[17]

In Nagaon also *ahu*, *bao*, and *sali* rice were extensively cultivated. As in Kamrup, acreage of rice cultivation in the district was expanding. In 1870–1 rice cultivation covered 78,373 acres but by 1875–6 it increased by another 38,876 acres. This figure is much lower than 1,31,728 acres shown in the return for the year 1849–50. The formation of the Naga Hills into a separate district and the transfer of some areas to the adjoining district of Sibsagar resulted in the decrease noted earlier. Indian corn was cultivated but not extensively. The Karbis were the main growers of the crop. Besides rice and Indian corn, various kinds of bean, *mati kalai*, *mug*, *khesari*, *musuri*, were also grown. Though the cultivation of jute was well-known, it was not a favourite crop among the peasantry. Rhea or china grass was cultivated by certain sections of people who made use of its fibre for fishing nets.[18] Official records do not suggest the use and cultivation of hemp and flax in Nagaon.

In Darrang *sali* rice was the staple crop. *Ahu* occupied a small percentage of cultivable lands. For sixteen years from 1850 there was a gradual increase in the area under rice cultivation. In 1850 it covered 1,45,109 acres of land and by 1866 it registered a downward trend, in 1870, the area under rice cultivation recorded 2,11,023 acres, the figures further went down to 1,82,172 acres in 1875.

The 'approximate area' under different crops in 1874–5 was as follows: Rice cultivation occupied 1,82,172 acres, mustard 3,644 acres, sugarcane 1,126 acres, *matikalai* 1,828 acres, *mug* 955 acres, *til* 116 acres, cotton 850 acres and jute 184 acres only.[19]

Ahu, *bao* and *sali* all the three varieties of rice were cultivated in the Sibsagar district. Other crops grown in the district were the Indian corn, *matikalai*, *mug*, *khesari*, *miri* or *arhar*, varieties of beans, mustards, sugarcane, jute, rhea grass and cotton. In Sibsagar the state of agriculture was officially described as 'very backward' considering the total area of the district and the area under actual cultivation.[20] It is necessary to record that a terrible murrain told heavily upon the peasant economy of the Golaghat sub-division in 1853–4. Dr. Long, the Civil Surgeon of Sibsagar reported to the government:

> At Kumar Gong, Golaghat and KachariHat I saw the paths and the fields strewn with skeletons. At Kachari Hat, where I found the disease, the air was tainted with the carcasses lying about, so strong was it filled with the effuvia that a copperish taste was very sensibly felt in the mouth in the neighbourhood.... I can state that in some of the homesteads visited by me every head of cattle in the place was attacked.[21]

According to the revenue survey (1875–6) the total area of the Sibsagar district was 2,855 sq. miles and out of this 2,181 sq. miles of land was marked out as cultivable, but the area under actual cultivation was 482 sq. miles, i.e. less than one-fourth of the available land.[22]

Large areas of fertile soil, sparseness of population and their 'excessively indolent habits' characterized agriculture in Lakhimpur. *Ahu* and *sali* were the two important rice cultivation of the district. In the years between 1850 and 1870 production of rice followed a downward curve. One reason for this was 'sacrifice' of agricultural land to tea cultivation. The government could foresee the total unwholesome effect of this trend and tried to improve upon the situation by supplying 'wheat, corolina, paddy, gram, potato and cotton seeds' to the cultivators in 1868 and 1869. As a result of these endeavours, the total acreage under actual cultivation bumped up from 61,490 acres in 1870 to 75,080 acres in 1875. Besides rice, the common pulses of the province, sugarcane, jute, rhea and a few more local varieties of fibres called *bar son barial*, *saru son barial*, *phonput*, *sonput*, etc., some of which had medicinal properties, were also grown by the people.[23]

During 1879–80, Sibsagar and Lakhimpur districts were free from epidemic diseases. But cholera, smallpox and fever finished off a large population in Goalpara and Nagaon. Though the figures for Goalpara are not available in the records, the number of deaths reported in Nagaon was 2,998. The state headquarters, disbelieved the statement and argued that it was 'probably far under the truth'. Cholera took an epidemic form in the Mangaldoi sub-division and the first seven months of the year 1879 as many as 3,342 cases of death were recorded. In Kamrup, cholera claimed 4,086 lives. Inspite of these demographic reverses, except Kamrup, there was neither a fall in land revenue nor contraction of agriculture. Extension of cultivation and assessment of leasehold grants on the expiry of their revenue free tenure led to the increase in land revenue in Darrang, Nagaon, Sibsagar and Lakhimpur. The term of twenty years of revenue-free settlement of land with the former Rajas of Darrang originated in 1859–60 having expired, the entire land was brought under resettlement. The resettlement records revealed that the ex-Rajas of Darrang had already resigned 2,512 acres of waste land to the government and alienated 3,115 acres of cultivated as well as wasteland to others who, again on their part, surrendered 345 acres of wasteland to the government.[24]

In Goalpara extension of cultivation in the Eastern Duars was evidential. Remeasurement of the *mauzas* in Binji and Sidli disclosed that the area under actual cultivation was larger than what had been reported to the government earlier. The revenue demand for the temporary settled estates went up by more than Rs. 10,000 in a single year from Rs. 73,383 in 1878–9 to Rs. 83,512 in 1879–80. The demand for the permanently settled estates remained fixed at Rs. 11,411 less than one-seventh of the amount noted earlier.[25]

The extension of cultivation in the remaining five districts was also significant. Except Darrang, the increase in the number of temporarily settled estates in a single year indicated the settled conditions of rural life. Yet, till then the peasantry by and large preferred short term annual leases to the long term ones. The increase in number of the estates will be found in the statement recorded by the revenue department of the government[26] (see Table 3.1).

In 1880 cholera took a heavy toll of lives in Sibsagar and Golaghat subdivisions. The year was infamous for the virulent form of cattle disease that swept past Cachar in the Barak valley and Darrang and Lakhimpur districts in the Brahmaputra valley. In Cachar the loss of cattle was so devastating that in some places the cultivators had to resort to the use of hoe. The loss in the Brahmaputra valley, as a whole, was inconsiderable and it could not reverse the trend of progress. But it was only an ephemeral respite.[27]

TABLE 3.1

District	*1878*	*1879*	*Increase*	*Decrease*
Goalpara*	14,731	14,485	–	246
Kamrup	137,231	138,826	1595	–
Nagaon	109,007	112,914	3907	–
Darrang	73,315	73,580	265	–
Sibsagar	83,267	86,508	3241	–
Lakhimpur	27,442	30,204	2762	–

Note: *Temporarily settled estates part of the district.

Successive murrains raged the Brahmaputra valley for three years from 1881–2. In 1881–2, a total number of 9,559 heads of cattle perished in Nagaon, 7,098 in Sibsagar. The loss of plough cattle had adversely affected cultivation leading to the impoverishment of the cultivators and drop in government revenue. The mortality of cattle in the Brahmaputra valley, according to the official reports, was 93,494 in 1883–4, it slightly came down to 91,091 in the following year. After a gap of one year cattle disease relapsed again and claimed 87,628 heads in 1886–7.[28]

It may be recalled that the Indian Cattle Plague Commission appointed in 1869 made some important recommendations. But how far those suggestions were taken note of by the local government and to what extent they were made known to the livestock rearers in Assam cannot be ascertained. Allan Octavian Hume, one of the moving spirits of the first session of the Indian National Congress also endeared himself to the Indian peasants by his sincere effort in this regard. Hume 'estimated the average annual loss of cattle in India by preventible cattle disease at fully ten million beasts...'.[29] As in other parts of the country huge loss of cattle was a great drain on the exiguous resource of the cultivator in Assam.

Public health also suffered whacking calamities in the years 1885 and 1886. Its memory went down for every future reference on the subject. Four categories of killing agent were identified, namely cholera, small-pox, fever (kalazar) and bowel complaints. In the Brahmaputra valley districts cholera claimed 3,411, smallpox 936, fever 43,341 and bowel complaints 8,081 lives in 1885. The corresponding figures for the same disease in the following year was 15,975.[30]

We do not have separate account of the ratio of birth and death per mile of population for the Brahmaputra valley for 1886–7. Including Cachar, Sylhet, Khasi and Jantia Hills, the ratio of birth and death in 1886–7 was 'much the same as in 1885–6, viz., birth 27:55 and death 27:77'.[31] Taking into consideration the official reports for the districts outside Assam proper on the general condition of public health we may conclude that the rate of death in the six districts was higher than the rate of birth.

DYNAMICS OF COTTON AND JUTE

The government made some effort to popularize the cultivation of cotton in Assam. By that time cotton had become a commercially important fibre crop in the western part of India. Though the use of cotton was well-known, its cultivation in the plain districts of Assam was almost nil. The hill tribes used to carry them down in the dry season and barter them for goods from the plains.[32]

The Cotton Committee constituted by the Agri-Horticulture Society (1820) found that the cotton grown in India was of inferior quality. From 1830 they started importing better seeds from America, Bourbon and Mauritius. The Englishmen were enthused by the very successful experiment of growing American cotton in Dharwar region of the Bombay Presidency. As a commercial crop it became popular with the peasants and acquired the brand name 'American Dharwar'.[33] In November 1857 the government collected four bushels of Brazilian and American cotton seeds for trial in Assam. The seeds were distributed among some English tea planters and local cultivators. Only the cultivators of North Kamrup, Darrang and the hill portion of Nagaon took interest in the cultivation of cotton. J.S. Ridsdale, a tea planter from Najira reported that although the seeds germinated well in their nursery he did not see any prospect of cotton in Sibsagar as he heard many cultivators say '*Kapahe pet Nabhare*'—cotton is no food.[34] That seemed to have been the general attitude of the cultivators.

The Secretary of State for India and the Viceroy in India were under pressure from the Manchester lobby to accelerate production and raise the supply of cotton to Britain. Manchester could no longer rely on the regular supply of cotton from America as that country was straining under the wounds of the civil war.[35] Moreover, the British merchants could obtain cotton from India at a cheaper rate. In a despatch dated 9 April 1870 to the Secretary of State, the Governor-General and Viceroy reported, 'Large sums were spent in former years, in attempts to improve its cultivation but with little useful result, owing to the mistaken system under which they were made. So, the home government was assured of renewed attention.'[36] The effect of the British cotton hunger was also felt in Assam. After three years, cotton cultivation covered 5,074 acres of land in Nagaon, the highest area in the province, Kamrup came second with 2,351 acres, Darrang and Lakhimpur had 850 acres each under cotton in 1874–5.[37] They seemed to have been the record figures.

Cotton cultivation in the Brahmaputra valley started dwindling and within next twenty years its cultivation in the valley as a commercial crop lost importance. It was continued in the hills portion of the Nagaon district, now called Karbi Anglong and the Garo Hills district, now under Meghalaya. The administration report for 1897–8 enlisted cotton as an article of import.[38] The export of cotton as recorded in the *Provincial*

Gazetteer of Assam, 1906, was based solely on the production in the hill areas noted above.[39] The disinclination of the cultivators to grow cotton was caused by two factors: the centre of cotton industry was Bombay and there was no easy communication with that city from Assam. The distance was done down by other attendent disadvantages, like transport cost, uncertainity of profit, etc. Secondly, the direct boost for production of a particular crop came from the local Marwari traders. There was no other agency to make for the stability of production of cotton which, besides strengthening a growing domestic industry could have been more profitable than jute. In fact, during the years 1880–95 cotton industry maintained an unwavering progress. The cotton mills employed 61,596 persons in 1884–5. Their number increased to 1,39,578 in 1894–5, whereas jute mills employed 51,902 and 75,157 persons respectively in the years noted above. Moreover, from a commercial point of view, jute was a fluctuating crop and compared to cotton, the demand for the products of jute industry was less stable.[40] But the peasants could have had no choice of their own. They merely responded to an external stimulus.

The necessity of a commercial crop was as much pressing for the traders as it was for the cultivators. Cotton proved to be an illusory charmer, jute seduced the cultivators of Assam. The cultivation of jute marked the beginning of regional specialization of agriculture in Assam.

The importance of jute as a cash crop became apparent in the last quarter of the nineteenth century. The use of jute for various domestic purposes like making of rope, twine, etc., was known in Assam but it was not quite extensive. With the growing facilities of river-borne trade, the Marwaris developed interest in this article of trade. Jute was grown more or less in all the plain districts of Lower Assam. Goalpara was the largest producer of jute. Its cultivation in the western part of the district spread only after 1881. By that time Bengal had already established itself as the largest producer of jute. By 1885, twenty jute mills were set up and jute industry acquired much importance. All jute mill owners then were Englishmen and they converted either side of the Ganga, from Calcutta to Chinsurah into the 'Dundee of Bengal'. Increasing jute production in Assam helped to get the best of it.[41] Thus, cotton failed in Upper Assam, jute triumphed in Lower Assam.

In 1897, the area under jute cultivation in the six districts of Assam was recorded as:

Goalpara	35,000 acres
Kamrup	400 acres
Nagaon	300 acres
Darrang	200 acres
Sibsagar	150 acres
Lakhimpur	100 acres[42]

The largest quantity of jute was exported from Goalpara. Boats carrying jute were usually registered at Sukchar and Manikchar, below Dhubri. Some boats left the district via Godadhar and Sankos rivers and avoided registration. Jute grown in some area like Jamadar Hat and Manikchar had specialities that attracted the traders.[43] We quote the figures of export of jute from Assam for some select years[44] (see Table 3.2).

These figures show that the export of jute was growing steadily. More export denoted more production, and more production indicated expansion of agriculture and a flow of immigration. Jute minimized the importance of mustard as a commercial crop, nontheless it paved the way for commercialization of agriculture in Assam. The sandy riverine land in Lower Assam which was very sparsely cultivated came under jute cultivation permanently.

It has already been noted that some boats escaped registration, so the actual quantity of jute exported from the valley was higher than these figures. The record of the steamer agent at Guwahati shows the following figures in *maunds*:

1894–5	51 *mds.*
1895–6	1,702 *mds.*
1896–7	982 *mds.*

But the volume of export in *maunds* from Barpeta during the same years was higher and on the ascending order:

1894–5	1,022 *mds.*
1895–6	1,228 *mds.*
1896–7	1,743 *mds.*[45]

The climate of Assam, the large tracts of sandy alluvium on both sides of the Brahmaputra, facilities for steeping the mature crop to extract the fibre and for conveyance by boats and steamers, all combined to give impetus to jute cultivation and trade. Compared to rice or *matikalai*, jute required more labour. The agriculture department thought that shortage of labour might pose a problem. It was mostly the Muslim cultivators of Bengal who excelled in growing jute.

In Bengal jute was grown in two types of land, high and dry tracts where the crop was immune from the routine damage by floods and the deltaic alluvious. Though jute cultivation and trade took firm roots in the province they did not extend over the hilly tracts. As labour was more expensive in Assam, the cost of jute cultivation was higher than that of Bengal. Unless the cultivator did it himself, engaging hired labour even at the final stage of harvest left no profit for him. The Assamese peasantry till the 1890s remained by and large unresponsive to the growing importance of jute as a cash crop. A government official bewailed, 'It cannot be predicted that, by putting a few days extra labour in the year, he could double his income from land by substituting jute for *Ahu* rice.'[46]

It was the understanding of the government that traders might advance money to the ryots on jute as they did in case of mustard, but the system of giving advances on jute crop was 'apt to lead to numerous evils, and should, therefore, always be deprecated'. The state government strove to spread the cultivation of jute but at the same time they saw to it that the production of food grain did not fall. The government ultimately came to the conclusion that without immigration and reclamation of waste land there was slight prospect of jute growing in Assam.[47] Encouragement to immigration of Muslims into Assam from the eastern districts of Bengal was carefully given on this consideration. They are the unsung heroes of reclamation and agricultural recycling. Within a short period they improved the mode of agriculture in Assam.

The Government of India was too eager to ensure export of agricultural commodities to Britain. The opening of the Suez Canal in 1869 reduced the export cost of goods to England by 30 per cent per cubic ton. This stepped up the export of mainly three products—cotton, rice and wheat. Assam was geographically not suitably located to take advantage of the situa-

TABLE 3.2

Years	*From the Brahmaputra valley (in maunds)*
1880–1	59,249
1885–6	1,63,185
1890–1	2,25,742
1895–6	2,79,113
1896–7	3,48,332

tion. The taxation policy of the government was framed to boost export. Until the end of the First World War almost all agricultural commodities except rice enjoyed exemption of export duties. Absence of such duty on jute till 1922 kept the operational cost of the traders at the minimum.[48] So, production loan for jute was no problem even in the rural areas.

MAUZADAR: A MIXED BLESSING

The ryotwari system where each cultivator could hold land as a separate estate under the government seemed to have had given impetus to the peasantry. The condition of peasantry in the permanently settled estates was far from satisfactory. The zamindars could not gear up the peasantry in the prevailing set up and usually they implored the government to grant them remission. Upon enquiry the government was constrained to give them large remissions almost every year.

The network of revenue collection which was evolved for the temporary settled areas worked well. Land assessment and proposals for settlement were made by the mandals who, in those days, were appointed by the mauzadars. The monthly salary of a mandal in 1880–1 was Rs. 6. As a matter of policy, the mauzadars were appointed from among the rich and respectable families of every district. Though they had their own tale of woes, they were men of consequence in the society. As commission agents they had a fair income to lead a comfortable life. There was not any fixed size of a *mauza*, so there was no fixed commission. Understandably, as a class of gentry they had to keep up a uniform appearance, which all of them could not afford from their real income. As a result, there were financial bunglings and discrepancies of record. The District Collectors were equally unsparing and dismissal was a frequent punishment meted out to the mauzadars. Their total number in 1880 was 345, next year it came down to 340.[49]

Let us take a glimpse at the position of the mauzadars in so far as their monthly commission was concerned. Our statement shows the number of mauzadars and the amount received by them as commission during 1881 (see Table 3.3).

Of the 57 mauzadars whose income from commission was less than Rs. 20, 37 belonged to the Lakhimpur district. As commission agents the mauzadars belonged to different categories. More than half of them enjoyed respectable social power; a substantial section of the rest were somewhat better than peasant cultivators. In between, a good many

TABLE 3.3

Number	*Amount of commission*
200	Rs. 50 or more
30	above Rs. 40, but less than Rs. 50
25	above Rs. 30, but less than Rs. 40
28	above Rs. 20, but less than Rs. 30
57	less than Rs. 20[50]

mauzadars enjoyed both power and material benefits but suffered from a remarkable sense of inferiority when compared with and confronted by the higher mauzadars.

THE RICH AND THE POOR: FACE TO FACE

D.R. Gadgil suggested that three things, namely, the area under cultivation, the nature of the crops grown and the extent of the livestock may be accepted as 'the best standards of agricultural prosperity'.[51] But unfortunately, available statistics with regard to those standards were unsystematic and indefinite. However, they are suggestive of the broad trends of changes that were taking place. A systematic compilation of the agricultural statistics was started in our country only in the wake of the Famine Commission.[52]

The Famine Commission also issued a questionaire to the Government of Assam on 22 June 1878. The Government of Assam sent their reply to the Secretary, Famine Commission on 8 March next year. The report gives us more or less a total picture of the state of agriculture in the province. Though it was based on reports from the Deputy Commissioners of the districts, the correctness of the number of women in the families was, in any case, doubtful. Husbandman found no reason to conceal anything about his economic status but he would hardly let any government agency know about the exact number of the female members in the family.[53]

The few instances listed below would help to form an idea about the peasant holdings.

One Bhogram Medhi of Nagaon was an example of a rich cultivator who owned 48 *bighas* of land. His family consisted of twelve male members and at least four female members. After paying Rs. 27–12–3 as rent, he could spend Rs. 15 for hired labour and Rs. 40 for other necessities annually for things not produced on land. Owner of 40 bullocks, cows and goats, his movable property was valued at Rs. 300. Bhogram was free from any debt and he spent his surplus in ornaments and marriage ceremonies. Likewise, Nambari Sarma supported his twelve-member family with the income derived from his land measuring 35 *bighas*. He had to depend solely on hired labour for his work in the field. He spent Rs. 80 for hired labour and owned 52 cattleheads. He incurred no debt.

Ponaram Gogoi of Cherekapar, under Changmai *mauza*, Sibsagar owned 16 *bighas* of land and paid Rs. 10–6–0 as rent. The total number of members of his family including women was seven. Ponaram was an opium addict and admittedly, out of Rs. 90 which he spent annually for his family, Rs. 68 was spent on opium. He incurred debt. Kinaram Ahom of the same locality who owned 35 *bighas* of land maintained his fourteen-member family without incurring debt. He spent his surplus on marriage ceremonies and annual feast. Joga Dom of Jogania *mauza* was an example of a resourceful husbandman. He had 17 *bighas* of land and paid Rs. 10–2–0 as rent. He supported his ten-member family by earning extra income by leasing opium *mehals*. He had bullocks, buffalos, çows and a pony. For his farm and opium *mehals* he spent Rs. 193 for hired labour. The annual feast which he offered cost him not more than Rs. 11. He declared to have earned a net annual profit of Rs. 45.

Sukura of *mauza* Lakhimpur Sadiya was an example of a poor cultivator. Owner of 9 *bighas* of land, he could not support his four-member family from the income of his land. He had to earn extra income by selling his labour as a coolie or a carrier. Similarly, Poali of Modukhat *mauza* and Muruli of Tengakhat with 12 and 17 *bighas* of land respectively, incurred debts for marriage, purchase of bullocks, etc.[54]

The statistics of a few typical cultivators mentioned earlier do not admit of any definite conclusion. These select cases might have been presented to show that by and large the peasantry was contented and there was no cause for anxiety. Even though we may discount part of these favourable statements the life and conditions of Sukura, Poali and Muruli were better and tolerable compared to the plight of the marginal peasants in other parts of British India. Generally speaking, sight of emaciated cultivators like Hasim Shekh and Rama Kyborta or Poran Mandal, the apocryphal discoveries of R.C. Dutt and Bankim Chandra Chatterjee was a rarity in Assam.[55]

Let us remember that while talking about the 'profusion of blessings' of British rule, R.C. Dutt alleged that the ryots of Bengal were totally denied of those advantages.[56] But in Assam, in the absence of any single class of people to appropriate to itself whatever benefits the British rule could ensure, the peasantry had a fair share of them.

Nonetheless, the Assam Government report clearly sounded that in the event of a famine really breaking out, the north bank of the Brahmaputra, the north Cachar area and the hill portions of the Nagaon district would fall easy victim of it. The government opinion was never put to test as no famine broke out in Assam in the years that followed.

Those statistical accounts apart, the report is a mine of information. As stated earlier, rice still constituted the main food crop grown in the province, *matikalai*, *mug*, *kalamah*, and *masur dal* were also grown extensively.

Use of manure was known to the cultivators but they made limited use of it. Generally, sugarcane was manured. In Nagaon the growers used to manure tobacco. With no scarcity of cultivable land the peasants did nothing to increase the productivity of the land. Though area under cultivation was growing in all districts of the valley, the average productivity stagnated. As a result, there could have been no improvement of the peasant lot. They were used to produce the same crop from the same land annually; they were not accustomed to rotation of crop. Reclamation of *chapari* land was started about this time. But the effect of reclamation in one place was almost neutralized by resignation of land in another place. Yet the reclamation was welcome for the value of the produce of the land so reclaimed.

Reclamation of land was necessary for expansion of cash crop. In Nagaon *chapari* lands were in plenty and the cultivators thought that after the second or the third harvest the land became exhausted and was therefore allowed to remain fallow for the next two or three years.[57] The *char* areas of the Brahmaputra were brought under cultivation in the mid sixties of the nineteenth century. Cultivation of mustard seed in the *char* lands was remunerative. Jute substituted mustard seed in the *char* lands only after two decades. Cultivation of mustard seed was encouraged by the Marwari traders. They gave seed and cash in advance to the cultivators who were too willing to receive them even under bad terms of debt as it was the only cash crop in those days.[58] Without being sure of profit in such a pursuit the merchants were unlikely to make an investment. This became a common feature in all the important stations.

The scales were therefore tipped against the peasantry. As neediness was their common characteristic, the growers of cash crops were unable to hold out for a better deal. Moreover, the small unit growers had no source of market information, which, many years later, became the guiding factor for them. The question of 'forced commercialization' in agriculture in Assam could be examined in the light of some later developments from the thirties and not earlier.[59]

The productiveness of the people engaged in agriculture in Assam has had not been studied with scientific precision. But indolence, incapacity and inanity of the cultivators, real or otherwise, had been the refrain of administrators and social thinkers. Karl Marx argued that the 'productiveness of labour is fettered by physical conditions' like the bodily constitution of the man himself and the surrounding nature-fertility of soil and natural wealth in the instruments of labour such as wood, metal, coal, etc. When nature is bountiful she 'keeps him in hand, like a child in leading-strings'. It is nature again which kills his initiative to develop himself. Marx added, 'It is not the tropics with their luxuriant vegetation, but the temperate zone, that is the mother country of capital.'[60]

In the light of these formularies we may try to understand the working habit of the peasantry in Assam. R.B. Pemberton and William Robinson made a thorough study of the 'extraordinary fertility' of the soil in the province.[61] John M'Cosh too averred that the soil was very responsive to cultivation, and amply repays any labour and expense bestowed upon it by producing abundant crops.[62] Obviously, the traditional cultivation did not impose any hard work on the cultivators. It was not the necessity of hard work but the absence of it which fouled up everything. Thomas Mun, a London merchant observed that natural wealth in means of subsistence 'make people careless, proud and given to all excess' and natural wealth in the instruments of labour 'enforceth vigilancy, literature, arts and policy'.[63] In such a classification Assam could be placed in the first category. The life of the peasantry was easy and idyllic. They were hardly willing to get out of their groove, a structured inertia was the common trait of their life. As a class they had no passion for affluence, far less of better social tastes.

Pressure for revenue gave them a jolt. Agriculture was their only source of income. The traditional produce did not leave much surplus income. Soon the peasants found that cultivation of cash crop was the only answer. Mustard seed was the number one cash crop, jute came second and cotton a distant third. Cotton was later substituted by sugarcane. They found that possession of money could provide solution to all their worldly problems.

Dhan that is money enriched the Assamese vocabulary itself. New words, idioms and proverbs connected with money came into existence. The omnific power of money became apparent. The wisdom expressed itself in the adage '*Dhan hale son hai*'—'When you have money you can have gold'. It implies that any work can be done by means of money. People soon realized, '*Dhanei dharmar mool, dhan nahale jai jati kul*'—

Money is the root of all virtues and without money it is difficult to protect the purity of caste. They abused those who could not make proper use of money. The skinflints were said to have amassed money only to construct funeral parlour—'*Dhanere marisali saja*', they said. They looked at that with idle lust but never knew their onions. The first ever poem on money in Assamese was published in the summer of 1885. The poem *Dhan* shows the magic power of money in society. The next poem *Toka* came out after two months in the same journal. The poet declared that money, the most covetable and elusive thing of this world, is the root of many social ills.[64]

The poor were puzzled by the incomprehensible movement of money. They fretted at it saying '*Dhanalai dhane khede*', 'Money begets money'. They even suspected that money encouraged vice.

We are unable to offer any single economic explanation of stratification in peasant society. Surplus appropriation is no adequate answer. Prosperity depends more on habit and social environment than on any fortuitous factor. Low productivity in agriculture, imperfect land–labour ratio, lack of education and ideas, absence of creative drive, distance from the trading world were some of the reasons of general, perpetual poverty. The exceptions justified their exceptional ability and took full advantage of the institutional changes. More often than not they tended to go overboard and abused the system. There was no magic solution to the disparities. The result was multi-level stratification and persistence of poverty.

Introduction of cash crop was also the beginning of stratification of the peasantry in the Brahmaputra valley except the permanently settled areas of the Goalpara district where the original sin was the zamindari system. The stratification that was certain but not always sharp until the beginning of the twentieth century, was a complex process and the causative factors were also changing. Ownership of land itself was of little consequence for the peasantry. They were not willing to possess a single slice of unproductive land under revenue assessment.

They preferred short-term lease of land only to avoid tax on unremunerative land. Possession of such land was thought to be an act of folly. In the pre-British days there really existed various sizes of land-holding which continued uneffected. But consequent to the new revenue assessment, a bigger land-holding was very often considered a burden and not a benefit. Immoderate use of opium by a large section of peasant population made them an incorrigible disclaimer of economic motivation. Other common factors like foreign rule, lack of capital, lack of man-power and health, lack of honest administration, an exploitative land system, inheritance law, etc., came into play subsequently.[65]

AGENTS OF DESTRUCTION: *JUI, PANI, YUIN*

We have no doubt that an individual peasant economy was very often put down by fire accidents. But we are unable to produce hard evidence to show its magnitude. Together with epidemic, murrain and natural calamities the role of fire has to be taken note of seriously. Fire was a major destroyer of wealth in Assam. Racial memory has it that *jui, pani, yuin* (fire, water and white ants) were the three calamitous agents of undoing every single reserve of private wealth. In a moment we shall show that incidents of fire devastation were quite widespread but the reports that came in for the source of our information, mainly, the journal *Orunodoi* were all related to incidents at different towns and involving leading persons, bazaars and government offices. There is no reason to believe that fire accidents were confined to the towns because published accounts are silent about similar accidents in the rural areas. Those calamities went unreported and were hardly taken of note by the administration. In a situation where hundreds upon hundreds of peasants fell in arrears of land revenue and had, at times, forfeited their possessions for want of paltry sums of revenue, the impact of a single sweep of fire destruction can be more truly conjectured than accurately proved. Even within living memory, the sight was not uncommon where fire destruction had rendered many people homeless. Usually, fire was the result of some accident, but it could not be generalized. Crime records and contemporary accounts are present to inform us of the human role in making catastrophic use of it by one against the other.

In the absence of any systematic account of destructions by fire, we could cite a few example from the available records to explain our point. On the night of 12 June 1846, some miscreants set fire to the *gola* of Nandaram Keya at Sibsagar town. The fire could not be contained and as a result four *golas* were completely gutted.[66] During the Doljatra festival at Guwahati in March 1849, a spark from a cracker spread into a devastating fire and destroyed the residence and property of Rabindra Barua, Parbatia Phukan and their neighbours.[67] Another conflagration on 25 October 1849 gutted the Guwahati market.[68]

In early March 1853, there had been incidents of fire devastation continuously for six days from 17 to 22 *Phalgun* in different parts of Guwahati. On 20 *Phalgun*, the house of Balram Phukan, a leading personality of the town, caught fire which destroyed everything. The loss was estimated at Rs. 10,000. A casket containing articles of diamond, pearl, gold and silver was also stolen during the tumult.[69]

A series of fire accidents next month at Guwahati frightened people out of their wits. On 3 April a fire originating at Latasil market completely destroyed the market besides the residence of Ram Charan Sheristadar. After five days another fire at the same place burnt away everything of Nandiram Barua, Gera Bamun and their neighbours. On the night of 13 April, the residence of Manu Deka was wiped out. On 16 April, the house of Nilakanta Choladhora Phukan Sangmai caught fire. The British officer at the Guwahati Civil Station, with the help of his attendants and other persons tried to save as much as he could from fire. But the fire blazed up with a strong surface wind and reduced more than a hundred houses to ashes. Besides the loss of huge government property, Choladhora Phukan, Nityananda Phukan, Bidyadhara Pandit, Bhisma Sanjtola and others lost all their property.[70]

The house, goods and chattels of Urbidhar Barua were burnt down on the night of 16 March 1854 at Jorhat. After four days, Purna Sehanobis of Amolapatty, Sibsagar suffered the same fate. In June that year fire destroyed the grocery shop of Loma Kotai and the house of Sasadhar Daroga. On the Diwali night of 21 October 1854 the *gola* of Hunatram Keya caught fire, spread to the neighbourhood and reduced twelve *golas* of the locality to ashes.[71]

In April 1885, except three or four houses, the entire town of Dhubri was destoryed by fire. The schools, offices, Circuit House, government bungalows, the beautiful private houses—all were grist to the fire-mill.[72]

Fire research in our country was still a distant dream. We do not know what measures were taken by the government towards fire protection. No John Bull could have ignored the lesson of British history that the Great Fire of London in 1666 was one of the causes of Clarendon's unpopularity which led to his dismissal and impeachment. Samuel Pepy's *Diary* written between 1660 and 1669, published after more than a century and a half, in 1825, records his account of the Great Fire in London. '... So near the fire as we could for smoke; but all over the Thames, with our faces in the wind, you were almost burnt with a shower of fire drops....' We have not come across such an account of a fire accident in Assamese literature. But we can bring in a reliable image from the great novelist Saratchandra Chottopadhyay. In his novel *Grihadah* (House-Burning, 1917) we find:

Within a few moments it seemed as if he saw the end of the world. He jumped from the bed, opened the door, came out and saw that one side of the verandah of the kitchen and the room where Achala was sleeping that night blazed up. The flakes of fire leapt up high and reddened up the whole blackberry tree above them. When a thatched house catches fire in a village, it is sheer madness to make an attempt to douse it and nobody dares. People of the neighbourhood run about frantically to remove their belongings and livestock to safety and those away from it huddle up, the men on one side, the women on the other, express their vicarious grief, discuss the cause of the fire, enthusiastically assess the quantity of loss and keep watching until everything is burnt to cinders.[73] [translation ours]

Such tragedy occured hundreds of times and over hundreds of places. Fire, a hungry maw of misery consumed everything, including the proof of its consumption. Of all the three agents, fire was the most destructive.

Flood of varying intensity was almost an annual occurance of the rainy season. It is likely that people used to adjust themselves with it and it is no exaggeration to say that they learnt to live amphibiously. Blights, floods and drought resulted in considerable fall of harvest at times.

Of all the districts Lakhimpur was prone to regular and excessive floods. From 1852 onwards protective embankments were constructed by the government. Yet, at no time flood damage could lead to a famine situation. Floods in Kamrup never gave cause for anxiety. Setting up of some ten embankments by the government proved useful. There was a growing demand for such protective measures. In Kamrup, it was officially stated that the demand for labour was so much larger than the supply that famine could threaten the district only if 'at least three-fourths' of the principal crop got wasted by some calamity. Counteracting influences of flood and drought 'kept the district of Goalpara free from the scourge of famine. In Darrang, any fear of a famine due to flood or drought was 'inconceivable'.[74]

The district of Sibsagar experienced severe drought in 1857, 1870 and 1872 which had adverse effects on farm output. What was more feared by the administration, was not drought but the annual occurance of flood which could have led to famine situation.[75]

Though not directly connected with peasant economy alone, the earthquake of 12 June 1897 deserves a brief mention. Its memory as '*Bor Bhuikamp*'—the great earthquake, is said to have overshadowed the history of the administration of the year in all departments.[76] The earthquake occured after five in the afternoon. It was a repeated reference point for many decades to come.

In the administration report the impact of the earthquake was recorded thus:

> there was sharp vibration accompanied by a loud rumbling noise.... In the plains large tracts of land subsided and were covered with sand, the river banks crumbled and fell into the river, and the beds of the water. All masonry buildings within the area of extreme incidence were completely wrecked and bridges were shattered. Embanked roads were broken up like ploughed fields, and in many places subsided to a level with the adjoining country.[77]

The recorded number of deaths, including Sylhet and the hill districts as a result of the earthquake was 1542 which, even by the government's own admission, must be considerably 'below the truth'. R.B. M'Cabe of the Indian Civil Service died in the capital town of Shillong when the house he was in crumpled at the shock of earthquake. The 'gloomy accounts' of public health began to pour in there from all the districts. The flood that followed the quake damaged large areas of crops. The loss in the tea gardens as a whole, was minimal. 'But from whatever point of view it may be regarded, the losses sustained by the people of Assam in consequence of the earthquake must be considered to be immense, and among the wealthy and comparatively well-to-do the loss and suffering were acute.'[78]

Though most people suffered damage caused by white ants a few of them bothered to leave record of that menace. John M'Cosh left us a telling account of the white ants. For him it was a veritable 'plague'. He noted,

> white ants occupy a prominent place in the annual economy of Assam. In no part of India their ravages are more destructive, they devour the very house as they stand, from the main posts sunk seven feet under ground, to the last bundles of thatch upon the ridge.... The furniture required to be constantly looked after, the feet of a table or a chair may be eaten up though no outwards signs be discernible.

Observation by a British lady stationed at Lucknow and a news item published in *The Englishman* would make interesting reading. The British lady observed,

> The white ant is a cruel destroyer of goods where it has made its domicile, a real misfortune may be considered to have visited the house. They are the most destructive little insects in the world doing as much injury in one hour as a man might labour through a long life to redeem.

The port trustees of Bombay had tough time in tackling invasion of white ants. The port engineer found that if they were destroyed in one place soon they appeared in a different place. They could even drill holes through lime.[79]

Government officials took note of the damage of crops caused by locust. Occasionally the locusts made their appearance in alarming proportions. For example, in 1822, 'there was a wholesale destruction of harvests by locusts' in the district of Nagaon resulting in scarcity of food.[80] The ravage was not confined to the crops alone, the locusts ate up the leaves of all fruit and other trees which they found before them. A second blight was noticed in 1840. The third blight occured in 1858 when the ravage of locusts was aggravated by the appearance of other insects as well. Broods of locusts were noticed in the districts of Goalpara and Lakhimpur in 1863 but the damage they caused was negligible.[81]

It is a happy thing to recall that the province of Assam was unheard of in the annals of famine in India. But famine conditions were not wholly unknown. For instance, in 1858 a famine situation developed in Nagaon where crop failure due to drought in the previous year was aggravated by ravage of locusts and other insects. Those who had paddy in their store were unwilling to release their stock speculating higher price. But the government forced them to sell their stock. The time went down in public memory as *Bharal-Bhanga-Bachar*, the break-open-granary year.[82]

The weight of the great famine of 1865–6 in central and south India was felt all throughout the length and breadth of the country. The situation was worst in Orissa. Recalled by posterity as the *Na-anka-kala*, the contemporary historian Pyare Mohan Acharya left an account of the horror of the scene there. In Assam, of course, the impact was almost inconsequential. In the wake of the famine rice was selling at a price in Kamrup, Sibsagar and Nagaon. That was not due to any shortage of food but because of export to the deficit areas elsewhere.[83] There was an-other famine situation in the district of Kamrup in 1901. The ruler of Dwar-bhanga, Maharaja Rameshwar Singh donated Rs. 3,000 to the government towards relief of the people.[84] The Maharaja was then on a visit to the Kamakhya temple. He made liberal donations for other purposes also. The government and other sources were totally silent about the number of people, if any, mortally affected by the famine conditions noted earlier. Famine often leaves some people unaffected, the famine of 1770 in Bengal is a case in point. Though 'at least one third of the inhabitants of Bengal perished' in that famine, the cultivators were least affected by it.[85] In Assam, scarcity of milder intensity could not have taken toll of any life.

Until 1868 bullock carts were not known in Assam. Gradually, they came into use all over the Assam valley. Soon it was found that the local bullocks were not fit for carrying carts and so cart bullocks had to be imported. Bullocks from North-West Provinces were generally preferred in Assam. They were imported in the dry season and concentrated in some select *hats* of the districts.[86]

PEASANTS' PROTEST

Though a quarter of a century passed since Moffat Mills made his observations, the provincial government did not depart an inch from their point of view. 'The apathy of the people and not the want of land or poverty of the soil, is the cause of the backward state of agriculture in Assam' they maintained. The government was of the view that:

> the Assamese cultivator is very well off, and does not, probably work during the year two-thirds of the time that a Bengali or a Bihari cultivator will do.... There is little actual poverty in the Province, land is to had [*sic*] in abundance...the revenue assessment is light, and prices of labour rule high. The wants of people are few and their habits are not extravagant, but they are as a class improvident, and the consumption of opium induces indolent habits.[87]

These statements do not show what exertions were made by the government to improve upon the admittedly 'backward state of agriculture in Assam'. That large extent of land lay waste was true, but that was not always the sequel of 'apathy' of the cultivators. Demographic reverses due to epidemics and the huge loss of livestock due to recurring murrains told heavily upon the peasant economy. The *Assam-Bandhu* (1885) seems to corroborate certain views of the government. The journal held that in Assam land was fertile, the revenue was low and utilization of land here did not require high expenses as in the neighbouring state of Bengal. It further said that the population of Assam then stood at about twenty lakhs and by reclaiming waste jungle lands, a population twice that number could be maintained and enriched.[88]

We come across other point of view also. In an article in *Mau* (1886–7) a journal known for its well-informed and moderate views, the agriculture department of the government was criticized for its inactivity. It was alleged that scarcity of water was an impediment of agriculture in the state. But there was not even the slightest effort from the government to provide irrigation facilities to the peasants. Irrigation system by then became extensive in the western part of the country. Though it appreciated the government policy of importing bullock for the state it did not condone the impassivity of the directorate of agriculture. It was even argued that the abolition of the directorate would only benefit the state exchequer and 'it would be no loss for our ryots'.[89]

Facts do not bear out the repeated assertion of the government that the peasantry was contented under the British all through. In Assam the people welcomed a settled conditions of life brought in by their rule. They came to believe in the fairness of the rule of the Maharani (Queen Victoria) and likened it to the best form of government they could ever dream of. They had implicit faith in her and by invoking her very name, they believed, they could ward off any danger. Benudhar Rajkhowa recalled in his memoirs that the *dakwals* who used to carry mail to and from Dibrugarh from a mofussil station travelling through roads infested by wild animals told upon enquiry that they had no fear of death on the road. 'We are *Maharani's* men. Why should we fear? The tigers that prowl on the road make way for us as soon as they hear the jingling sound of our approach.' It is only an illustrative statement out of many of such stories. There is no motive of propoganda in such statements. They only reflect the agreeable ambience of the time.[90]

But their faith in the justness of the rule of the Maharani notwithstanding, the cultivators were not blind to their own interest. With the coming of the British rule they got used to payment of revenue in cash. Economy was not the virtue of the average cultivator in Assam. They supported themselves mostly by the produce of their own field. Cash transaction was limited. Mustard seed was the only important cash crop, minor domestic produce brought in cash very rarely. The growers were indebted to the local moneylenders. Demands of revenue and other expenses perpetually increased the cultivators' burden of indebtedness. The cultivators' transaction with his moneylender after the harvest was no better than a distress sale. So any proposal for enhancement of revenue by the government made the peasants' blood boil in their veins. The first organized protest which turned violent due to inept handling by an English officer took place at Phulaguri in the Nagaon district in 1861 against the 'prohibition of poppy cultivation' and rumours of imposition of taxes.[91] Phulaguri is an episode without any moral effect.

Peasants' anger found expression through other channels also. In early 1855 some discontented ryots of the Mangaldoi sub-division sent a petition to the Lt. Governor of Bengal complaining against their mauzadars. Earlier, one Somdhar Lahkar was the mauzadar. As he became old he entrusted the *mauzas* to his two grown-up sons, Maniram and Maheshchandra, with approval from the government. Maniram and Maheshchandra were haughty and oppressive and thereby antagonized the ryots. Upon inquiry by an officer called Captain Reynolds, the allegations against them were substantiated and both of them were dismissed. Besides, a criminal charge was framed against Maniram and after trial he was imprisoned.

Somdhar Lahkar alleged that the charges against his sons were got up by a family of Chatgaree Barua. A fresh inquiry was conducted by W.S. Hudson, Sub-Deputy Collector of Mangaldoi. Hundson reported to G.F.F. Vincent, Collector of zillah Darrang that the ryots he met stated before him that they would not accept the same mauzadars any more. The ryots further threatened that if any one of them was restored they would 'retire to live among the Bhooteah Hills'. Hudson ascertained that one Juggomohan Chowdry was the adviser of the ryots but he was not sure if Juggomohan had any improper influence over them inconsistent with his profession as a *moktar*. Hudson also gathered that Chandramal, the *patgiri* of Bhergaon was also trying to get settlement of the *mauzas*. There was a division among the ryots and Maheshchandra won over the majority faction. The newly organized ryots then demanded that at least one *mauza* should be restored to Maheshchandra against whom no criminal proceeding was drawn up. After hearing the opposite party the government conceded their demand. Next year some Kachari ryots of Mangaldoi and Kalai Gaon brought complaints against their mauzadars. Prompt action, however, mollified them.[92] These facts cannot be viewed in isolation. There was considerable tension in the rural life of north Kamrup and Mangaldoi areas where the peasantry had little opportunity for selling their produce for cash whenever necessary. That made the mauzadars' task more difficult. The more he came under the threat of dismissal from the government for his inability to pay his revenue on time the more he became nervous and ruthless. There was no scope of sudden change of fortune of either the ryots or the mauzadars. So, there were alliances and intrigues, pushing and shoving among them leading to the tensions. Proposal for enhancement of revenue in such situation only added fuel to the fire. The violent protest movement that swept north Kamurp and Mangaldoi in 1893–4 was the culmination of the tensions. The storm cloud thickened over the years.

The protest movement started at Rangiya in December 1893 and it came to a tragic end at Patharughat in January in 1894. Officially described as the 'Assam Riots' the resistance movement was put down by the government. The events took place at a dramatic speed. The movement was confined to some contiguous localities of north Kamrup and the western part of the Darrang district.[93]

The disquiet areas were located at a considerable distance from the trade depots. Rice, the only crop they produced was not yet a cash crop. Cultivation of mustard wherever existed, was negligible. To demand enhanced rate of rent in such a situation was like trying to draw blood out of stone. Discontent was not confined to the peasantry alone. Mauzadars and landlords were also hard-pressed. They took advantage of the peasants' anger and directed it against the government. A. Guha writes, 'the non-cultivating landowners—Brahmins, Mahantas and Dolois, the traditional rural elite apparently took the initiative and a leading role'. One landlord of Vyaskuchi was a 'notable leader' of the ryots.[94] Peasants' participation was therefore, inspired not spontaneous. It was more with bravado than conviction that they registered their protest.

We have already shown that there was no dearth of disgruntled mauzadars and mauzadars-in-waiting in Mangaldoi sub-division. It was matter of no surprise if they were on the look out for a chance to settle old scores. Judged by the outcome of the stir we may guess that the leaders had no vision, no idea about remedial justice. Yet they played a vital role in providing leadership and encouragement. As they were sure of the loyalty of the ryots they rode on the crest of their discontent. Popular historiography found it easy to invent momentous merits of the movement. Every Indian peasant movement produced a charismatic leader, the Assam movement none. The subaltern school of historiography is yet to fish out a hero. In the face of government repression the leaders disappeared. As soon as the movement became leaderless it fizzled out. The roar of the outburst metamorphosed into a quiet bubble.

It is necessary to explain as to why the incidents at Lachima (Kamrup) and Patharughat (Darrang) failed to stir the imagination of the educated minds. It will be seen below that they were not insensitive to hardship of the peasantry. They were not loath to criticize the government when necessary. Possibly they knew the movement by their leaders for whom they had little or no sympathy. They suspected that once concessions were secured then it was every man for himself.

The peasantry had genuine grievances but they could do very little towards their redressal. Some issues needed long-term solution, a reversal of the social order; some of such issues were taken up by the Ryot Sabhas, the Assam Association and later by the Indian National

Congress. These issues became a part of the national movement for freedom.

So far historians are unanimous in their understanding of the peasant uprising in Kamrup and Darrang. But a close reading of the record, one may argue, lends itself to a different interpretation. The peasantry was angered by the increase of revenue rates; more than them, the revenue-hike was resented by the non-cultivating rural gentry, because they had been pleading for a total exemption of land revenue. The Assam Land and Revenue Regulation 1886 introduced an elaborate tenancy system, tightened the loopholes and brought all and sundry under a common code. The traditional landed gentry secured concessions but they wanted more. They did not welcome the Regulation and if possible they would have been up in arms to resist it. The Regulation is still the *Manu-Samhita* of land rights in Assam. These disgruntled men were waiting for a chance to wreak vengeance on the government and they struck at the right moment. They issued an injunction and instigated the peasantry to move forward though they did not show their hand. The peasantry could not ignore their command because they were the source of credit in the village. Those who made money hand over fist at the cost of the ryots appeared as their saviours. The peasantry played right into their hands. They opened their mouth, the scheming landlords and priests spoke through them. Unlike popular wisdom one refuses to see it as a straight fight of the peasantry against the government. There existed, in fact, three, not two contending parties. The report (1894) of M'Cabe, Deputy Commissioner of Kamrup, brings it out clearly:

> The ordinary village Panchayet, originally constituted as an authority on social matters has developed into the mel or assembly, not only of the members of a village but of whole of the inhabitants of even one or more Tehsils. These mels are governed by the leading Dolois or Gossains and by the principal landholders of the district.

A. Guha speaks of their 'leading role', but their role was essentially diabolical. In the face of government repression the peasantry stood their ground, made sacrifices but the 'leaders' betrayed them and disappeared. Their proxy resistance broke down.[95]

Left to themselves the peasantry resorted to ingenuous modes of protest. James C. Scott explains with suitable contemporary evidence that malicious gossip, tales, slander, anonymous sabotage, character assassination, nicknames and rumours constituted symbolic resistance of the peasantry. They also resorted to the Brechtian form of class struggle with foot dragging, dissimulation, false compliance, desertion, pilfering, feigned ignorance, slander, arson sabotage, etc.[96]

The resistance was offered not against the government alone, their target included the government agents and others who identified themselves with the power of the state. Desertion as a form of protest was known in Assam since the days of the Ahom rulers. Let us recall Purandar Singha's tragedy. Following instruction from the supreme government Purandar abolished 'capitation, house and hearth taxes' and had to depend solely on land revenue. The rates had to be raised, but the 'fishermen, braziers, weavers, goldwashers and potters of Upper Assam' immediately left his territory to defy the orders and avoid taxes. 'The real cause of desertion of the ryots' the Commissioner confirmed, 'was the exorbitant extortion'.[97]

Migration of peasants from one district to another continued for the entire period of our study. The most common feature of such migration was that the peasants always moved from a fully settled revenue unit to areas of little administrative interest. The sparsely populated areas in the districts of Darrang and north Lakhimpur absorbed a large number of such migratory peasant population. The uninhabited foothills of countless hills of the province allured a large number of marginalized peasants. Those who moved houses had no reason to be happy about the social order which failed them. James Scott reminds that symbolic protest make no headlines so we cannot produce evidence to show that such plebian protest was ever really made. Their search for a better future symbolized their disdain for the present condition.

Nicknames were not unknown. Lakshminath Bezbaroa's Bhempuria was in all probality a nickname picked up from real life. Bhempuria was a characterless, corrupt, rapacious and conceited mauzadar of the British age. He was unpopular but nobody dared to open his mouth against him because of his connection with the government.[98] After 1894 there was no outburst of peasants. But they did not fully reconcile to the British rule either. In fact, they provided the mainstay of the freedom struggle in Assam.

We have no dependable means to ascertain the different components of the peasant movements noted above. Nor can we measure the intensity of anger of the participating groups. We cannot ignore the fact that in a period of less than forty years of the legal and institutional changes driving deep into the society, the peasantry ceased to be a unipartite body. The first brood that came into focus were the agricultural labourers. A section of the peasantry thus broke into the labour market for the first time.

AGRICULTURAL LABOURERS

The question of agricultural labourers in Assam was taken note of for the first time in 1878 in the wake of the Famine Commissioner's queries. Until the abolition of slavery the slaves served as field labourers. After their formal release some of them might have stuck to their old masters and continued to work for them as before.

Being able to own property, house, goods and chattels the people so released acquired a new status. The emancipation was not followed by a settlement scheme and so many of them remained absolutely landless. That cultivable land was available and in abundance had no meaning for those who were no better than driven cattle of their masters. The change of legal status did not automatically change their way of life. A big chunk of the agricultural labourers came from this class. This is our assumption though we have no means to test its validity. Disease of men and cattle, calamities of flood and fire, lack of cheap credit facilities and wiles of moneylenders contributed to the impoverishment of the peasantry. They swelled the ranks of agricultural labourers. Unlike today, absolute landlessness was not the only factor of their becoming labourers. They alternated as peasant proprietors and agricultural labourers. Uncertainity of engagement and income told its own tale.

In the early years payment of wage to the labourers was made both in cash and in kind. The nature of employment differed from district to district. In Goalpara, for example, working people, entered into a contract to give their services in lieu of money lent to them by the employers.

TABLE 3.4

District	*Agri. Labourers*	*Horse Keeper*	*Masons*	*Carpenters*	*Blacksmiths*
Goalpara	6–10	7–10	13–18	16–20	15–20
Kamrup	6	9	12	12	12
Darrang	6–7	8–10	15-20	12–20	8–10
Nagaon	6–7	7–9	8–20	15–30	15–25
Sibsagar	6–8	7–10	12–17	12–17	12–17
Lakhimpur	8	9	20	15–20	16–18

TABLE 3.5

District	*Rice obtainable for a Rupee in 1878*	*Salt obtainable for a Rupee in 1878*
Goalpara	14 *seers*	8 *seers*
Kamrup	14 *seers*	8 *seers*
Darrang	10 *seers*	6 *seers*
Sibsagar	11 *seers*	6 *seers*
Nagaon	13 *seers*	7 *seers*
Lakhimpur	9 *seers*	6 *seers*

In such cases they had no bargaining power at all. In Nagaon, labourers were usually engaged for a month or a year. The monthly system was more popular in other districts.

We produce in Table 3.4 the rate of monthly wage of an able-bodied agricultural labourer in 1878. We have also listed the wage of some other categories of private service (figures in rupee, anna, etc.).[99]

It becomes clear from the Table 3.4 that the agricultural labourers were the most low paid people. Skilled services secured twice or even more amount given to them. Labour rates were lowest in Kamrup and highest in the Lakhimpur district. The condition of the agricultural labourers was further worsened by the absence of opportunity for continuous employment round the year. Price situation was unpredictable which went sometimes in favour and sometimes against the labourers. As we presently see in Table 3.5, there was a slight rise of daily wage in the next 4 or 5 years but the prices of rice and salt were falling. We have already noted the monthly rate of wage above and let us now consider the price situation.[100]

The statement shows that rice and salt were comparatively cheaper in Goalpara and Kamrup, but costlier in Lakhimpur and Darrang.

The 1881 Census put the total number of people engaged in agriculture as land proprietors, tenants cultivators and agricultural labourers at 17,55,656, out of which 26,413 or 1.5 per cent were agricultural labourers. We can draw only tentative conclusion from these figures as they included the statistics of the Surma valley and the Hill districts.[101] Anyway, though the number was small at that time to attract the attention of the administrators, their emergence sounded a note of alarm.

By 1880s agricultural labourers emerged as a distinct labour force in all the districts. The daily wage record of such labourers in the subdivisions for the years 1882 and 1883 are taken up for our

TABLE 3.6

Sub-Divisions	*Daily wages in 1882*	*Daily wages in 1883*	*Rice obtainable for a Rupee*	
			1882–3	*1883–4*
1 Dhubri	4 *annas*	4 *annas*	20 *seers*	16 *seers*
2 Guwahati	4 *annas*	4 *annas*	18 *seers*	16 *seers*
3 Mangaldoi	4 *annas*	3–4 *annas*	20 *seers*	22 *seers*
4 Tezpur	5–7 *annas*	6–8 *annas*	15 *seers*	18 *seers*
5 Nagaon	4–6 *annas*	4–6 *annas*	16 *seers*	15 *seers*
6 Sibsagar	4–6 *annas*	4–6 *annas*	16 *seers*	15 *seers*
7 Dibrugarh	6 *annas*	8 *annas*	15 *seers*	11 *seers*
8 Golaghat	6 *annas*	6 *annas*	not available	
9 Jorhat	3–6 *annas*	4–6 *annas*	not available	

Note: In most of the cases the quantity of rice obtainable for a rupee includes a few *chataks* in addition to the *seers*. We have noted only the *seers* as these figures are good enough to suggest the price pattern.

analysis. We have also noted the price of rice for those years (see Table 3.6).[102]

From Table 3.6 we can see that the daily wage of an agricultural labourer fetched 5 *seers* of rice in 1882 but 4 *seers* next year. Again, except for Mangaldoi, Tezpur, Jorhat and Dibrugarh the daily wage remained the same in other sub-divisions and barring Mangaldoi the three other towns recorded slightly higher wage. Though daily wage was rising in Mangaldoi and Tezpur but the price of rice was falling. In Dibrugarh the rate of wage rise was nearly equal to the rate of price rise. In Guwahati, Nagaon and Sibsagar price of rice had gone up but there was no change of wage rate. Though rice was the staple food, its price variation did not have quick effect on labour rate. Price of salt remained almost the same for the years. One rupee fetched 11 *seers* of salt in Dhubri, Barpeta and Guwahati, 8 *seers* in Mangaldoi, Tezpur, Nagaon, Sibsagar and Dibrugarh and only 6 *seers* in North Lakhimpur.

A significant aspect of agricultural population as it transpired from the Census Report of 1901 was the rise of cultivating tenants, farm servants and field labourers. The figures in Table 3.7, though they include statistics of the Surma valley, point up the trends.[103]

The increase in the number of cultivating tenants in the three districts of Darrang, Sibsagar and Lakhimpur was phenomenal. It was, the government thought, 'due to a practice which is growing up amongst the Assamese of leasing out the land lying near a tea garden to the

TABLE 3.7

Occupation	*Population in 1891*	*Supported in 1901*
Cultivating tenants	1,041,520	1,740,906
Farm servants	24,352	40,215
Field labourers	11,145	51,961

coolies'.[104] But the dependence of larger population on these occupations had some other implications. They set in motion four irreversible trends: (i) pressure on cultivable land, (ii) fragmentation of land holding, (iii) immigration of peasant population into the province, and (iv) growing landlessness and poverty of the peasantry. A tension in social life thus became inevitable. So long as agriculture remains the mainstay of Assam's economy, the tension is ineluctable. The Assamese cultivators looked upon the *char* lands as the domain of Hades, a gloomy nether world and shunned them.

The Census Report of 1901 showed that 87 per cent people of the Brahmaputra valley were engaged in agriculture, 82.6 per cent in the Surma valley and 84.6 per cent in the hill districts. Compared to the census figures of 1891, the average percentage (84.6) was higher by 21.4 per cent than Bengal, 26.4 per cent than Bombay, 28.9 per cent than Punjab, 25.8 per cent than Madras and 24.8 per cent than the all India average.[105]

LITERATURE ON AGRICULTURE

No account of agriculture and peasantry in Assam is complete without a note on literature on agriculture. Much like the first printed history of Assam, the first book on agriculture in Assam was also written in Bengali by Kefayat Ullah, Sadar Munsiff of Guwahati. Published in 1853, the book *Krishi-Darpan* was written for the benefit of the Assamese cultivators at the instance of Captain Rowlatt, Collector of Kamrup. The book gave instructions on tilling land, selection of seeds, rearing of livestock and it discussed the utility of crops like wheat, barley, peanut, jute, cotton, flax, tobacco and some vegetables. The monthly journal *Orunodoi*, in the following year, while introducing the book to its readers made an appeal to the inhabitants of Assam to make use of the book to improve agriculture and thereby increase their income.[106]

Narayan Sarma Barua (1868–1938) was the pioneer of agricultural science in Assam. He was the son of Rosheswar Sarma Barua who owned several tea gardens. In recognition of his endeavours, Narayan Sarma Barua was honoured with the Rai Saheb title by the government.

His Assam Nursery opened in 1891 at Lahing in the district of Sibsagar was perhaps the first of its kind in the province. He might have borrowed the idea of such a nursery from the tea planters. He published the first part of his *Asamiya Krishitatwa* in 1909. It was a voluminous work and was favourably reviewed in *Banhi.*[107] The author wrote about the deplorable conditions of agriculture in Assam and offered suggestions for improvement.[108] Two years later, he collected the traditional maxims on agriculture *Asamiya Krishi Vasan* with the sole object of introducing them to the new generation of cultivators and putting them in good use. He rightly deserved praise for his scientific spirit in preparing one Rain Table for the year 1911. It is no small credit for a person from the non-agricultural community to have stressed the importance of pluvial variation for the growth of agriculture. Narayan authored a third book entitled *Asamiya Krishi Daul.* It was, in fact, a permanent calander with exhaustive suggestion for daily work round the year.[109]

Another important work on agriculture in Assam was done by Bharat Chandra Das in 1909. His *Asamiya Kheti* contained eleven chapters in all running into 248 pages.[110] Srikanta Choudhury wrote *Krishi Silpa Vigyan.* The book was serialized in the *Sadiniya Asamiya* of Chandra Kumar Agarwala. As the name suggests, the author discussed the problems of agriculture and industry together. There was plenty of reading in it.

SOME EXPERIMENTS

There was tangible administrative drive towards all round development of agriculture. It was the thrust area of government policy. The state government introduced monthly scholarship at the rate of Rs. 20 for students desiring to take up higher training in agriculture. Willing students, after selection, were admitted in the agriculture college at Sabour, Bihar. 'Hector *sali*' was an important variety of paddy grown in both the valleys of Assam. It derives its name from Mr. G.P. Hector, the Economic Botanist of Bengal who had set up the Karimganj Farm for experiments in rice. He selected three pure varieties of *sali* rice and his prescription had done well.[111] Hector *sali* was also known as *Indrasali.* Narayan Sarma Barua developed what he called George *sali* named after the king of England. Both these varieties of transplanted paddy secured success.

Experiment in potato was carried on in Upper Shillong. Potatoes 'were first introduced into the Khasi Hills in 1830'. Within a brief period it became the principal crop there and other highland tracts. Calcutta market swallowed huge annual export of potatoes from the Khasi Hills. In 1915, the summer and winter crops taken together, the total output of potatoes grown was 1,411 *maunds*. Ferguson of Dhamai Tea Estate collected some 20 lots of seed from St. Andrews University and donated them to the Upper Shillong Farm. Another fruit experiment station was set up at Shillong under the supervision of C.H. Holder. Varieties of apples were produced in the station.[112]

Cultivation of superior varieties of sugarcane was started in 6 centres in Kamrup and 16 in Sibsagar. The agriculture department used to organize demonstration of sugarcane-crushing mills. The three roller-iron sugarcane-crushing mills were at first owned by the government and they were let out on hire during the crushing season. The sugarcane growers came to appreciate the utility of this new technique and they started buying the mills for their own use and for hire.[113]

The government engaged some honorary correspondents for the department of agriculture. They took active interest in experiments and kept the government informed of the progress. These correspondents had a pivotal role in the expansion of agriculture. Babu Jnan Chandra Roy of Baithalangshu was such a correspondent for Nagaon. In 1915–16 he cultivated about one-third of an acre of sugarcane with B-147 and 376 varieties supplied by the government. The cane grew about 14 ft. long and were very thick. About 43 *maunds* of *gur* were obtained from the cultivation. It was some sort of a record. Debeswar Sarma Barthakur was the correspondent for Sibsagar. He was the owner of the Thakurbari Farm at Haloguri. Debeswar Gossain of Barpathar was an enterprising grower of sugarcane. He started a sugarcane farm at Badlipar. He 'continued to work his small sugar factory and made a good profit'. Debeswar Gossain was successful in growing Barbados and Mauritius canes 'acclimatized at Jorhat'. Pitambar Saikia, mauzadar of Khowang, Lakhimpur, promoted paddy cultivation. The other Correspondents were: Lalit Mohan Dutta (Dhubri), Dinesh Chandra Chakraborty, manager Gauripur Estate (Goalpara), E.P.R. Gilman of Borduar Tea Estate (Kamrup), K. Rahman (Guwahati), Tayab Ali (Sonapur), Jatindra Chandra Maitra (Tezpur), Pratap Narayan Choudhury (Khata, Nalbari), Baikuntha Narayan Barua (Panitola, Lakhimpur), Chandranath Sarma Pandit (Palasbari) and Bhagadutta Hazarika, mauzadar (Dharamtul).[114]

K.C. Sarma wrote on the imported cows. A large number of cattle were annually imported into Assam from western India. But they did not survive long. There was always lack of enough care. Sarma's suggestions that the cowsheds should have raised floor, the cows should have grazing fields, etc., only underlined the ignorance of the peasant community of the elementary knowledge of cattle rearing.[115]

Improvement of livestock was in the agenda of the agriculture department. It was rightly noticed by the government that the local 'weedy cattle' was not useful either for plough or for milk. The department imported sires from Bengal Cattle Farm. Accordingly, breeding bulls were imported and sold to the public. The Government of Bengal supplied the bulls from the Rangpur Farm. They also sent a few selected yearlings.[116]

ELITES' ATTITUDE

It has been the general tendency of some scholars to present the educated Assamese elites in poor light with regard to their attitude towards the ryots. But our queries reveal a different picture. *The Statesman* dated 21 May 1886, published quite a long letter from 'An Assamese' of Jorhat. The correspondent, in all probability was Jagannath Barua. The correspondent gave the lie to the charge that the elites were out of any compassion for the peasantry. The letter was addressed to focus the plight of 'the poor dumb ryots... of the neglected province in the farthest corner of the Indian Empire....' The government, it has already been noted, favoured long-term leases of land for the peasant proprietors but the peasants considered the long-term leases as tedious burden on their back and they opted for annual leases instead. The settlement policy of the government to cut down the annual lease facilities drastically was looked upon by the Jorhat correspondent as 'deprivation of their rights'. Nor did he agree with the repeated assertion of the government about the happiness and improved condition of the peasantry of Assam. 'The wrong impression' of the government, he felt, could not be uprooted unless 'the famine makes a periodical visit to the province like other parts of the empire'. But the government never had to face that famine-test. The correspondent remarked that beneath the veneer of contentment lay the real agony of the ryots. The same pathetic sight repeated itself every year. There the ryots stood friendless and powerless and it seemed as though they were born to suffer the rack-rent. Then came his rebellious assertion; 'I say the ryots are in no way better off....' In a single sentence he brought into focus the plight of the ryots;

Ah what an affecting scene it is to see the parents seperated from their children whose services they pledge in order to get a loan for escaping the government liability and how many a ryot incurs debt on this occasion at an exhorbitant interest such as has no ending, and such as brings ruin upon himself and his family, it is needless to say.[117]

No man without sympathy for the ryots could have made such observation.

With the growing role of money in daily life the moneylenders appeared on the scene. Moneylending was an unregulated business down to 1934. The Marwari traders who reached out to the interior parts of the province and set up their depots took to moneylending as a subsidiary occupation. In Kamrup, there were a large number of Assamese moneylenders. Moneylending was a thriving business everywhere. Though the Census Report of 1891 recorded the total number of professional moneylenders in the Brahmaputra valley as 1791, their real number was more than that. There were disguised moneylenders in the villages. Transactions were made on good faith and mostly without any document. The very nature of the transactions did not leave any scope of documentary evidence. Administration (judicial) reports of the nineteenth century rarely made mention of litigation arising out of moneylending. Moneylenders were a stable source of agricultural finance and they played a major role in agricultural economy. Loans were contracted even for unproductive purposes. From some writings of Kamalakanta Bhattacharyya we gather that the moneylenders had an effective network and proper means to realize their loan amount.[118] Rate of interest varied from place to place and from season to season. The moneylenders adopted flexible methods of operation to make themselves acceptable to the loanees. Loanees had to mortgage movable or immovable property such as land or land documents, ornaments, utensils, etc. Cases were not rare when peasant loanees failed to redeem the mortgage and lost their mortgaged property for ever.

It is possible to agree with Hori in Premchand's *Godan* who reflected over the implication of loan in the family economy of a peasant: 'A loan was like an unwelcome guest, who, once in the house dug himself into a permanent fixture.'[119]

The general characteristics of the Assamese people were noticed by some observers from outside the state and at time they expressed their opinion about them which were not always found favourable by the elites. For instance, a correspondent of *The Statesman*, who went unnamed, in a letter to the editor, published on 26 August 1891, referred to some rumours made by what he called 'your Allahabad contemporary' (*The Pioneer*) and defended in so many words the 'indolence' of the Assamese. The correspondent suggested that there was no necessity of hard labour. 'In Assam the peasant simply scratches his field with his primitive plough and the result is that a bumper crop is produced.' The element of complusion during the rule of the Ahom kings, he argued, kept them active. 'Under British rule no such forced labour has been exacted, and this fact no doubt encouraged the growing slothfulness of the people. Being under no obligation to labour and being well fed by the bounty of their fields, they were perfectly contented to live a lazy life' he argued. That the peasantry was far from 'perfectly contented' was borne out by the quick sweep of peasant unrest in parts of Kamrup and Darrang districts two years later. Three things, spread of education, civilizing effect of the British administration and increase of wants, the letter pointed out, had 'gone a great way towards inducing them to leave off their sluggish habits and set to an active life'.[120]

Within a fortnight, another letter written by U.N.B. from Calcutta appeared in *The Statesman*, on 8 September 1891. The 'U.N.B.' could be none other than the spirited Upendra Nath Barua of Jorhat. Though it was not specifically mentioned, U.N.B. wrote his letter in support of the earlier one by the unnamed correspondent. Referring to 'a rabid article in the columns of the *Pioneer* abusing the Assamese in unmeasured terms', U.N.B. lamented 'the paucity of opulent and professional men' in Assam. He found criticism of 'the poor and defenceless Assamese easy and common' and alleged that none had taken up 'the question earnestly and practically as David Hare did in Bengal'. In the same letter U.N.B. referred to an article published in the *Planters' Gazette* about a year before, 'suggesting some harsh and despotic measures to be adopted by the government for the removal of the ingrained laziness of the Assamese'. He was in no mood to lose sight of the 'progress the Assamese have made under the auspices of the English Government'.[121] A good fund of elites' sympathy was therefore always in reserve for the peasantry.

NOTES

1. P. Sinha, *Nineteenth Century Bengal: Aspects of Social History*, Calcutta, 1965, p. 13.
2. For details, see M.S. Randhawa, *A History of Agriculture in India*, Delhi, 1982, Vol. III.

3. Anandaram's memorandum is contained in Appendix J in A.J. Moffatt Mills' *Report on the Province of Assam*, Guwahati, 1984, pp. 93–132. For his remark on agriculture, p. 102.
4. Ibid., p. 103.
5. Ibid., pp. 103–4.
6. Ibid., p. 104.
7. P. Sinha, loc. cit.
8. G. Barua, *Anandaram Dhekial Phukanar Jivan Charitra,* Guwahati, 1971, pp. 79–82, Mills' Report, op. cit., p. 104.
9. Mills' Report, loc. cit.
10. Published in April, *Orunodoi*, edited by M. Neog, Guwahati, 1983, pp. 128–31.
11. M.S. Randhawa, op. cit., p. 62.
12. Ibid., p. 72.
13. Ibid., p. 73.
14. Ibid., p. 75.
15. Ibid., pp. 64–6, 82–3, 109–15.
16. W.W. Hunter, *A Statistical Account of Assam*, Delhi, 1982, Vol. II (hereafter Hunter), pp. 17–18, 54–5.
17. Hunter, Vol. I, pp. 45–6.
18. Ibid., Vol. I, pp. 190–2.
19. Ibid., pp. 125–8.
20. Ibid., pp. 251–2.
21. B.N. Chaudhury, 'British Rule in Assam (1845–1858)' (unpublished thesis) London, 1956, Ch. 2, p. 24.
22. Hunter, op. cit., p. 253.
23. Ibid., pp. 369–73.
24. *Report on the Administration of Land Revenue, 1879–80*, Shillong, 1881.
25. Ibid.,
26. Ibid. The increase in the number of estates was due to ryotwari settlement system and the holding of each cultivator was counted as a separate estate. Evidently, the ryotwari system gave boost to agriculture in Assam.
27. *Report on the Administration of Land Revenue, 1880–81.*
28. Worked out from the *Reports on the Administration of Land Revenue* for the years 1881–82, 1882–83, 1883–84, 1884–85 and 1886–87.
29. Randhawa, op. cit., pp. 161–2.
30. *Report on the Administration of Land Revenue, 1886–7.*
31. Ibid., p. 21.
32. J. M'Cosh, *Topography of Assam*, Delhi, 1986, p. 30.
33. Randhawa, op. cit., p. 76; and K.L. Tuteja, 'Cotton Improvement Programme in Dharwar in Mid-nineteenth Century', *IHC Progs*, 1990.
34. Foreign Dept. Consultations (NAI), 19 March 1858, Nos. 34–7.
35. For details see Randhawa, op. cit., pp. 175–7.
36. Quoted in Randhawa, op. cit., p. 177.
37. Worked out from Hunter, op. cit., Vols. I and II.
38. *Administration Report on the Province of Assam 1897–8*. Part II B, p. 94.

39. *Provincial Gazetteer of Assam*, 1906, p. 64.
40. D.R. Gadgil, *The Industrial Evolution of India*, Delhi, 1982, pp. 75–8.
41. S.K. Mukhopadhyaya, *Banglar Arthik Itihas* (*19th century*), Calcutta, 1987, pp. 93–4. Also Randhawa, op. cit., pp. 133–4.
42. *Report on the Jute Cultivation in Assam*, Shillong, 1898, p. 10.
43. Ibid p. 8.
44. In some years the volume of export came down, for example, in 1883–4 it was 84,589 *maunds*, in 1886–7 it was 95,216 *maunds*. These two years were particularly notorious for calamity in agriculture in Assam which resulted in crop failure and fall in export. All figures have been reproduced from the *Report on the Jute Caltivation in Assam*, Shillong, 1898, op. cit., pp. 6–7.
45. *Report on the Jute Cultivation*, op. cit., p. 11.
46. Report of B.C. Basu, Asstt. Director, Dept. of Land Records and Agriculture, quoted in *Report on Jute Cultivation in Assam*, Shillong, 1898, pp. 14–15.
47. *Report on the Jute Cultivation in Assam*, 1898, loc. cit.
48. S. Bhattacharya, *Aupanibesik Bharater Arthaniti*, Calcutta, 1989, pp. 51–2.
49. *Annual Report on the Administration of Land Revenue in Assam 1880–81*, pp. 20–5.
50. *Report on the Administration of Land Revenue in Assam*, loc. cit.
51. D.R. Gadgil, op. cit., p. 66.
52. D.R. Gadgil, loc. cit.
53. Based on a note entitled 'Assam Famine Relief and Famine Prevention' in a brittle condition. Some portions of the text, page numbers and end notes mutilated (NAI).
54. These accounts have been collected from the note mentioned in note 53 above.
55. R.C. Dutt, *The Peasantry of Bengal*, Calcutta, 1980, pp. 157, 161–71, also see 'Bangladesher Krisak', in *Bankim Rachanabali*, Calcutta, 1988, pp. 289–98.
56. R.C. Dutt, loc. cit.
57. See note 53.
58. Ibid.
59. The situation of forced commercialization in Bengal has been discussed by S. Bhattacharya, op. cit., pp. 56–8.
60. K. Marx, *Capital*, Moscow (n.d.), Vol. I, p. 481.
61. R.B. Pemberton, *Report on the Eastern Frontier of British India*, Guwahati, 1966, p. 76.
62. J. M'Cosh, op. cit., p. 5.
63. Quoted by Marx, loc. cit.
64. See *Assam Bandhu*, Guwahati, 1984, pp. 116–18 and 187–9. For aphorism on money see Benudhar Rajkhowa, *Asamiya Khandavakya Kosh*, Guwahati, 1980, pp. 132–3.
65. Resignation of land for fear of tax burden was common to both the poor and the rich peasants. We have shown in Chapter 1 above that the government took serious notice of that tendency but it was unable to offer any remedy. Also see, A.J. Fonseca (ed.), *Challenge of Poverty in India*, Bombay, 1969, particularly

the articles by B.N. Ganguli, pp. 3–10; John Hicks, pp. 11–22 and P.D. Ojha, pp. 25–47.

66. *Orunodoi*, edited by M. Neog, p. 41. Guwahati, 1983.
67. Ibid., p. 319.
68. Ibid., p. 375.
69. Ibid., pp. 929–30.
70. Ibid., p. 960.
71. Ibid., pp. 1108–9.
72. Rameswar Sen, *Atmakahini*, Santipur (WB), 1932, p. 344.
73. For Samuel Pepys' *Diary* see W.J. Long, *English Literature*, Delhi, 1978, pp. 252–5; and J. Canning (ed.), *100 Great Books*, Delhi, 1987, pp. 232–3. For extract from *Grihadah* see *Sarat Rachanabali*, Calcutta, 1989, Vol. II, p. 507.
74. Hunter, *A. Statistical Account of Assam*, Vol. I, pp. 54, 135; Vol. II, p. 71.
75. Hunter, Vol. I, op. cit., p. 258.
76. *Report on Administration of the Province of Assam*, 1897, p. i (Summary).
77. Ibid., p. 1 (2).
78. Ibid., p. 1 (3).
79. J. M'Cosh, op. cit., p. 52; M.H. Ali, *Observations on the Mussulmans of India*, Delhi, 1975, p. 260 and *The Englishman*, 9 February 1887.
80. Hunter, op. cit., Vol. I, p. 197.
81. Ibid., Vol. I, p. 376; Vol. II, pp. 70–1.
82. G. Barua, *Anandaram Dhekial Phukanar Jivan Charitra*, op. cit., pp. 139–40.
83. *The Cambridge Economic History of India*, Vol. II, p. 231. For the account of the famine in Orissa, see, H.K. Mahtab, *History of Orissa*, Cuttack, 1960, Vol. II, pp. 446–7. Also Hunter, op. cit., Vol. I, pp. 54, 258, 397; Vol. II, p. 71.
84. *Usha*, edited by Padmanath Barua, Vol. II, p. 70.
85. N.K. Sinha, *The Economic History of Bengal*, Vol. II, Calcutta, 1968, pp. 54, 61.
86. Note on 'Assam Famine Relief and Famine Prevention', Introductory part (page numbers destroyed, NAI).
87. Introductory remark from the note 'Assam Famine Relief and Famine Prevention' (note 53 supra).
88. 'Amar Manuh', in *Assam Bandhu*, 1885, pp. 132–3.
89. 'Rajaswa Committee', in *Mau*, Guwahati, 1980, pp. 68–71.
90. B. Rajkhowa, *Mor Jivan Dapon*, Guwahati, 1969, p. 21.
91. K.N. Dutt, *Landmarks of the Freedom Struggle in Assam*, Guwahati, 1969 pp. 28–9.
92. Fort William Judl. Progs., 7 June 1855, Nos. 14–16; 31 July 1856, Nos. 26–8.
93. H.K. Barpujari (ed.), *Political History of Assam*, Guwahati, 1977, Vol. I pp. 88–102.
94. A. Guha, *Planter-Raj to Swaraj*, Delhi, 1977, p. 54, also see his footnote.
95. A. Guha, ibid.; K.N. Dutt, *Landmarks of the Freedom Struggle in Assam*, pp. 36–7, also see P. Barthakur, *Swadhinata Ranar Samsparsat*, Dibrugarh, 1968, pp. 12–13.

96. J.C. Scott, *Weapons of the Weak*, Delhi, 1990, pp. 27 and 282.
97. H.K. Barpujari, *Assam in the Days of the Company*, Guwahati, 1980, p. 126.
98. L.N. Bezbaroa, *Works*, Guwahati, 1988, Vol. I, pp. 653–5.
99. Note on 'Assam Famine Relief and Famine Prevention' (note 53 supra), p.13.
100. Ibid., p. 14.
101. *Report on the Census of Assam, 1881*, Calcutta, 1883, worked out from the 'Professional Group', Class IV (Agricultural)
102. *Annual Report on Land Revenue Assam, 1883–4*, Shillong, 1885.
103. *Census of Assam, 1901*, Delhi, 1984, Vol. I, Subsidiary Table VIII, p. 175.
104. Ibid., pp. 162–3.
105. Worked out from the statement, para 210, ibid., p. 153.
106. *Orunodoi*, May 1854 op. cit., p. 1139.
107. *Banhi*, Vol. 1, No. 5, 1831 *Saka* (1909).
108. *Usha*, Vol. 3, 1831–2 *Saka* (1909–10).
109. *Bani*, Vol. 2, No. 6, 1833 *Saka* (1911).
110. A review note on the book was published in *Usha*, 1832 *Saka* (1910), p. 128.
111. Introductory remark in the *Report of the Agricultural Dept. Assam* for the year ending on 30 June 1916, Shillong, 1916
112. Ibid., p. 3.
113. Ibid., pp. 4–5.
114. The names of all those Correspondents have been collected from the *Report of the Agricultural Dept. Assam* for the years ending on 30 June 1916 and 1918.
115. K.C. Sarma, 'Amar Kheti', *Banhi*, Vol. 2, No. 5, 1832 *Saka* (1910).
116. *Report of the Agricultural Dept. Assam* for the period from 1 July 1918 to 31 March 1919, Shillong, 1991, p. 9.
117. *The Statesman*, 21 May 1886.
118. *Kamalakanta Bhattacharyya Rachanawali*, Guwahati, 1982, pp. 22–3.
119. Premchand, *Godan*, Bombay, 1984, p. 76.
120. *The Statesman*, 26 August 1891.
121. *The Statesman*, 8 September 1891.

CHAPTER 4

The Changing Social Spectrum

THE CONSOLIDATION of British rule in Assam and its administrative and economic integration with the rest of India opened up new avenues of socio-economic change.

BOAT AND MAN

Boats were the most important means of transport in the nineteenth century Assam. Boats were to Assam what camels were to western and horses to central India.[1] The coming of boats into use in large numbers in Assam was an event of this period. Use of waterways by common man for their day-to-day work was not in vogue. It was only among certain communities that the rich as well as the poor possessed boats of some kind or other. David Scott found that as an agricultural country Assam could have exported rice but for want of suitable boats.[2] John Butler who was given an assignment to Saikhowa, in the extreme north-east corner of the valley in 1844 had to 'track up against a rapid stream' to reach his destination.[3] He completed his journey by 'west country boats'. Those boats are said to be 'heavy' and they were seldom met with in Upper Assam; *Khel-nao* or pleasure boats measuring 'about fifty feet long and three and a half feet wide with a grass roof over a portion forming a sleeping berth', etc., were of course available.[4]

The 'west country boats' referred to by John Butler above were indispensable for the traders to take full advantage of the waterways. Like horses and camels, boats were extensively used during the Mughal period. In the late sixteenth century 'some 30,000 boats plied in Kashmir and some 40,000 in the sarkar of Thatta'. The British traveller Ralph Fitch is stated to have travelled from Agra to Satgaon 'in the company of one hundred and four score boats'. William Finch noticed many boats on the Ravi near Lahore. Boats were built to suit the two different river systems of the Sindhu and the Ganga. Ludovico de

Varthema, an Italian adventurer, saw various types of boats in the Malabar and Konkan coasts and wrote about them.[5]

Though Assam could not draw upon advanced technology of boat-building, large number of boats were constructed nonetheless. Of them, the war-boats were particularly effective and famous. The boat-builders designed varieties of boats keeping in mind the suitability of their use in different river-systems. Swarnalata Baruah has rightly said, 'An abundant supply of timber woods made it possible for the Assamese to build numerous boats, both in the ancient and in the medieval times.'[6] Use of boats by the ruling elite in early medieval Assam was extensive. The Tezpur Copper Plates of King Vanamaladeva of the ninth century give us an account of the boats owned by him. As his capital city was on the banks of the Brahmaputra, all his boats were stationed there. The Tezpur inscription reads:

> The boats, like harlots, display the bodies, embellished with varieties of ornaments. They wear jungling bells like small girls. They get their speed accelerated by hard strokes like the women of Karnata. Like prostitutes they had chowries. They have red teeth like the damsels of the harem of Ravana. They are extremely speedy as if they are consorts of Pavana. They charm one and all like the beautiful women of Daluha. Like dancing girls, their trembling increase with the approach of dancers. They always desire to remain in a higher position of water....[7]

Though we may discount a part of the literary flourish, it is beyond doubt that different types of boats were built in Assam for different purposes. We may cite here a few common names which were known to the people living during the period of our study. They were: *choranao, chuchianao, holongnao, khelnao, marnao, mayurpankhi, paltoranao* and *pansai or dinga.*[8]

The tea planters also made use of the country boats in Assam as they found the steamer service unsuitable because of its high transport cost. Second, the limited availability of steamers compelled the tea suppliers to maintain and develop their own system of transhipment. The Assam Company, for example bought iron boats of its own.[9] Without the river transport facilities growth of tea industry in the second half of the nineteenth century would have remained a well-nigh impossibility. S.B. Medhi has remarked, 'the river transport enabled the tea industry to take root in Assam more than half a century before the advent of long-distance railway communications'. Down to the year 1908–9 the river transport covered 50 per cent of total export and 41 per cent of imports.[10]

In Assam boats were used for conveying post. It was maintained by a relay system with persons at fixed points to carry the post from one station to the other. The Calcutta post took about one week to reach Goalpara, another three days to Guwahati and next three days to Biswanath. The return post by the downstream took much less time.[11]

The government too maintained boats for their own purpose. But it was mainly the demands of trade which buoyed up the boat building industry.

With the upward trends of trade, an elaborate network of river traffic became necessary to keep pace with it. It was a safe, easy and reliable system. The government found that the system could be developed in Assam almost free of cost. The big rivers were navigable round the year though their branches could be used only during the rainy season. The inter communication between the vital trading posts, however, remained unaffected even during the dry season.

The Brahmaputra river was truly 'the great natural highway between Bengal and Assam'.[12] Until the coming of the days of the steamers as a regular service in 1861 boats were the only means for carrying goods and passengers between Calcutta and Assam. Even after the steamers were introduced the importance of boats did not decline as the steamer service was infrequent and it could not cover all the stations.

Water traffic provided livelihood to a large community in the river-side town of Goalpara. W.W. Hunter spoke of the 'poetry of Indian river names' and cited the examples of the Swaraswati, Swarnarekha, Swarnamati, Chitra, Haringhata, Karnaphuli, etc.[13] The names of the rivers of Goalpara too lend us a touch of poetry. They were the Manas, Gadadhar, Suvarnakos, Champamoti, Jingiram, Jinari, Kaladarni, Krishnai, Haripani, Dudhnoi, Tipkai and Bomnai.[14] Of them only the first three rivers were navigable by big boats throughout the year, the others were navigable during the rainy season only.

Guwahati, Barpeta and Palasbari were the three important centres of river-traffic in the Kamrup district. The Brahmaputra was the core of the system which nourished the life-strings of the minor rivers of the district, namely, the Manas, Chaulkhowa, Pagladia, Pahumara, Kaldiya, Kulsi, Naonadi, Boraliya, Bornadi, Lakhaitara, Digaru, etc. Though these were not navigable by big boats round the year, native crafts were engaged to keep up the flow of import and export.[15] In fact the bulk of the river-borne trade was carried on by native cat boats.

Biswanath, Tezpur and Mangaldoi were the three riverside towns of the Darrang district. Native boats were extensively used in these stations. It has been worked out from the record of the trade registration that in a period of twelve months from October 1875 to September 1876 the import and export of goods to and from the district amounted to 21,822 and 7,500 *maunds* respectively and that the entire waftage was run by boats.[16]

In Nagaon there were only two trading posts connected by river traffic, the district headquarters town of Nagaon and Raha. The confluence of the Kalang, Kapili and Dimal rivers near Raha helped it to grow in importance. Raha was the channel through which passed cotton, lac and Indian-rubber produced in the Naga Hills and north Cachar. The business was monopolized by the Marwari traders who used to store them along with the local goods during the winter season and put them all over to Guwahati when, at the onset of monsoon, the rivers rose to upbear the large boats. Some other rivers namely the Kalong, Kapili, Nanai, Sonai, Leteri, Jamuna, Kiling, Deopani, Dimal, Borpani and Dhansiri were navigable for medium sized boats during several months of the year. It was estimated that there were 'about a hundred and ten smaller rivers and streams in the district navigable during the rainy season by boats of two tons burden'.[17] Obviously, export or import trade could have had no necessity of a large fleet. Boats were used by the small traders for buying and selling local vends. Regular fishing and hunting habits of the people, made boats indispensable. At times boats were used for harvesting crops.

Golaghat and Jorhat were the two important river traffic stations in the Sibsagar district. Though there were only two depots the river-borne trade was not negligible. Various sizes of boats maintained the intercommunication. River traffic of Golaghat included export of rice and import of piece-goods and copper. Jorhat, connected by the Disai river imported cotton and woolen goods and exported silk and raw cotton. The rivers navigable by boats of 4 tons burden throughout the year were the Dhansiri, Burhi Dihing, Disang and Dikhow. Boats with half of that capacity could sail on the Kakodonga, Disai, Kaila, Janji, Dwarika and Dimau rivers during the rainy season.[18]

Dibrugarh, Sadiya and Jaipur were the notable riverside stations in the district of Lakhimpur. Almost the entire trading community who lived by river traffic resided in these three places each situated at the junctions of two or more rivers. Until recently the very name Lakhimpur brings to our mind the image of an artificial union of three tracts of flat land sandwiched by hogbacks and interspersed with an uncommon river system. The question of navigability of the important rivers of the district, namely, the Dibru, Buri-Dihing, Tingrai, Sisi, Subansiri, Lohit, Dhol, Ranganadi, Dikrang, etc., cannot be covered by a general description. Different kinds of boats and canoes had to be used even in the course of a single river depending on the current and other obstructions.[19]

It is not difficult to ideate from the above account that boats did play a major role in the economic life of the community. For some they were a daily helpmate and for many, a binding companion in their struggle for existence. The growing use of boats enlivened the boat making industry. Boat making was quite a challenging craft but there was no dearth of skilled hands. During the Ahom rule a particular official called Naobaicha Phukan was in charge of the guilds which were responsible for making and maintenance of the royal fleet. There were grades of boat-rowers and their services were drafted in accordance with the rank of the dignitaries travelling by boat.[20] The British abolished the guild system. The right of making or of possession of boats as of necessity was thrown open to all. A thousand and one men lived by working on boats at different stages. Unfortunately there are not enough records to tell us the entire truth. It comes upon us as a surprise that they suffered a total neglect in Assamese literature. They came from the lower rungs of the caste and social hierarchy and lived beyond the ambit of the literary culture. They were ignorant, unorganized and inarticulate. Their be-mused existence was matched by a harmless insouciance of the men of literature.

But whether anyone took notice of them or not they made a good showing in a massive economic activity. Happily, folk literature bears some testimony to their existence and occupation. The boatman used to sing songs when merchants set out for their business tour, or fishermen went fishing or when the boatmen themselves took part in boat race. The boats which daily spread on the rivers like a school of whales could be seen no more but its memory survives in the songs. All songs were rhythmically suited to the stimulating movement of the oars.[21]

Lakshminath Bezbaroa casually called to remembrance the use of boats in the second half of the nineteenth century. His direct concern was neither the boats nor the boatmen. His father, a munsiff, on transfer, travelled by boat with his family from Nagaon to Barpeta in 1864. Again, after the retirement of his father from service in 1873, they shifted from Guwahati to their home town Sibsagar. The journey by two wherries took some 22 days.[22]

In his study of the *Mediterranean World* Fernand Braudel spoke about the 'crests of foam that the tides of history carry on their strong backs', he further believed that the sea itself was the greatest document of its past history.[23] A study of the rivers of Assam may also provide clues to the understanding of the socio-economic fabric of the past. For Braudel the sea was everything, it provided unity, transport, the means of exchange and intercourse among nations. The rivers also played a similar role in Assam.

The river system governed the settlement pattern, farming and crop selection habits. The rivers were the highways of communication and commerce; unifiers of history, men and measures; straighteners of identity, language and culture. Their broadness was the index of the Assamese mind and the meanders symbolized their self-defeating waywardness. Rarely a source of worry, every river of Assam was an object of worship. The river was the promoter of urbanization and destroyer of moronic exclusiveness. By denying themselves the sight of the beauty and broadness, the later generations may have brought upon themselves the curse of ignorance. Open the rivers and you open new opportunities.

The exact number of people engaged in various works connected with boat cannot be ascertained. The census figures are also of little help in this regard. For instance, the Census Report of 1881 recorded only four persons as boat owners and seven as boat builders in Assam. The same report gave an occupational break up of men which showed 69,404 as fishermen, 3,744 as carpenters and 571 as timber dealers.[24] The carpenters did not include people engaged in construction of houses. They were enumerated as builders and masons. In a seperate explanatory paragraph a total number of 7,600 persons had been shown as boatmen including laskars.[25] The number of fishermen recorded above does not give us the real picture. Largely guided by caste consideration the female members were also recorded as fishermen.[26] Again, timber dealers invariably included dealers in dug-outs and boats. Likewise, the exact number of boat builders in 1891 cannot be ascertained but, we are told, four-fifths of them combined the occupation with agriculture.[27]

In 1901, boat building was the exclusive occupation of 1823 persons. Another 1,094 cultivators reported to have had practised it as a subsidiary occupation. The cart owners, drivers and boatmen together numbered 38,591.[28]

Over and above the anomalies of enumeration and compilation of specific occupation pattern, our analysis gets diluted because of the fact that the figures of the two Surma valley districts were also cast up in the statistics. Taking everything into consideration and making allowance for some marginal error, we may conclude that in the period of half a century from 1870 not less than forty thousand people depended on boats for their livelihood. In terms of percentage of population they constituted a mighty little but in terms of volume of business and as a part of forest activities, they did really matter.

Speculative capital also poured in bit by bit. In Eastern Duars, for example, the Boro people received cash in advance from the traders and supplied them boats. Though their principal occupation was agriculture, they were tempted by ready cash. They felled the trees in the forest, shaped them into dug-outs and got them ready for sale in the rainy season. Half the proceeds of the boats went to the shopkeepers as interest for money advanced by them, the other half was the share of the boat makers, who still remained liable, however, to the moneylending shopkeeper for the principal amount given in advance in the first instance.[29] The poor tribals were thus exposed to the wiles of the loan sharks.

Until 1883 there was no system of registration of boats at any entry or exit point in Assam. In that year, registration of boats was made compulsory. The duty was assigned to the Divisional Forest Officer at Dhubri. The registration records provide us with dependable statistics regarding export of timber and other forest produce from Assam to Bengal. The number of boats exported during the years from 1883–4 to 1893–4 totalled 16,386, on the average 1,490 boats were exported yearly.[30] The highest number of 2,812 boats were exported from Assam in 1893–4. Since then there was a gradual decline in export of boats, the figures for the next four years were 1886, 1712, 875 and 410 respectively.[31]

The export of huge number of boats from Assam was worked upon the demand for boats in Bengal and those were mostly made of the durable variety of timber, the *sal*. Secondly, the boat making industry, once a thriving business in Calcutta, Chittagong and Sylhet, was slowly going down in the later part of nineteenth century.[32]

Investment in this sector became unprofitable and it gradually petered out. But the need of the common men could not be fully satisfied by the steamers, cart roads and railways. They opened their eastern window craned their necks out and discovered a land of promise. It was not only an endless source of supply of their essential means of transport, but also of every other single item of common menage like logs, posts and pieces, bamboo, canes, reeds, thatching grass, etc. Every poor soul knew this as much as he knew his God or Allah.

The importance of boats in the economic life of the people of the low lying districts of eastern Bengal and Assam could be suitably illustrated from the writing of Nirad C. Chaudhuri. He has given us a telling account of the very common means of transport in its heydays. His account holds good equally for all the rivers and river-boats of Lower Assam. Before the introduction of railways into the jute supplying areas, an elaborate system of boat traffic kept the flags of native skill flying. In his well-known autobiography, Nirad C. Chaudhuri spoke about 'a little river' of his home town Kishorganj in the district of Mymensing. The river filled out in the rainy season and then the frogs, the leeches and large crowd of peasants in search of fish became its unfailing allies.

> Last of all came the boats which were the sight of the season we loved best. Every year they came like migratory birds, in twos and threes for the first few days and then in larger numbers.... They were always kept spick and span, for as the boatmen were in the habit of saying, 'The fortunes of boat and wench alike depend on the make up.' All those things went on like unalterable laws of the Medes and the Persians until 1942 when thousands and thousands of these boats had been ruthlessly destroyed at the time of the Japanese invasion scare....[33]

Recent research has also shown that burning up of more than twenty-six thousand boats and diversion of another twenty thousand to unreachable destinations, lest they fell into the hands of the Japanese in 1942, was a contributing factor of the great famine of Bengal next year. The single panic—scared act had cut into the very lifeline of food transportation in many districts.[34]

This 'non-mechanized' transport system continues to play a significant role in Bangladesh even today. Bangladesh cannot dispense with her country boats any more than she can change her geography.

FABULOUS FOREST

It did not take much time for the British to realize that forest could be an unending source of revenue. So they quickly established their exclusive control over the flora and fauna of the province. Until 1878 the government had no policy for conservation of forests though forest and forest activities attracted their attention even in the early fifties of the nineteenth century. The association of the indigenous population with the forest was confined to collection of wood for house-building, boat-building and other materials of daily necessity including fuel logs, thatch, reeds and canes.

Forest activity had the possibility of absorbing a large number of people. But the people did not take any advantage of this new area of economic activity. Neither there was initiative of the government nor of the merchants from outside the province to involve them. Yet, the volume of trade was increasing and the area of operation was expanding without hindrance. The merchants from Bengal in particular feasted on it. Thus began commercialization of forest in Assam.

The legacy of the colonial economic order was nowhere more apparent than in the exploitation of mineral and forest resources of Assam. Traders and speculators, both Indian and foreign, made investment and earned good profit. The government encouraged investment and gave the investors all protection, as they were interested in the continuous flow of revenue. The income effects of those diverse economic enterprises on the local economy was almost nil. We have no definite information about the employment pattern of merchant houses or the trading companies, yet it would not be unsafe to conclude that the local recruits, no matter how big or small was their number, had only subsidiary roles. The surviving scene does not hint at any other possibility. The absence of a commercial class in the province created room for external capital to flow in. Commercial capital was followed by industrial capital and the forest of Assam offered them golden quarries ad infinitum.

Catching elephants for domestication was an old practice. During the Ahom rule it was not open for all. Pratap Singha, the Ahom king had the ambition of becoming the owner of one thousand elephants and assuming a title of pride, 'Gajapati'. Though his ambition remained unfulfilled he raised a small township near Jorhat known to this day as Gajpur—a town of elephants.[35] There was considerable research on elephants. The *Hastividyarnava* prepared in the early eighteenth century is a living testimony of it.

The *Hastividyarnava* was prepared under the royal patronage of the King Siva Singha and his Queen Ambika Devi. The work was entrusted to one Sukumar Barkayastha. The text of the treatise was full of rich and colourful illustrations done by Dilbar and Dosai, both of whom were Muslim painters. P.C. Chaudhury who edited the *Hastividyarnava* and translated the text into English is of the view that some of the illustrations would excel even the modern compilations made by G.P. Sanderson and G.H. Evans. Distinct features of 12 types of male and 6 types of female elephants have been discussed in the work. Sukumar Barkayastha had drawn heavily on some earlier works in Sanskrit.[36]

We could not ascertain exactly since when, after the coming of the English, the export of elephants from Assam to the other parts of India started. At the beginning there was no restriction on catching elephants for trade, the government threw it open to every kind of private enterprise. All that the government did take care of was the realization of levy at the rate of Rs. 10 on each elephant exported from Assam. The annual return of this levy often reached upto Rs. 6,000 which implies that no less than 600 elephants were exported annually. The actual figure, however, was higher than this as many traders avoided the payment and secretly left the province by the northern Duars. The government ignored the evasion 'because it was considered politic to encourage the hunting of elephants rather than to restrict it'.[37] With the abolition of all transit duties at Goalpara the tax levied on export of elephant was also done away with.

The government was yet to evolve a policy on elephant catching and trade. The Government of Bengal called for the views of F. Jenkins, the Commissioner, who in turn invited the opinions of the District Magistrates. They were divided in their opinions. Some of them favoured the idea of imposition of tax on elephant catching. Anandaram Dhekial Phukan supported this proposal. He suggested that tax might be imposed either on the *koonki* (the trained female elephant used for catching the wild calves) or the newly caught elephants. There were others who resented the idea of imposition of any tax. They argued that taxation might discourage elephant catching and a growing number of elephants meant a growing 'menace'.[38]

Lieutenant F.G. Eden of the Assam Light Infantry Battalion was then in-charge of government *kheddah* or the Elephant Catching Operation. Particular localities were earmarked for government operations. Eden collected information with regard to the varieties of elephants and their nature of habitation. Eden identified three distinct kinds, 'castes' as he called them, of elephants, namely *Coomahs*, *Dooarsala* and *Maraga*. Eden was in favour of putting strict restrictions on private catching. On the contrary, Jenkins did not find it advisable to throw any check in the way of hunting elephants except in the vicinity of the government *kheddahs*. Termination of all hunting right might lead to public resentment. Secondly, he noted that for the hill tribes trade in ivory was an inalienable privilege and murder of foreign hunters who invade their area of operation was too common to ignore. 'In my judgement', Jenkins concluded, 'the better plan would be for the government to abandon their own hunting altogether and to make arrangements to buy at fixed and liberal prices all elephants caught by private hunters'.[39]

But the Governor-General Lord Dalhousie did not fully concur with the views of Jenkins. In a lengthy note '*kheddah* in Assam' Dalhousie displayed his keen interest in the matter. He directed that 'elephant catching should not be attempted among the Rengma, Lotah and Angami

Nagas'. He could see through the demerits of private catching 'not because great numbers are so caught, but because those partial operations disturb and drive away the animals from their grounds and render the efforts of the government establishment ineffectual'. Dalhousie was fully aware of the demand for Assam elephants. He noted that the province of Pegu had already imported 150 elephants from Assam and 'many more are wanted there. The new office of the Lt. Governor has just created a fresh demand for 80 more elephants which cannot be supplied.' By abandoning the *kheddah* at that stage as suggested by Jenkins, the government would have to depend on private hunters. Dalhousie had no difficulty in getting his own way.[40]

Next to boats, elephants were the most useful means of communication for the rich. Besides the government officials, the mauzadars, the planters, the contractors and the *satradhikars* used to keep them.[41]

The free-to-hunt-and-catch policy continued till 1874. After 1874–5 new regulations came into force. The government created elephant *mahal* or operational partition in the districts and the right of elephant catching in those tracts was sold in auction. The open season allowed to the lessee was for six months in a year from 1 October to 1 April. In addition to the auction money he had to pay a royalty of Rs. 100 for every elephant captured. The government reserved to itself the right to purchase all elephants from the *mahal* owner on payment of Rs. 600 for each elephant.[42] These measures brought some discipline into the matter and the well-known appellation. *Hati-dhani*, i.e. rich in elephant wealth came into vogue since then. There were many who made their pile out of this. Notable among them were Bhagyamalla Barua, Gangagobinda Phukan, Earl Grey, Kingsley, Radhakanta Phukan, Dhanbar Gam, Sadhanchandra Hazarika, Lankeswar Gohain and Manik Hazarika.[43] There were hunters who earned fame and money by shooting game of elephants. Tarunram Phukan (1872–1938) was the prince among them. His charisma as a barrister, a political leader and a hunter was unparalleled. Phukan's shikar accounts are full of evocative descriptions.

Outside the plain districts, Garo Hills was an important centre of elephant hunting and trade. Hunters from Purnea, Rangpur, Mymensing, etc., came to Assam and captured elephants in the jungles freely.[44] Recollecting his childhood days, Benudhar Rajkhowa tells us about an Englishman called Parsell whom he visited with his father. He was in all possibility a lessee under the new forest regulation. Parsell kept some thirty wild elephants in his stable. He chose only the fast elephants for his work and did not like to keep the calves. To get rid of them the mother and the calf were taken to the river, the calf shot down and thrown into the river.[45] Sadhanchandra Hazarika owned a large fleet of elephants and it was so believed that nobody knew their exact number. The very sight of his menagerie made people speechless. Pageantry was the hallmark of Sadhanchandra, who was later made a Rai Bahadur. Benudhar writes that it was as if the extravaganza of Sadhanchandra proclaimed the power of the British Government.[46]

With the opening of forest for commercial exploitation a tribe of woodcutters appeared. Though drawn from agricultural background, they fell in love with the forest and tried to make it a home away from home. The woodcutters were neither dealers, nor agents of the traders, as such they had no share in the pie. The woodcutters of Bengal were joined by the Boro, Rabha, Garo, Rajbansi and Hajong labourers. They were driven into the forest by the magic power of money. Every year, about six hundred boats came from Sirajganj, Dacca and some other stations of Bengal for purchase of timber.[47]

We have given an account of the export of boats earlier. Besides boats, the export of other forest products too calls for our attention. The export figures for the first eleven years of registration, from 1883–4 to 1893–4, are reproduced in Table 4.1.[48]

The export figures for the next four years suggest a different pattern. Generally speaking, except logs, there was a rise in export of other materials. Though we have no definite information as regards the high demand for logs by the government in the early years and the gradual fall in demand later, in all probability, it was related to the construction of railways. Construction of railway lines was given a boost by the New Guarantee system evolved by the government after 1880. From 1882 to 1900 the 'construction went on rapidly, averaging 744 miles per year'.[49] There was every possibility of the government demand fluctuating for this and other reasons, but public demand for the essential materials of

TABLE 4.1

		Average
Logs	5,39,813	49,074
Posts and pieces	34,40,391	3,12,762
Bamboos	2,10,435	19,130
Canes	53,74,754 bundles	4,88,614
Reeds	7,38,790 bundles	67,162
Thatching grass	35,483,946 cft.	32,25,813

TABLE 4.2

Materials	*1894–5*	*1895–6*	*1896–7*	*1897–8*
Logs	30,102	19,197	30,344	31,141
Post and pieces	3,18,022	3,73,343	3,64,624	3,13,485
Bamboos	17,907	20,640	14,327	5,600
Canes	6,10,041 bundles	9,25,085 bundles	8,50,801 bundles	9,72,244 bundles
Reeds	71,072 bundles	63,493 bundles	72,432 bundles	37,160 bundles
Thatching grass	22,77,244 cft.	2,517,133 cft.	1,183,953 cft.	513,203 cft.

house construction was on the rise. Four districts of Assam had their share in the export materials. Boats and dug-outs went from Goalpara and Kamrup (the dug-outs from Garo Hills district, at present under Meghalaya, found market in the same channel); logs, posts and pieces went from Goalpara and Kamrup; bamboos from Kamrup; canes from Lakhimpur, Sibsagar, Kamrup and Goalpara; reeds mainly from Kamrup; thatching grass from Kamrup and Goalpara. Apart from the near destinations of Rangpur and Mymensing, those materials were carried down to the interior parts of eastern Bengal like Bogra and Pabna.[50]

So, there was no let-up of the oppressive drain on forest resources. Evasion of government notice to avoid revenue payment was common. As the Table 4.2 shows, the recorded figures were in no way less staggering. Since our interest is on the volume of export, we have combined the figures for government and private supplies.[51]

It is obvious that though boats and elephants played a vital role in the socio-economic life of the people, they could not provide the infrastructure of modern economic development. They could only play a subsidiary role. The impetus came from cultivation of tea and exploration of petroleum. As thousands of boxes were needed for the export of tea, it gave boost to the lumber industry in the state. The role of the government to propel business activities in mineral resources was limited. They could foresee that the talents of the local people if any, could at best be drawn upon agriculture and handicrafts. They had no entrepreneurial ideas or experience.

The point is whether the government took any step to take the province out of the medieval morass. Shortage of population was a permanent obsession with the government; they thought that more population meant higher demand and higher production. Whatever might have been the sympathies of a particular Commissioner or a Lieutenant Governor, decisions of the supreme government on financial matters were determined by hard economic realities. The dominant economic philosophy of the government was free trade and until the First World War there was no shift of policy.[52]

Before we take up tea, petroleum, coal, etc., for discussion, we should like to put briefly the two different views on the limited role of the government in the economic arena.

L.C.A. Knowles, the leading economic historian, stated that: (i) England could have done much more towards the economic growth in India had she 'not believed so thoroughly in laissez faire for herself and for other', but at the same time, he reminded, 'a policy of government development is expensive, and it would have meant increased taxation to be paid by the peasant...and (ii) that, "sense of values" the English had differed greatly with the Indians' whose outlook in life is essentially 'non-economic'. Knowles studied the question of economic development of the overseas empire of the British and discerned these limitations of the economic situation. But Knowles' assumptions did not reveal the whole story. A.K. Bagchi blames the rulers for what he called the 'paralysis of will' caused by a conflict between understanding and practice of economic policy. He also asserts that government did not believe 'in complete laissez faire for India outside the fields of investment in railways and irrigation'.[53]

In Assam, however, the entire field of industrial economy was kept open for the champions of laissez faire. The provincial government did not take any active role in the development of petroleum and coal industries. We cannot ignore the fact that though in India modern industries namely coal mining, railway construction, jute, cotton, etc., began much earlier and various labour and factory legislations came into force before the birth of the Indian National Congress, the Government of India created the Department of Commerce and Industry as late as 1905 only.[54] So, until then, it is obvious, the government had but very little role in the growth of modern industries in our country. Then how could things be different in Assam? Even the objective conditions for developing manufacturing industries similar to Madras or the United Provinces were absent in Assam.

LOVE FOR CHINESE LABOUR

The new economy had two most essential requirements, namely, labour and capital. The government knew that if they could ensure the supply of labour, capital would take care of itself. In the period under review, we notice that the government never made any attempt to organize capital. Their attempt would have led to more tax burden on the peasants. But they left nothing to chance as far as the question of labour was concerned.

The interest of the government was most likely aroused by John M'Cosh. From 1837 he was exploring the possibility of a route from Assam to South China.[55] Again, in 1861, he wrote an article 'On the various lines of overland communication between India and China' which was published in the *Proceedings of the Geographical Society of London*. Of the five routes he knew and talked about he favoured the Patkai–Bhamo–China route.[56]

The necessity of such a route was further emphasised by Clement Williams, Agent to Chief Commissioner, British Burma in 1864. With the characteristic zeal of an Englishman he estimated:

> There are forty millions of people waiting to be clothed with British piece-goods, and to be furnished with the handiworks of all the manufactories of England, and ready to give, in return, silk, tea and the most valuable of the useful and precious metals, from mines that European skill would make many-fold more productive than now.[57]

China, the British thought, could be an unending source of labour supply. Though the Anglo-Chinese relationship had come under strains in the wake of the Opium War the economic hardship of the Chinese people was too widespread to be overlooked. When exactly the idea smote them could not be ascertained. But we gather from a report of Col. Jenkins, the Agent to the Governor-General, sent to the government of Bengal on 30 April 1860 that 'repeated attempts had been made by Col. Vetch, Col. Hannay and Captain Holroyd, the officers of the frontier district of Upper Assam. They spared no effort to establish a free communication with the northern Burmese posts across the Patkai range. Bhamma, Moogkoom were some of the important posts regularly visited by the Chinese traders.' But every attempt of the officers failed. Jenkins was of the view that the line of communications as desired should be worked out by the British Commissioner of Pegu.[58]

But the Government of India was apparently not satisfied with the report of Jenkins. They kept insisting on finding out a dependable line of communication with China, more specifically, Yunan to draw 'surplus population' from there. Jenkins wrote to the government in Fort William that there were no American missionaries in Assam who were familiar with the frontier tracts through which a route to Yunan could be located. The only person who had intimate knowledge of the intermediate countries between Assam and China was Col. Hannay. But Hannay passed away in the meantime. Jenkins expressed the hope that the exploration could be taken up in the following season by Captain H.S. Bivar or his subordinate military officer. Jenkins further recollected the successful expedition of Col. Wilcox in 1828–9 when he passed the line of the eastern range. The account of his travel was published in the transactions of the Asiatic Society. Jenkins assured the government that in view of their friendly relations with the Khamptis and other tribes inhabiting the border, fresh attempts could be made without any difficulty.[59]

When the officers were given to understand the strong desire of the government they took up the matter with earnestness. Captain H.S. Bivar observed that the 'expediency' of the proposal to ask 'the surplus populations of Yunan in China to immigrate to Assam was self-evident, both as to the interest of Assam and to the benefit which Chinese immigrants would derive from settling in a country so congenial to them'. Bivar noted that opening a road to Yunan would not be an easy task but if they could overcome the difficulties the results would be very rewarding. Captain Bivar attempted to give precise information as to the routes and their distance. From Makum a frontier post of the Lakhimpur district, the distance to Yunan, he said, would be between 250 to 300 miles and could be covered in 23 days. He, however, apprehended resistance from the Nagas, the Singhphoes and also of the Burmese Government against immigration of Chinese labour to the British territory. Since the country between Assam and Yunan was a *terra incognita* the first step to clear the route would be a simple geographical exploration. But parallel investigation and testing of possibilities were simultaneously going on almost without the knowledge of the provincial government. Baron Otto des Granges, for example, advanced the idea of a direct trade route from Calcutta to China via Sylhet, Kalanga Ghat, Manipur, Monfoo, etc., in 1846. He calculated, as the crow flies, the Chinese province Yunan and Agra lay at an equal distance from Calcutta. But his idea did not find favour with the government.[60]

A CANAL FROM KARACHI TO SADIYA?

The canal-wizard Sir Arthur Thomas Cotton of Madras Engineers who had a brief stint of service, as colonel, in Bengal (1858–62) and studied the water communication system of the Ganga valley, prepared a scheme to open a communication between Assam and China.[61] He proposed the route leading from Calcutta by the Brahmaputra and then across to the Yang-tse-Kiang. He estimated that the distance to be covered by land routes between the two rivers would be 300 miles. He found his scheme more workable than that of Captain Osborne who suggested that the communication should be opened through Burma proper, from Bhamo to the Chinese province Yunan. Col. Cotton was of the view that a steam-boat canal of about 100 miles of length connecting the Sutlej and the Ganga would result in a permanent water communication from Karachi to Sadiya. On the Chinese side, he reported, there was a communication line by the Yang-tse-Kiang, the grand canal and up to the Howang Ho covering a length of 3,000 miles. With the proposed land carriage of 300 miles, Col. Cotton emphasized, 'there would be continuous inland water carriage of more than 6000 miles'.[62] Had this scheme ever materialized the geo-politics of north-east India would have been quite different.

Col. Cotton suggested that in order to materialize his scheme the government should collect all the necessary information in England and that a competent person should be sent to Sadiya to explore the land route and lastly, the Consul at Sanghai or some special agent should be directed to gather information regarding the navigability of the rivers on the Chinese side. The Governor-General confidentially asked Col. Hamilton Vetch to examine the scheme of Col. Cotton and to report to the government. Col. Vetch reported that the country lying between the river points on either side was 'exceedingly mountainous and rugged'. But he suggested that field investigation should be followed up and carried deep into the Chinese territory. He was of the opinion that Dibrugarh and not Sadiya would be the most suitable starting point to explore a land route to China.[63]

Col. Henry Hopkinson who took over the charge of the Commissioner and Agent to the Governor-General after Jenkins in February 1861, totally differed with the assessment of his immediate predecessor and of Captain Bivar. He thought that the problem of scarcity of labour could not be adequately solved by importing Chinese labour as the wage rates in Assam were low. Thousand of Chinese and Shan labourers found their way to Pegu and the Tenasserim and Martaban provinces. A Shan labourer could easily earn Rs. 10 a month and a Chinese labourer much more there. A tea plantation labourer got Rs. 2–8–0 a month in Guwahati and in Dibrugarh where labour rates were supposed to be the highest, the labourers were paid at the rate of Rs. 4–8–0 per month. Hopkinson pointed out that the sources of supply are much nearer at hand and more abundant than they are in Pegu, Tenasserim and Arracan and that Rs. 10 a month was a highly attractive rate 'to inundate Assam with labour from Bengal'. Hopkinson wanted that working in tea plantation would ensure as high wages as the working of teak forest in Burma but the tea planters used to pay their labourers about a half of what they really deserved. Under these circumstances, 'even if an easy and safe route from Yunan were established', Hopkinson observed, 'the idea of Chinese immigrants coming to settle or work for hire in it cannot be reasonably entertained'.[64] Love for Chinese labour thus vanished into the thin air and the idea of a Karachi–Sadiya canal was also shelved for ever.

ISLAND OF CHANGELESSNESS

Communication is perhaps not the word to relate the absence of it. There was no awareness either of its absence. Generations of men and women lived out their lives in one village or within the first or the second village next to it connected by a common field. There was no necessity of movement from one place to another except under compulsion of a political or natural calamity. The villagers lived in cooperation for their survival against unbelievable odds.

Caste was an important element of village formation. But men belonging to different contiguous castes used to live in one village in perfect peace and harmony. Variation in occupation pattern related to caste had no effect on their attitude towards life and death. Caste was not a force of social affiliation in Assam. Caste codes were honoured without any social discomfort. Beyond the contours of the village existed what may be described as village centres or local functional units. Those units were linked to a *hat*, a river port, a mart or a temple town. But for these opening facilities, the villages would have been islands of changelessness.

Changes in the rural society were slow, because change meant the break of man's daily contact with the land, water and air. The appeal of the sight and sound of his known environment was not easily lost in him. Villagers went by the ancestral wisdom that a small fish near at hand is better than a big one at a distance. Inseparable association with and commitment to their kith and kin constituted a sacred duty comparable to an obeisance to the Ganga. This is the essence of the thing we call the rural spirit.

Two constants of the rural spirit, viz., (a) a belief in the unity of interests and (b) an attitude of resignation helped the people to hold their own against winds of change. The bhakti movement purged their heart of many prejudices but its long-term effects were not entirely propitious. In the absence of a free flow of fresh blood the dynamism of the movement was lost. Fetishism got the better of it and life was interpreted only in religious terms.

It taught them the lesson of quiet resignation and self-denial which robbed them of their natural urge for exertion and love for individuality; it smothered their instincts of doubt and debate and ingrained in them an uncanny belief in the unity of social and economic interests in the community, it made knowledge the domain of a few and any venture into it an offence; it discouraged zest for life: by implication, zeal for competition, and greed: by implication, surplus production; it was unable to appreciate differentiation of labour and skill. The results were cynicism, insularity and immobility. The society was badly in need of a big push.

Unmindful of the changes around, some people dug their heels in and wallowed in their ignorance. Take for instance, the travel diary of C.T. Metcalfe, Chief Civil Officer with the Right Column, Dooar Field Force, of December 1864. Metcalfe had the stunning experience of motionless life in the ruling family of Bijni. To his great surprise, Metcalfe found that the common people were ignorant of the localities of police stations. They rarely used public roads. 'We passed through the villages of Kaljar and across a branch of the Manas to the village of Hoglebari', Metcalfe noted, 'country entirely given over to jungle, with only a few traders here and there of mustard cultivation'.[65]

The officer marched through the village of Borogaon to Raha thana, situated on the bank of a branch of the Manah. The stream was the boundary between Binji and Kamrup. From there he went to Bijni. The account of his visit to Bijni on Tuesday, 27 December 1864 could be best reproduced in his own words:

> Bijnee is a miserable collection of huts, without fort or Bazar or any pretension to a large village. The Rajbari consists of a brick wall enclosing some fifty thatched houses. I know of no such desolute position in Bengal as that of Bijnee....

Rani Apeswari, a 'concubine' of the late ruler Amrit Narayan, was then putting up her show. The Sheristadar of the Rani was a Bengali who expressed his 'inability to supply any provisions of any kind'. In spite of the wretched condition of the ruling family, Metcalfe was shocked to hear that the Rani had a big horde of slaves and they numbered 1,400. It was not the violation of law, since slavery was abolished in 1843, but the very thought of taking the burden of one thousand and four hundred souls by the Rani for no apparent necessity of hers that made his hair stand on end. The slaves in fact were the models of unproductive wastrels who used to hang around every man of means and were well content with a piece of cloth and a morsel of food. They seemed unwilling to set up as independent families. They remained happy with their parasitical existence. It took a long time, before they became conscious of their right to private property and lawful gains. They were not conscious of the world around them.

From Bijni C.T. Metcalfe and his party went to Sidli. There also he gathered no better experience and found the zamindar of Sidli 'totally ignorant' of the most essential information. The zamindar solely depended upon his assistants whom Metcalfe found to be 'guilty of gross falsehood'.[66]

Change depended on the development of communication systems and the degree of capitalist penetration. The government developed the water transport system almost free of cost. The implementation of the need-based road construction plan of the PWD and the Local Boards was hamstrung by shortage of finance and labour. Comparatively, railways had a better record. Beginning with the two short distance lines of Dibru–Sadiya Railway (1882) and Jorhat Provincial Railway (1884), came up, the most important of all, the Assam Bengal Railway (1895), the Eastern Bengal Railway connecting Dhubri with Calcutta (1902), and the Simaluguri–Naginimara (1917) and Chaparmukh–Silghat (1920) branch lines. A few tea garden feeder tramways built during these years strengthened the railway network.[67]

SAVINGS BANK

There is little information about the savings bank. Whatever evidence survives admits of a disjointed account of their existence and business. The savings banks were the pioneer banking institutions introduced by the government in Assam in the early seventies of the nineteenth century. Before the coming of the bank the upcountry traders carried on the banking functions with due sanction from the government. There were popular small trading houses in and around the tea gardens. Because of them banks came late into the tea districts of Sibsagar and Lakhimpur.

Except for Sibsagar and Lakhimpur, savings banks were established in all the district headquarters by 1872. The savings bank at Tezpur in the district of Darrang was opened on 3 July 1871 and in the period of nine months that followed ending in March 1872, a total of 29 persons were found to have had opened accounts with the bank. Of them, 16 were Bengalis, 8 Assamese and 5 Europeans and some of them were bank employees and their total deposit stood at Rs. 2,928–8–0. The provincial government reported to the government at Fort William that private traders gave higher rate of interest to the depositors than the bank. Whatever be their numbers, all the depositors lived in the same town. The report contained a remark on money circulation in the rural area which must not be taken as a comment on the district of Darrang alone, it was a representative statement on the prevailing situation in all the districts. The report said:

> Money in the interior was but little known seven years back, bargains being made in kind and even at present it is too much of a valuable novelty, to be entrusted to the care of others at the rate of 3¾ per cent per annum.[68]

The Nagaon savings bank was opened on 1 May 1872. In three months, up to 30 July, five persons opened accounts with the bank and their total deposit amounted to Rs. 97 only. Even after two years, transactions in the bank did not show any sign of improvement. Upon enquiry from the Chief Commissioner of Assam as to why banking function did not flourish in Nagaon as it did in the other districts, the Deputy Commissioner reported,

> the Omlah and well to do natives prefer investing their surplus cash in the purchase of land and immovable property to depositing it in the bank. The better class of agriculturists too, either invariably buy land or gold ornaments, such as necklace, earrings and bracelets with their savings or surplus cash.[69]

The scope of surplus cash with the government employees and the cultivators was limited. Whatever saving was possible the people were unwilling to deposit in bank. Deposit of cash and other valuables with the traders was a common practice. In sending the report quoted above the Deputy Commissioner stated that he was unable to find out which class of people were the depositors in the other districts. Without any supporting evidence we may guess that men variously connected with the tea gardens increased the number of depositors in the other districts. The common men had their small savings stashed away in the loft or in bamboo conduits.

When the government went on opening the banks and took care to see that they thrived, the Issue Department of the Assam Treasuries knocked them cold. It appears from record that without the knowledge of the Commissioner Henry Hopkinson, the Issue Department started issuing Rs. 5 notes by 'cutting the notes in half and sending one set of halves at a time'. The department took this step so much as to impress upon the government the ignorance of the common men of the use and proper care of bank notes. The department however, clarified that those who preferred whole notes could get them pasted. Hopkinson reported the matter to the government of Fort William with his strong disapproval of the new method of issuing cut-notes. He observed that under the law the whole notes were the legal tenders and said, 'I really doubt if a man could be obliged to take a silver rupee in two halves'. He also cried down the paste-if-you-like authorization of the department. He noted,

> It is all very well to say that people who require whole notes can paste the halves together, but the paste or other cohesive mixture has yet to be discovered that will hold notes together anywhere on the eastern side of the Bay of Bengal...and the note paper itself will not bear perpetual repasting in this climate.[70]

What really irked Hopkinson was that the prestige of the provincial government was at stake. What could be a bigger disgrace for the British than their inability, after so many years of uninterrupted rule, to infuse into their subjects the elementary knowledge of use of money? Hopkinson, therefore, remonstrated, 'The adoption of the cut-note plan by the Issue Department suggests a slur on the executive which it does not deserve.'[71] Hopkinson's objections were too strong to be ignored and the practice of issuing cut-notes stopped immediately after. We are not sure if this practice was adopted anywhere else in India.

DISCOVERY AND DEVELOPMENT OF TEA

Tea is the most precious legacy of the British rule in Assam. It was a popular beverage in Britain right from the seventeenth century. The Assamese have no such long memory of tea. There is a vague conjecture that some people used the extract of dry pounded leaves of tea growing in the wild. But people in general took to the habit of drinking tea as a matter of daily routine only in the mid-nineteenth century. Though tea could not conquer the opium addicts of Assam it soon became a respectable component of Assamese culture.

In the discovery of tea the Assamese had no important role. After the discovery came the period of experiment and development. Tea was a metaphor for adventure, it 'called for courage, endurance and fortitude and withal some of the gamblers' instinct to take a chance with the unknown'.[72] Though they lacked the spirit of adventure, the Assamese were not bad learners and before the turn of the century the ambitious few among them began a new chapter of life with tea.

It serves no purpose to criticize the flow of private British capital. The foundation of modern industry in Assam was laid by foreign capital. Government policy alone could not provide motivation and direction for investment. Without adequate cooperation, the government policy meant nothing. For instance, the government tested the possibility of lac and rubber as commercial crop and they met with encouraging response. The hill portion of Nagaon and the Kamrup district would have been the prolific quarries of lac and the districts of Darrang and Kamrup promised good rubber. The government made it known that the prospective investors would receive the same liberal treatment as the tea planters did. But no speculator cared to sniff out. The government projects doddered for some time and then died a natural death.[73] Capital serves marvellous imagination, abhors asinine indulgence and never responds to desultory venture.

Long before the discovery of tea, Robert Kyd visualized the importance of the flora in Assam as an article of commerce. Robert Kyd, though a soldier by profession, earned reputation as a horticulturist. He was the father of the project of Royal Botanical Garden in Calcutta. On 1 June 1786 he wrote his first letter to the Governor-General suggesting the establishment of a Botanical Garden. Referring to his travels in Assam about ten years earlier, Robert Kyd reported that he 'stumbled on a tree the unusual foliage of which attracted' his attention. He took a few plants from Assam and ascertained their identity as the 'Cassie or true Cinnamon tree' of an inferior quality. The name of Robert Kyd does not appear in the list of the early European visitors or writers or merchants who traversed Assam. But his communications with the Governor-General conclusively prove that he had visited Assam and without doubt the western part of it and large areas in the foothills of Bhutan. Kyd hoped that his discovery would be 'the means of awakening the nation at large to a sense of the inestimable treasures which we already hold in our extensive dominions in this part of Asia'. He advocated a policy 'to reject such unprofitable parts of our empire as have already proved useless burden'. Kyd reminded that the collection and cultivation of such flora were not simple things of curiosity or of luxury but that they could 'prove beneficial to the inhabitants as well as the natives of Great Britain' and that in good time they would result in the extension of national commerce.[74]

The Ahoms called Assam '*Mungdung sunkham*'—the Land of golden gardens. Certainly they were charmed by the variety of green vegetations and the scenic beauty of the hills and plains. Robert Bruce, a British merchant, came to Assam in 1823. It was then writhing in agony under the Burmese. In the course of his itinerary Bruce came to know about the existence of tea plant from a Singpho chief. The matter was taken up with all seriousness by Robert's brother, C.A. Bruce.[75] The information of the Bruce brothers was enough to arouse the English spirit of optimism and they cashed in on them. Though it must go on record that Joseph Banks, a naturalist was the first Englishman to give encouragement to cultivation of tea in India as early as 1788.[76]

In 1834, William Bentinck, the Governor-General of India, appointed a twelve-member committee to examine the possibility of introducing tea cultivation. This came to be known as the Tea Committee, G.J. Gordon was appointed Secretary. On his departure to China Dr N. Wallich acted as Secretary.[77]

The communications of the Tea Committee deserve careful consideration. The committee 'with feelings of the highest possible satisfaction' reported that 'the tea shrub is beyond all doubt indigenous in Upper Assam.... We have no hesitation in declaring this discovery...to be by far the most important and valuable that has ever been made on matters connected with the agricultural or commercial resources of this empire.'[78] The Governor-General was delighted. He 'sent a commission of thirty persons to Assam among whom were doctors, experts in botany and geography'.[79] In fact, this was an extension of the Tea Committee. Gordon brought a few manufacturers from China and started work. By the end of 1837 they sent the first consignment of 46 boxes of Assam tea to Britain. It appeared in the English market as the first imported 'British tea'. The tea brokers of Britain declared that the tea was 'capable of competing with that of China'.[80]

As an article of trade tea was no more 'a speculation' but 'the certainty of a fair profit'. It ultimately destroyed the monopoly of China. The achievement of the British merchantile enterprise was considered 'no less than the brilliant achievements of her Nelson and her Wellington...'.[81] The Bengal Tea Association was formed by some European and Indian capitalists in 1838. They received encouragement from the Governor-General Lord Auckland. In England, the Assam Company came up in February 1839. Within a year the Bengal Tea Association merged itself with the Assam Company. The entrepreneurs were tempted by the tales of the territory 'flowing with milk and honey'.[82] It will be useful to record that private venture and speculations surpassed the government efforts and the tea industry became out and out a private enterprise. By 1840 the government opted out of it.

Once the government ascertained the possibility of tea cultivation they declared an open sesame to investors and gave them a free run of the province. They declared a set of waste land rules, applicable to the five districts of Assam proper, to induce capital investment. The rules were revised from time to time. A look at those rules will show that nothing could have been more inviting than the easy terms offered to the prospective planters. The first set of rules was declared in 1838. To constitute every grant as an economic holding it was laid down that the minimum area of grant shall be 100 and the maximum 10,000 acres. One-fourth of the entire grant shall be revenue free and no revenue shall be charged for the remaining three-fourths for the first twenty years. At the end of twenty years revenue shall be assessed at 9 annas per acre for three years and at Rs. 1–2–0 per acre for next twenty-two years. Thus the lease granted for 45 years would come to an end. Next came the rules of 1854, better known as old Assam rules. The minimum area of a grant was raised from 100 to 500 acres. One-fourth of the entire grant shall be revenue free and no revenue shall be charged for the remaining three-fourths for the first fifteen years. For the next ten years revenue to be assessed at the rate of 3 annas per acre and at the rate of 6 annas per acre for seventy-four years more to cover the lease period of ninety-nine years. Every grant was subject to re-survey and re-settlement after the expiry of the lease term.[83]

These rules did not specifically debar non-Europeans from the privilege of taking up lands for cultivation of tea, but in practice, their claims were usually ignored and rejected. The district authorities pursued a policy of discrimination. Here is one example of such discrimination. Ramjay Bhattacharjee in early 1856, applied for a grant of jungle land somewhere in the district of Sibsagar. The District Collector, C. Holroyd refused to consider his application. Ramjay then brought the matter to the notice of the Commissioner, Col. F. Jenkins.

The Commissioner found that though such restrictions were not clearly expressed in the rules, yet 'the exclusion of all but European capitalists from the benefit of the Rules, and the cultivation of such articles such as sugar, tea, coffee, indigo, etc.', had hitherto been practised. He took up the matter with the Board of Revenue and pleaded with them to do away with the restriction if there was any. The Board saw reasons in his plea and removed the restriction. Such remedial action notwithstanding, racial discrimination did not die out.

The Lt. Governor promptly acted on it. It was laid down that waste land grants in future should be given to Europeans, Assamese, Bengalees and others, 'without destruction, and the cultivation of whatever produce the grantee may think proper'. Following this, Jenkins suggested C. Holroyd to accept the petition of Baboo Ramjay Bhattacharjee. Thereupon, Holroyd, to quote his own words, 'called on the Baboo for Kabooleut to the effect that he will not settle on the grant any ryot of neighbouring villages, now paying rent to the government, but that he will induce foreigners to settle down and thus I trust we may introduce an improved system of agriculture, and obtain the services of a race of men possessed of more energy than the Assamese in general'.[84] By 1861, four public companies, twenty private companies and thirty-eight individual proprietors, seventeen of them Indian, were growing tea in Assam.[85]

Another set of rules came into effect from 1862. Under these rules, except under special circumstances, grants were brought under a limit of 3,000 acres in a single and compact tract of land.

Grants were also sold by public auction at the rate of Rs. 2–8–0 per acre, in exceptional cases the price could go up to Rs. 10 per acre. Inspite of great care there were ups and downs in tea cultivation. In the middle of sixties, one tea planter noted, 'the Companies and private plantations had to stop work. The coolies to whom they owed several months wages had to be dismissed.'[86] But soon the things were looking up. From 1869 its progress had been rapid and regular. Yet, it will be worthwhile to remember that Assam did not turn out to be a 'second California' as many of the speculators fondly believed.[87] It was but natural that the European planters were loyal and loving friends of the Raj. The Ilbert Bill controversy in 1883 stimulated their racial arrogance. The anti-Bill campaign gained momentum in England following the first Assam Dinner which led to the formation of a London unit of the European and Anglo-Indian Defence Association. In Assam their sound of fury was not strong enough to waken racial hostility of the people.

As soon as the tea industry fully recovered from the depression, new companies sprang up. They obtained land grants from the government and started plantations. It is worth recalling that the tea gardens employed a large number of local people in the beginning. Up to 1870–5, they constituted the major part of the total labour force in Assam. The growing number of tea gardens compelled the planters to look for some stable source of labour supply. In 1859 there were only little over fifty tea gardens in Assam. In 1869, 24 plantations came up in the Kamrup district; 110 in Sibsagar in 1870; 46 in Darrang in 1871; in Lakhimpur the number rose to 112 in 1874; and in 1872, 27 came up in Nagaon.[88]

When the tea industry felt itself fully secured, the Indian Tea Association turned its attention to the development of its scientific side. In 1900 a scientific department came into existence. The Government of Bengal and Assam also contributed grants-in-aid towards the working of the department. Dr H.H. Mann and Dr G.D. Hope were appointed scientific officers who served for the first decade. 'The rapid growth in productivity and the improvements in quality which ensued owed much to their advice, whilst improved machinery and factory technique produced a high standard finished product.'[89]

PETROLEUM AND COAL

Next to tea, petroleum and coal were the two important discoveries of the British in Assam. Though not completed, preliminary investigations in that direction were conducted by some British army officers, among whom mention must be made of Major A. White at Nampong (1837), Lt. W. Bigge at Namrup (1837), Captain F. Jenkins at Borhat and Makum (1838), Captain H. Vetch at Makum (1842) and Captain P.S. Hannay at Namchik Pathar (1845). Of them all, P.S. Hannay might have struck a rich deposit of petroleum. He recorded his exciting experience of noticing 'muddy pools in a constant state of activity, throwing out with more or less force white mud mixed with petroleum'. He also noted, 'At times there is an internal noise as that of distant thunder, when it bursts forth suddenly with a loud report and then subsides'.[90]

But it was W.G. Wagentrieber, an Austrian fortune-seeker who could be called the real discoverer of petroleum in Assam. Wagentrieber's application to the District Collector of Lakhimpur praying for lease of some petroleum wells situated in the district contained the first chapter of the story of petroleum in Assam. Before making the application Wagentrieber visited some wells of the district and assessed their rich potential. He was particularly attracted by the wells situated at Makum, Namchuk and Bapoo Poong. He stated that the wells were exposed to ravage and waste caused by wild animals and stray vendors of the crude who used to collect small quantities from the wells and never cared to protect the source. He was told by the people living in those areas that oil could be procured only during rainfree months of December, January and February. But Wagentrieber expressed his hope that by adopting proper steps the work could be carried on for a much longer period of the year. He also prayed for permission to work up the coal-beds in the neighbourhood.[91]

The District Collector of Lakhimpur was not aware of the wells mentioned by Wagentrieber, yet he recommended to the Revenue Commissioner of Assam to provide encouragement to him. But at the same time he gave a note of caution. He believed that the elephants frequented the wells for salts and not for petroleum. Bapoo Poong was an important post of elephant *kheddah* set up by Lt. Eden who was in charge of the government *kheddahs* in Assam. Search for petroleum must not interfere with the catching of elephants in that area. Wagentrieber should be given exclusive rights to work there without any hindrance to elephant catching. Namchuk was a remote point and the Collector was of the view that it would not be an easy task for Wagentrieber to protect his exclusive right there even if that was accorded. He favoured a lease of the Makum spring 'on any terms that may appear most encouraging to the lessee'. In the event of other petroleum springs coming to their knowledge and not discovered by Wagentrieber until then, 'the encouragement to the party first engaging in the speculation' should be continued; also the Collector suggested that for a time, three years or so no other application should be entertained. He favoured exclusive right to Wagentrieber to work up the coal-beds. The Revenue Commissioner, Lt. Col. Jenkins was too enthusiastic about the proposals. In fact, he was inclined to grant longer lease in favour of the applicant as the latter would have to make larger investment in sinking wells at the springs and any lease for a shorter period might entail him loss. Besides, he recommended that W.G. Wagentrieber should be allowed to work the coal with the understanding that in case the coal should be required by government he should surrender the quarry with a liberal compensation for any money expended in making roads to the mines or in other measures to render the quarries approachable or workable.[92]

From an additional report of the District Collector, Captain Dalton, it further appears that the quantity of petroleum usually collected was 'not more than from 20 to 30 *maunds* in the course of a year, that the only use made of it was by government officers and Europeans as a preservative from the attack of white ants...'. As the Assamese did not use it at all, there remained some surplus which was sold out to some traders who, in turn exported them outside the province. At the time of making these queries Dalton found that one Bengali trader, Ramjay Majumdar by name, had been carrying on the export trade without obtaining any valid title to do so. The cost of petroleum was also low. In June 1854 one *maund* of petroleum cost the Collector only four rupees including freight to Dibrugarh.

The Government of Bengal ultimately endorsed the recommendations of Col. Jenkins to grant the lease of the springs. But the lease of Bapoo Poong was given on the condition that Wagentrieber's operations would not disturb Lt. Eden's elephant catching. The monopoly of the coal beds was not granted to him but the government accorded him full permission to dig coal until further notice.[93]

We have this part of the story of Wagentrieber's adventure on record and nothing more. We presume that in spite of all the concession he received from the government, he could not materialize his dreams and his plans were never commercially successful. In any case, his was a low-key launch and nobody took any notice of his work or his winding up of it.

In 1865, H.B. Medlicott of the Geological Survey of India visited the eastern most part of Assam to report on the coal deposits of the area. During his tour he came upon by chance oil seepage at Makum. He recommended experimental digging. The Government of Bengal was not very keen on going ahead with the suggestion. The work was finally carried out by one Mr Goodenough of the Maclillop Stewart and Company on the either side of the river Dihing. Goodenough's efforts were a success and on 26 March 1867 he collected 300 gallons of oil from a well at Makum. S.N. Visvanath who has given a reliable account of oil in Assam observes that the 'well at Makum was the first successfully mechanically drilled well in Asia'. A tea planter called S.E. Peel also furnished information about the rich deposits of coal and petroleum in the Margherita area. Investigation on scientific lines was also carried out by other British nationals, namely, H.H. Godwin Austen (1874), T.W.H. Hughes (1874) and F.R. Mallet (1876). Their work greatly contributed to the geological knowledge and we are told, 'by 1880 the foundations for the understanding of Assam geology had been well and truly laid'.[94]

The extremely limited measure of success of all these efforts, from the native gatherer or vendor of petroleum to the individual efforts of W.G. Wagentrieber, Goodenough and others to derive raw produce of oil and coal for commercial purpose led to the conclusion that without developed technology and much larger capital, production of these goods was not feasible. The growing number of tea gardens, on the other hand raised the demand for coal. In the meantime, construction of railways in other parts of the country had revolutionised the communication system. Assam did not lag behind.

The Calcutta based Coal Committee took notice of the coal-fields of Assam but it was unable to organize mining. The Assam Tea Company (ATC) had carried on some mining operation around Jaipur. The real start was given by M/s William Malcolm and Browne Wood, a coal and timber company. In 1850, it 'entered...into agreement with the chiefs of Namsang and Kongan Duars for the liberty of cutting timbers and working coal within their lands on payment of Rs. 60 a year to each clan'.[95] After four years the ATC purchased the mining rights of the Malcolm and Wood Company.

The success of the ATC encouraged other speculators to join the race. Oblivious of the line of control, the speculators often forayed into the Naga Hills and raised disputes. In 1873, the Government of India imposed the Inner Line Regulation prohibiting people to travel beyond the line without permission from the government. In 1880, the Governor-General in Council exempted the ATC from the purview of the Regulation. But the company worked to meet their own requirements only. The largest concentration of coal was however located around Makum. The entire credit of the development of the Makum (Ledo) collieries goes to a British mining engineer, George Turner of the AR & T Co.[96]

The formation of the Assam Railways and Trading Company in London in 1881 was a timely event. It was on to a good thing at the right moment. The founders of the company could well imagine the prospect of such a company that would undertake construction of railways and then make use of them for its own trade. Timber and coal, the two major requirements of construction and operation of railways, the promoters of the company knew, were in abundance throughout the entire zone of its choice. Thus the AR & T Co. became the forbear of some economic novelties in Assam, it introduced railways, worked up petroleum and coal as articles of ever increasing trade and geared up tea and timber industries. The AR & T Co. was an instant success. But it felt 'that the profitable development of the oilfields could best be secured by a separate organisation'. Very soon the AR & T Co. had given over its 'petroleum interests including the Makum and Digboi Concessions' to the Assam Oil Company floated in 1899 with a capital of $ 310,000. Though the managing boards of the companies were different, they had one common Chairman. Accordingly, Lord Ribblesdale, the Chairman of the AR & T Co. became the first Chairman of the Assam Oil Company with its headquarters at Digboi. Another enterprise called Assam Oil Syndicate (1893) was also engaged in exploration of oil and it set up one small-sized refinery at Margherita and Digboi oil was transported there by rail wagons. The Assam Oil Company purchased the rights of the Assam Oil Syndicate and began construction of the Digboi refinery in 1900 which was completed the next year. The first consignment of kerosene produced there was 'symbolically' released to the market in December 1901. There was now genuine native oil for the lamps of India. The Margherita refinery was closed in 1902.[97] Petroleum and coal gave impetus to urbanization of Digboi, Duliajan, Ledo and Margherita.

All these undertakings with British capital promised the dawn of a new era in the field of industry. Unlike tea, the very nature of their operation did not leave any scope for native participation. It is equally intriguing to find that the native society took no notice of those novelties. They seemed to have remained as dull as lead to the discoveries brought about by the foreigners. Even the educated people did not react in a conspicuously different way. The absence of positive response to the new situation had far-reaching consequences. The pathological aloofness subsequently turned into a curse. By their impassivity and regressive mental attitude they made themselves persona non grata there. Such painful realization came, but it came very late.

That a handful of Assamese stuck to tea was the only silver lining. Petroleum and coal reserves are not inexhaustible. Reports have it that they may run well into the twenty-first century, not beyond. But so long as the mother earth survives, tea has a chance, unless destroyed by man.

In an interesting study Henry Hobhouse has identified six plants—quinine, sugar, tea, cotton, potato and coca which he argues, have changed the history of mankind.[98] As commercial plants they involve huge labour and capital, high gear technology and cut-throat competition, They call for tremendous state effort to keep the vagaries of the production barons within limit. Of the six plants, the British sincerely tried to introduce cultivation of tea, cotton, and sugar in Assam. But the old non-economic habits of the people remained in place and the attempts did not succeed fully. The Assamese were half-hearted about cotton and sugarcane.

There were few who realized the importance of the big changes. On 30 May 1891, an unusually long letter entitled 'Growing importance of Assam' appeared in *The Statesman*. The correspondent was 'K.L.B.' from Calcutta. We have strong reason to beleive that 'K.L.B.' was none other than the later-day historian Kanaklal Barua (1872–1940). K.L.B. wrote, 'Gradually the little and rather out of the way province of Assam is gaining more and more importance in the fields of industry. Its extensive tea plantations and coalfields worked with British capital under British supervision have proved to be sources of profit to the capitalists and have very properly raised the little province to the position of the more important commercial centres of the empire.' The land and river communications having been improved, he stated with pride, 'thousands of foreigners are annually overcrowding the valleys of Assam. The factories are not only replenishing the pockets of the British merchants, but are also providing employment to a large number of the starving people of Bengal and Chota Nagpore.'

K.L.B. was hopeful of the large natural potentialities of Assam. He wrote, perhaps more truly that he knew, that besides the Makum Coalfields there were 'many other coal mines in the province, while the prospect of working out petroleum looks very bright'. He emphasized the need of scientific knowledge to make use of the resources. He expressed his belief that there were 'various other gifts of nature to Assam which, for want of capital and industry, have, as yet, remained in an undeveloped state'. But he regretted that inspite of 'so many fields of occupation from which intelligent and industrious men can reap advantage, the Assamese are perhaps the poorest people in India'. He asserted that opium was at the root of their poverty. His remark that the Assamese were the poorest people of the country is debatable but the fact that the new situation offered big opportunities for the willing hands cannot be denied. K.L.B. saw things in an uncommon perspective and had a clear opinion about it, but he was too young and lonely to inspire the people to opt for such unconventional occupation or to make positive response in every possible manner.[99]

The Government of Assam was fully aware of the good works done by the AR & T Co. Henry Cotton, the Chief Commissioner of Assam wrote to the Government of India on 24 September 1898, 'Without the great work of the AR & T Co. there would have been no Borjuli Tea, no Margherita settlement, no Digboi oil and no Makum coal.' Lord Curzon, the Viceroy, visited the area on 7 March 1900 and observed, 'I find here a most interesting and enterprising corner of Her Majesty's Dominions.'[100]

NOTES

1. For the importance of horses and camels in the economic life of the people, see *The Cambridge Economic History of India*, Delhi, 1984, Vol. I, pp. 350–1.
2. N.K. Barooah, *David Scott in North East India*, Delhi, 1970, p. 105.
3. J. Butler, *Travels in Assam*, Delhi, 1978, p. 2.
4. Ibid., pp. 7–8.
5. *The Cambridge Economic History of India*, Delhi, 1984, Vol. I, pp. 350–2.
6. S.L. Baruah, *A Comprehensive History of Assam*, Delhi, 1985, p. 438.
7. See M.M. Sharma, *Inscriptions of Ancient Assam*, Guwahati, 1978, the original Sanskrit text, pp. 99–100, English translation, pp. 103–5.
8. Cf. H.D. Phukan, *Assam Buranji*, Guwahati, 1962, pp. 108–9.
9. S.B. Medhi, *Transport System and Economic Development in Assam*, Guwahati, 1978, pp. 19–20.
10. Ibid., pp. 26–7.
11. J. M'Cosh, *Topography of Assam*, Delhi, 1986, p. 82.
12. W.W. Hunter, *A Statistical Account of Assam*, Delhi, 1982 (hereafter Hunter) Vol. II, p. 22.
13. Hunter, *The Imperial Gazetteer of India*, London, 1881, Vol. IV, p. 155.
14. Hunter, Vol. II, pp. 201.
15. Ibid.,Vol. I, p. 18.
16. Ibid., pp. 141–2.
17. Ibid., pp. 174–5.
18. Ibid., pp. 128–9.
19. Ibid., p. 298.
20. H. Barbarua, *Ahomar Din*, Guwahati, 1981, p. 539.
21. B. Datta, *Goalpariya Lokagit Sangrah*, Jorhat, 1974, pp. 172 (12), 186 (13), 342–4; L. Gogoi, *Asamiya Lokasahityar Ruparekha*, Golaghat, 1968, pp. 133–6.
22. L.N. Bezbaroa, *Works*, Guwahati, 1988, Vol. I, pp. 2 and 15.
23. F. Braudel, *The Mediterranean and the Mediterranean World*, London, 1981, Vols. I & II, p. 21.
24. *Report on the Census of Assam for 1881*, Calcutta, 1883; worked out from the list of Professional Class III and Class IV.
25. Ibid., paragraph 218, p. 120.
26. Ibid., paragraph 223, p. 122.
27. *Report on the Census of Assam for 1901*, Delhi, 1984, Vol. I, para 223, p. 167.
28. Ibid., p. 165.
29. Hunter, op. cit., Vol. II, p. 131.
30. Worked out from an exhaustive report of Mr Campbell, Divisional Officer at Dhubri included in the *Progress Report of Forest Administration in Assam* for 1893–94, Shillong.
31. Worked out from the *Progress Report of Forest Administration in Assam* for the years 1893–94, 1894–95, 1895–96 and 1897–98, Shillong.
32. S.K. Mukhopadhyay, *Banglar Arthik Itihas*, Calcutta, 1987, p. 82.

33. N.C. Chaudhuri, *The Autobiography of an Unknown Indian*, Bombay, 1979, pp. 4–5.
34. S. Bhattacharya, *Aupanibesik Bharater Arthaniti*, Calcutta, 1989, p. 69.
35. P.C. Chaudhury (ed.), *Hastividyarnava*, Guwahati, 1976, p. v.
36. Ibid., pp. v–ix
37. Extract from the Report of Col. Jenkins, dt. 17 May 1854 to the Govt. of Bengal Foreign Dept. Political Consultation (NAI), July 1854, No. 36.
38. Foreign Dept. Political Consultation (NAI), July 1854, No. 37.
39. Ibid.
40. Foreign Dept. Political Consultation (NAI), 22 September 1854, Nos. 25–31.
41. B. Rajkhowa, *Mor Jivan Dapon*, Guwahati, 1969, pp. 15, 34. Also see T.N. Sarma, *Auniati Satrar Buranji*, Majuli, 1975, pp. 236, 267, 269, 298.
42. Hunter, op. cit., Vol. I, p. 109.
43. Benudhar Sharma, *Tokora Bahar Kuta*, Guwahati, 1987, p. 288.
44. Hunter, op. cit., Vol. II, p. 145.
45. Rajkhowa, op. cit., p. 8.
46. Ibid., p. 15.
47. Hunter, op. cit., Vol. II, pp. 26–7.
48. Worked out from the *Progress Report of Forest Administration in Assam* for the years from 1883–84 to 1893–94, Shillong.
49. V.B. Singh, *Economic History of India (1857–1956)*, Delhi, 1981, p. 333.
50. From the report of Campbell quoted in note 30. Also see *Progress Report of Forest Administration in Assam*, 1895–96, Shillong.
51. Worked out from the *Progress Report of Forest Administration in Assam* for the years 1894–95, 1895–96, 1896–97 and 1897–98, Shillong.
52. A.K. Bagchi, *Private Investment in India*, Delhi, 1980, p. 19.
53. Ibid., p. 20.
54. Ibid., p. 50.
55. J. M'Cosh, *Topography of Assam*, Delhi, 1986, p. 11.
56. D.K. Chakraborti and N. Lahiri, in *Man and Environment*, Vol. X, 1986, p. 128.
57. Quoted in D.K. Chakraborti and Lahiri, op. cit., p. 130.
58. Foreign Dept. Progs (NAI), Part 1, January 1861, Nos. 11–16.
59. Ibid.
60. See 'The Assam-Burma Route to China', by D. K. Chakraborti and N. Lahiri, in *Man and Environment*, Vol. X, 1986, pp. 123–8. Also a report by Mihir Mukherjee, in *The Statesman*, 3 December 1996.
61. Son of Henry Calveley Cotton, Sir Arthur Thomas Cotton (1803–99) became a legend in his own life time. Sir Proby Cautley, the architect of the Ganga Canal was a contemporary of Arthur Cotton. The two cult figures of north and south India locked horns in an interesting debate, as though to rob each other's 'claim to immortality'. Cotton stressed on low cost and Cautley on optimum functioning. (Sir Arthur Thomas Cotton was not related to Sir Henry Cotton 1854–1914, the former Chief Commissioner of Assam.) Ian Stone's *Canal Irrigation in British India* (Cambridge South Asian Studies) is a scholarly contribution to the study of the historical importance of the canal irrigation system of India (U.P.).

62. Foreign Dept. Progs. (NAI), Part A, July 1861, Nos. 460–1.
63. Ibid.
64. Letter of H. Hopkinson to the Govt. of India, dt. 3 July 1861. Foreign Dept. Progs. (NAI), Part A, September, Nos. 8–10.
65. Travel Diary of C.T. Metcalfe, from 20.12.1864 to 27.12.1864. Foreign Dept. Progs. (NAI) Pol. A, February 1865, Nos. 125–34.
66. Travel Diary of C.T. Metcalfe, op. cit., from 28.12.1864 to 30.12.1864.
67. Medhi, op. cit., Ch. II, pp. 40–2, Ch. III, pp. 56–65.
68. Assam State Archives Record. Letters Issued to the Government of Fort William, Vol. 47, No. 1473.
69. Ibid. Also see J.N. Bhuyan, *Uwalijoa Nathir Para*, Nagaon, 1991, pp. 114–15.
70. *Assam State Archives Record*, Vol. 47, Letter issued to Govt. of Fort William, No. 1315
71. Ibid.
72. H.A. Antrobus, *A History of the Assam Company*, Edinburg, 1957, p. 11.
73. G.N. Gupta, *A Survey of Resources and Industries of Eastern Bengal and Assam, 1907–8*, Shillong, 1908, pp. 81–4, 137.
74. *Fort William India House Correspondence*, Vol. XIII, see Introduction by P.C. Gupta (ed.).
75. William Robinson, *A Descriptive Account of Assam*, Delhi, 1975, p. 136.
76. R.K. Renford, *The Non-official British in India to 1920*, Delhi, 1987, p. 52.
77. Antrobus, op. cit., p. 16.
78. Tea Committee's report cited in W. Robinson, op. cit., pp. 137–8.
79. C. Becker, *History of Catholic Missions in North-East India*, Shillong, 1980, pp. 35–6.
80. W. Robinson, op. cit., p. 139.
81. Ibid., p. 14; cf. H. Hobhouse, *Seeds of Change*, London, 1999, pp. 155-8.
82. H.K. Barpujari, *Assam in the Days of the Company*, Guwahati, 1980, pp. 245–6.
83. Hunter, op. cit., Vol. I, pp. 50–1.
84. Fort William Revenue Progs., May 1856, Nos. 28–30.
85. R.K. Renford, op. cit., p. 57.
86. Becker, op. cit., p. 38; cf. Renford, op. cit., p. 54.
87. Becker, op. cit., p. 244.
88. Worked out and summarised from Hunter, Vols. I & II.
89. R.K. Renford, op. cit., pp. 70–1.
90. S.N. Visvanath, *A Hundred Years of Oil*, Delhi, 1990, p. 17.
91. Fort William Revenue Progs., 27 July 1854, Nos. 16–18.
92. Ibid., Letter of Jenkins to the Board of Revenue, Lower Provinces, 14 March 1854.
93. Ibid., Letter of William Grey, Secy. to the Govt. of Bengal, 25 July 1854.
94. Visvanath, op. cit., pp. 10–14.
95. S.K. Barpujari's essay in S. Bhattacharya (ed.), *Essays in Modern Indian Economic History*, Delhi, 1987, pp. 200–1.
96. Ibid., pp. 205–6.
97. W.R. Gawthrop, *The Story of the Assam Railway and Trading Company Limited*, London, 1951, p. 47; Visvanath, op. cit., pp. 19–20.

98. Hobhouse, op. cit.
Note: The book has a lot of good quqtes such as:
'It is unlikely that the problems created by the use and abuse of these six plants will be solved quickly, if at all. They have each created some grit in the oyster of the world's social balance, but few pearls subsequently emerge from the grit. But there is always hope that pearls may one day be found, as well as the more sanguine aspiration that hope may triumph over experience.'
99. *The Statesman* 30 May 1891.
Note: Kanaklal left for Calcutta for higher studies in 1888, stayed there till 1894 and returned home as B.A.B.L. He contributed important historical articles to the magazine *The Indian Culture*. The letter to the *Statesman* above could have been written only by an Assamese like him.
100. Quoted in S.N. Visvanath, op. cit., p. 20; cf. P. Gohain Barua, *Asamar Buranji*, Guwahati, 1976, p. 165.

CHAPTER 5

The Origin and Growth of the Assamese Middle Class

A COMPOUND PRODUCT

THE EMERGENCE of the Assamese middle class in the second half of the nineteenth century was the permanent and positive legacy of British rule. Unlike other social classes such as the priests, the peasants and the pensioners of the old nobility, the middle class had no inseparable link with the past. They had no nobiliary pride in them. In a sense, they marked a rupture with the past.

Scholars have studied the social roots of the Assamese middle class with visible enthusiasm.[1] They have contributed to our understanding as far as they go. Our enquiry leads us to certain conclusions which are at variance with others.

Though the emergence of the middle class in every state of India as a formidable social force is directly related to British rule, their social roots varied from state to state. Let us consider their position in two vibrant regions of British India. In Assam, as a social category, the middle class was at the top of the social hierarchy. But in nineteenth century Bengal, according to the social historian S.N. Mukherjee, the middle class really belonged to the middle rung. At the peak was the *abhijata bhadralok* class which comprised big zamindars, merchants and top administrators and who controlled land and capital market. Below them was the *grihastha bhadralok* or the *maddhyabitto sreni* (middle class) and it 'accepted the leadership of the *abhijata* and imitated their life-style'.[2]

In Punjab (1849–1947) the middle class was not a single social category. Its identity had to be located, according to the perceptive researcher Sukhdev Singh Sohal, in terms of 'classes' and they sprang from different sources. The well entrenched among them was the commercial middle class which consisted of moneylenders, bankers, brokers, etc. The strong footing of the commercial middle class can be presumed from a random selection of some facts: (i) Moneylending was a thriving business in Punjab even before the annexation. In 1872–3, about 2,500 moneylenders paid income tax. Between 1881 and 1901, the total number of moneylenders and money-changers went up from 43,000 to 1,82,000. (ii) The number of joint-stock companies rose from 50 to 155 between 1901 and 1913. The National Insurance Company of Amritsar, the People's Bank, the Amritsar Bank, the Hindustan Bank and the Doaba Bank came into existence. (iii) From 1860 onwards began a thriving export trade of food grain to Europe and other parts of India. Paradoxically, 'the agrarian middle class' comprising mainly the 'subsistence oriented cultivators' had a fragile existence. The landlord was a later entrant. (iv) Next in importance to the commercial middle class was the industrial middle class which received impetus only after the First World War. The professional middle class sprang from the common fount of 'western education and training'.[3]

Obviously the term middle class covers a broad spectrum of social and economic categories possibly with antagonistic interests within itself. Compared to Bengal and Punjab, the Assamese middle class had a narrower social base and it had to follow an uncommon trajectory. By bringing in the examples of Bengal and Punjab we are trying to emphasize the distinctiveness of the Assamese middle class.

Among the scholars, Manorama Sharma tried to pinpoint the social roots of the Assamese middle class. She says:

> One line of social roots of the Assamese middle class can, therefore be traced back to early British revenue officers, the most important of whom were the *Mauzadars* because of their numerical strength, their affluence and social importance. The other line of these roots must be looked for in the other important social institution of the time—the Vaishnava *Satras*.[4]

But we are unable to reason it out as to how these two institutions could provide grounds for the emergence of a new social class. On the face of it, they were less fertile than other areas. Emergence of the middle class was primarily an urban phenomenon. In nine cases out of ten the chiefs of *satras* and the mauzadars lived out their lives in the villages. They were not brought up on urban bread, though they were obliged to maintain close links with the district or sub-divisional towns. Towns attracted them a little later.

What was the real situation of the two institutions? The British established their control over Lower Assam before the Treaty of Yandaboo (1826). Upper Assam came under their control after the treaty. By 1853, the British Government in Assam was fully settled with a uniform system of general administration for all the districts of the Brahmaputra valley. On revenue matters, so far as the Lower Assam was concerned, the government showed some flexibility and allowed the old system to continue, which meant the rule of the zamindars in Goalpara and those of the choudhuries in Kamrup. In Upper Assam the government introduced the ryotwari system which created the mauzadars almost in a parallel situation with the choudhuries though their legal incidence were not the same.[5] Leaving aside their tale of fluctuating fortunes, the choudhuries and mauzadars were the men of consequence, of wealth, power and prestige in the villages. From 1872 the choudhuries came to be known as mauzadars.[6]

The mauzadars were the necessary adjuncts of the ryotwari system. As commission-agents they were under the control of a hierarchy of revenue officers. They could not take their privileges for granted. We have shown in Chapter 3 that very often their fate hung in the balance. Manorama Sharma herself suggested from a contemporary description that by 1886, 'the *Mauzadars* were no longer given the importance and respect which was given to the early *Mauzadars*'.[7] It is difficult to locate who the 'early mauzadars' were and what was the quantum of their 'importance and respect'. Maniram Dewan's petition submitted to A.J.M. Mills, 33 years earlier, did not give any favourable account of them.[8]

Padmanath Gohain Barua, in one of his successful plays, *Gaonburha* (The Village Headman) depicted a true picture of the rural society in the early phase of the British rule. (It was a textbook for the M.A. course in the University of Calcutta.) One mauzadar, a familiar character of the village had a strong presence in it. As then everyone knew, most of all himself, as son of a resourceful mauzadar, what it meant to be a mauzadar in those days. The mauzadar did command little respect and loyality; he often evokes pity. His peace of mind, nay, every moment of existence is haunted by fear of the inspecting sahib. His fortune's wheel might turn any moment from bad to worse.[9] At best he lived a life of dazzling uncertaintly.

The District Gazetteers of Assam, 1905 listed 288 *satras* in the province. Satyendra Nath Sarma incorporated a list of 380 *satras* with the names of their founders and approximate date of foundation.[10] Of those 380 *satras*, large numbers were established in the seventeenth century. The eighteenth century also saw the establishment of many *satras*. But only 4 *satras* were founded in the nineteenth century, they were Gonamara (Nagaon), Dharmapur (Goalpara), Nahira (Kamrup), and Nasatra (Sibsagar). The *satra* institution suffered severely during the Mayamoria rebellion and the Burmese invasions when 'some *satras* were destroyed totally and properties of others were looted or set on fire'. Though with the coming of the British in 1826 'may *satras* were revived and restored to their former position' their influence on the people began to wane. Sarma remarks, 'The impact of western civilization and the growth of nationalistic ideas amongst the people have stood on the way of its further expansion and the process of gradual decadence has already set in.'[11] Dying trees bear no fruit. The nineteenth century saw the eclipse of about one hundred *satras*, but it registered the rise of the middle class.

The sympathetic account of S.N. Sarma leaves us in no doubt that the best days of the *satra* institutions were over. On their own they cannot rise again. They gave a rich religious literature, revived and popularised the art of classical music and dance, introduced dramatic performance, encouraged handicrafts and introduced the art of manuscript painting. The newly evolving society had newer requirements which the *satras* could no longer supply. The new reality was the very explanation of their 'decadence'. No decadent institution could produce men who were destined to dominate the thought and action of a larger community in a new situation. Nor that role was expected of the *satras*. The higher ideals which inspired the establishment of the *satras* by some savants in the sixteenth century had become relics of the past, the establishment of the new *satras* was not always guided by noble intention; lust for money, power and prestige also went with it. They ceased to be the agents of social and spiritual progress and became sad symbols of cultural inertia. Indira Goswami depicts the guilt and misery of life in such a *satra* in her celebrated novel *A Saga of South Kamrup* (1993). Moreover, the inner and outer accoutrement of the *satras* of Upper Assam greatly differed from those of Lower Assam. In the *satras* of Upper Assam the *satradhikar* or the chief priest lived a life of pomp and grandeur but in Lower Assam the chief priest led a spartan life.[12]

Barring a few *Brahma Samhati satras*, the moral and material output of the 380 *satras* were too insignificant. Likewise, more than 300 mauzadars of the valley could give no good account of themselves. They began to gain social importance in the wake of the nationalist movement, mostly as loving and loyal friends of the British. As a class they acquired political importance after independence. The institutions therefore could do no wonders for anyone. Fame, resource and influence of the principal *satras* like Auniati, Dakhinpat, Garmur, Kuruabahi, Kamalabari, Kaihati, Pat Bausi, Byaskuchi, Bardowa, Barpeta, Sundaridiaya, Dinjay, Bhawanipur and Ahatguri were of little use in the emergence of a new society. Indifference to modern opportunities and vanity of birth, so characteristic of traditional values were grafted on to new seductive impacts of education and service, though on a subsidiary plane. Like elsewhere in India, certain traditional values entered the total sensibility of Assamese middle class.

The old value system continued to occupy the pride of place in the *satra* institutions and there was no reform movement to change them. The Gandhian movement of the thirties touched off the outer fringe of the institution. The assertion that 'the *satras* helped in the emergence of the early educated elite in Assam and hence in the emergence of a middle class'[13] therefore, flies in the face of simple truth.

We are not denying that the substratum of pre-modern society is carried on as a heavy baggage by a new society with modern values. This strange burden of the past carried by the dynamic present is an instructive area of investigation. But the past and its husk culture only determines the local specificities of a new middle class. In no way it may be said that the new values are born out of an atrophied society and decomposed values.

Likewise, the resource to give Western education to their sons and make them qualified to take part in the colonial administration was not limited to the two categories of people alone. They were open for wider sections of people and in reality they had utilized the resource and opportunities. The 'revenue officers' enjoyed no particular privilege to call for seperate attention from those others in the employ of the government.

The Assamese middle class was the compound product of colonial bureaucracy, English education and tea industry. It is indissoluble. Though the three components played mutually supportive role, the social formation of the class was flexible and it was capable of absorbing newer elements. It was a process, not an event.

Compared to the large number of persons produced by the colonial bureaucracy, English education and tea industry, as we shall presently see, the *satras* and mauzadars produced, in the period of our study only six persons who may truly be said to have had arrived. Of them, Dattadev Goswami (1818–1904), Hemchandra Goswami (1872–1928) and Pitambar Dev Goswami (1885–1962) hailed from three *satras* of Upper Assam and Abdul Majid (1867–1924), Ghanashyam Barua

(1867–1923) and Padmanath Gohain Barua (1871–1946) came from mauzadar families.[14]

COLONIAL BUREAUCRACY

We may now discuss how the three components noted earlier contributed to the making of the new social class. Apparently, the sources are not related to each other, but in some cases men belonged to one category could very well fit into the other. A person who had started his career in one profession might have ended up in some other, or the profession of one generation, was not appreciably looked upon or taken up by the next generation.

We have used the term 'colonial bureaucracy' strictly to mean the native ingredients of colonial bureaucreacy. Setting up of a creditworthy if not altogether popular administrative machinery in Assam in the thirties of the nineteenth century was no small challenge for the British. But they overcame the hurdles and built up a durable administrative system. In its early stage, people without formal education or with little knowledge of English were picked up and trained in police and civil administration. Jaduram Deka Barua (1801–69), Haliram Dhekial Phukan (1802–32), Jajnaram Phukan (1805–38), Dinanath Bezbaroa (1813–95), Harakanta Sarma Majindar Barua (1815–1902), Anandaram Dhekial Phukan (1829–59), Gunabhiram Barua (1834–94), Hemchandra Barua (1835–96), Madhabchandra Bardaloi (1847–1907), Rajanikanta Bardaloi (1867–1940) and Kanaklal Barua (1872–1940) are names to conjure with by every researcher of social history of Assam.[15] For their livelihood each one of them took service with the colonial government and each of them served his turn perfectly well. Our point of consideration is not their British connection but their contributions to the Assamese society. In an age when Bengali clerks were repeatedly accused of skittling out the Assamese and conspiring against their language, their getting into government service though small in number, had positive results.

The undisputed fact was that each of them gave a good account of himself in different ways. Singly or collectively they instilled vigour into the heart of a stolid people, gave them self-assurance through examples of their own lives, consolidated their language, discovered its literary heritage, created new social values, generated undying enthusiasm for education and cleared the way for a new cultural awareness and nationalism. Layer after layer deposit of the memories of their achievements created new aspirations and shaped a collective will that tried to assert itself. It was the middle class which gave voice to that will and its voice was heard. By 1874 when Assam became a Chief Commissioner's province it secured a solid footing and could arouse a feeling of admiration for themselves in the minds of the people.

We would make a brief survey of what they did to commend themselves. Jaduram Deka Barua was the first lexicographer of Assamese language. A knowledgeable man of his age, he contributed articles to Bengali journals like *Samachar Chandrika* and *Samachar Darpan*. He opposed the *sati* system and supported widow remarriage and himself married a widow.[16]

Haliram Dhekial Phukan is immortalised by his *Assam Buranji* (1829) written in Bengali. Writing about the history of early Bengali prose, Sajanikanta Das concluded that the *Assam Buranji* authored by Haliram may be marked out as the first printed original history written in Bengali. Sukumar Sen also agreed with the views expressed by Sajanikanta and he further observed that by the standard of that time the prose style was extraordinary.[17]

Jajnaram Phukan was attracted by Western education and the Brahmo faith. He was supposed to be the first Assamese who learnt English by his own effort. An acquaintance of Raja Rammohun Roy, Jajnaram's rebellious spirit found peace with Brahmoism and he became a *fidus Achates* of Rammohun.[18]

Dinanath Bezbaroa was a conservative Sanskritist, but later he realized the utility of English education and changed his opinion. He founded an English school at Lakhimpur. On his death *The Statesman* put on record these words which he really deserved, 'He was a living history of reference on all subjects social, religious and political, of the time of the kings of Assam.' He took 'the lead in all matters of public interest', said the *Times of Assam*.[19]

Harakanta Sarma Majindar Barua learnt Sanskrit and had working knowledge of English, Persian and Hindi. He lived through the best and worst years of the nineteenth century and his selective instinct faithfully served him when he set about writing his autobiography. The book, *Sadaraminar Atmajivani* is a mine of information and a running commentary on the time and events as the author lived and saw them from 1815 to 1890.[20] We have noted in Chapter 3 that the earliest book on agriculture in Assam was written by Kefayat Ullah. Published in 1853, that was perhaps the first book on agriculture written in any Indian language by an Indian. J.C. Marshman published his two-volume work on agriculture in Bengali in 1831 and 1836.[21]

Anandaram, Gunabhiram and Hemchandra were the pick of the bunch. It is easy to identify them as followers of the ideals of the Enlightenment. Anandaram was a pathfinder of his people. He was inspired by the industrial progress of England. At that time the term industrial revolution was not in vogue. The secret of England's progress, Anandaram believed, was education. He introduced the names of Oxford and Cambridge to the children of Assam.[22] A hungry frequenter to the bookstalls of Calcutta, he himself wrote *Asamiya Lorar Mitra* (The Friend of Young Assam) in Assamese though until then it was not the medium of instruction. This three-volume work established him as the father of modern Assamese prose.[23] Worship of learning was the central theme of his writings.

Anandaram singlehandedly created a linguistic consciousness and generated among the people a love for their own language. The moral influence of his endeavours became gradually perceptible. The American missionaries, namely, Rev. O.T. Cutter, Rev. Nathan Brown and Dr Miles Bronson first took up the cause of the Assamese language. But it was Anandaram who provided the backbone of the movement.[24] The generation that followed him set the style and tone of a literary movement. Almost every Assamese student took upon himself the task of making some literary contribution as a pious duty. The temper of the chase was complex and at times bitter but it was pursued in a spirit of openness. Althroughout his life Anandaram kept himself unspotted from the world.

Long before M.K. Gandhi was adorned as the Mahatma, the only Mahatma known to the people of Assam was 'the Mahatma Anandaram'. This adoration shows the feeling of the early elites for him.[25] Destiny denied him a long life or even much productive leisure, yet his life gained an inner momentum. At a guess, one would say, overwork killed him. Anandaram had a vision and a prayer for the all-round development of Assam. Though his prayer was never fully answered he left a strong moral influence on posterity. The voice of Anandaram became the voice of the Assamese people. For them he was, in every sense of the term '*enfant the son siecle*', a son of his century.

Gunabhiram's reputation as a writer rests upon his biography of Anandaram. He made his mark as a historian also.[26] His relevance to the contemporary society was surely not for these works alone. His other writings proclaimed the approach of a social storm. Gunabhiram's ideational proximity to Iswarchandra Vidyasagar and commitment to womens education, widow remarriage and Brahmoism showed that he was ready to challenge the tenets of the traditional society. Assamese prose truly 'became in his hand a weapon of strength and beauty'.[27]

Hemchandra Barua was a solitary rebel. He lampooned the vices of the old society but did not associate himself with any social movement of his time. It does not surprise us when we consider the academic projects he worked through. Otherwise, how could a collectorate clerk have raised the palladium of his language? He exemplified a type of man not known before. He was a man of wide sympathies with a high level of intellection. He was uncompromising, but always urbane and humane. He kept an ear to the ground but reveted his eyes on Bengal where epoch-making changes were taking place.[28]

Madhabchandra Bardaloi put emphasis on the cultural identity of the Assamese. Wide recognition of the heritage was expected to give Assam the necessary facelift. Since he could not look for help anywhere, he forked out his savings and brought out the *Ramayana* translated from Sanskrit to Assamese by Madhav Kandali, an erudite pre-Sankardeva poet. Madhabchandra's work of collecting the old Assamese manuscripts was carried on by the students.[29] A clerk at the district Cutcherry, Ratneswar Mahanta died at the age of 29, so he could not come to much as a writer. Yet we notice the early glimmerings of nationalist thinking in his essays. He talked up the legend of Jaymati to glorify Assamese womanhood, he brought to focus the martyrdom of Maniram Dewan and asserted that the English took a savage vengeance on him.[30]

A clerk at the Public Works Department, Lakhiram Barua brought in a fresh air of hope through his philharmonic talents. The virtuoso created an environment for music in Shillong, Dhubri, north Guwahati and Tezpur.[31] His fame marched with great eclat. Many people came forward to enrich Lakhiram's repertoire. They produced oratoriq, pastorale, idyll and humorous compositions.[32]

Rajanikanta Bardaloi established novel as a literary genre in Assamese. His important novels were written while he was still in government service. His stable readership allowed him no rest. Rajanikanta's literary triumph was a great asset of self-assurance for those who felt that the question of nationality was essentially a question of language and literature. It also gave the middle class a point of pride in its potentiality and a sense of fulfilment.[33]

Hemchandra Goswami and Kanaklal Barua had been casting about their role as promoters of patriotic history-writing since their college days in Calcutta. It was based on a pride in the past which relieved their pain of the present. They might have been influenced by Rajani Kanta Gupta and Nikhil Nath Roy who promoted patriotism in Bengal through historical literature. Their pretty long association with the British, as government servants, could not soften their zeal. Both of them were closely associated with the Kamrup Anusandhan Samity, the first research organization of the state, since its inception in 1912. They were successful awakeners of past history and their discoveries in the field of pure history and literature produced a receptive audience.[34] It is therefore, no surprise that there were other scholars to follow them.

All these men are remembered today not for the positions they held under the British but for what they did inspite of them. Without them, there can be little doubt, the British administration would have run smoothly, but Assam would have remained poorer.

ENGLISH EDUCATION

By English education we mean the Western system of education introduced by the British. Till the end of the nineteenth century opportunity of education in Assam was limited to the high school only. The Cotton College in Guwahati was started in 1901. The college fulfilled the immediate aspirations of the middle class, the common man also welcomed it as a happy augury. They looked upon it as the sacred cow of the Brahmaputra valley.

Compared to Bengal, the process of growth of the educated middle class was slow in the province. Sending of children to Calcutta for school and college education had begun even before the establishment of the Calcutta University in 1857. Anandaram Dhekial Phukan was the first child sent to Calcutta for education. There were some others who followed him. All of them could not complete their education. Our survey shows that those who were born roughly within fifty years of annexation of Assam and were educated in Calcutta, laid the foundation of the Assamese middle class. Education gave them opportunities for diverse careers. Until a few decades to come they could not constitute themselves into distinct professional groups. So, the middle class of the late nineteenth century Assam was an amylic amalgam of people of different professions or trade perhaps not yet conscious of their own strength.

Notable among those who went to Calcutta for education were, Anandaram Dhekial Phukan, Priyalal Barua, Gunabhiram Barua, Haribilash Agarwaḷa, Madhabchandra Bardaloi, Sibram Bora, Radhakanta Handique, Jalnur Ali Ahmed, Fatik Chandra Barua,

Anundoram Borooah, Gobinda Chandra Bejbaroa, Jagannath Barua, Manik Chandra Barua, Golap Chandra Bezbaroa, Bolinarayan Bora, Radhikaram Dhekial Phukan, Phanidhar Chaliha, Arangashah, Amrit Bhusan Deb Adhikari, Upendra Nath Barua, Gunjanan Barua, Lambodar Bora, Ramakanta Barkakati, Satyanath Bora, Debicharan Barua, Lakshminath Bezbaroa, Ratnadhar Barua, Budhindra Nath Bhattacharyya, Abdul Mazid, Chandra Kumar Agarwala, Ghanashyam Barua, Rajanikanta Bardaloi, Chandrakamal Bezbarua, Sonaram Choudhury, Padmanath Gohain Barua, Swarnalata Barua, Sarala Barkakati, Benudhar Rajkhowa, Hemchandra Goswami, Kanaklal Barua, Chandradhar Barua, Hari Krishna Das, Nabin Chandra Bardaloi, Radhanath Phukan, Lakhiprova Bora, Tarunram Phukan, Kaliram Medhi and Jnanadabhiram Barua. Three other seminal figures, who were born before the end of the century, too, cut their wisdom teeth in Calcutta. They were Suryya Kumar Bhuyan, Banikanta Kakati and Krishnakanta Handique. Two sisters, Sudhalata Duara and Sukhalata Duara who happened to be the first Assamese woman graduates also studied in Calcutta.[35]

Calcutta was the first school of the Assamese middle class. A learner's sojourn in the heart of renascent Bengal was a pilgrimage, a journey from ignorance to wisdom and a mutation of the self. Calcutta gave them intellectual stimulation and strength to their moral fibre. The youth in their efforts to discover the self discovered Assam. Surely, they were the faces of hope.

Our list above does not include all who went to Calcutta and studied there. But those mentioned were the persons who constituted the cream of the Assamese society. They spread out in different fields with diverse professional commitment. Majority of them entered government service, some took to tea plantation and trade, some set up as lawyers, a few preferred jobs of school teachers in Assam and even in rural Bengal. Though the scope of engineering and medical education in India and abroad was extremely limited, Assam too had her representation in those professions. New professions brought in new experience which added new colour and taste to their life.

They are the typical examples of, to quote K.B. Neuschel, 'the many formally educated men and women in Third World countries who routinely cross the "boundary" between their traditional village cultures and westernized professional lives in urban centers, alternating modes of communication and, it seems, personality type as well'.[36] In Assam, this class was easily identifiable. As a class it is torn between two value-systems and therefore, unable to develop a compact personality; courage and creativity coexisted with masochistic instinct and blurred vision.

Those green shoots of new Assam achieved treedom in due course. Under their lengthened shadow Assam came to terms with the situation of the early twentieth century. There were few others like Hemchandra Barua, Gangagobinda Phukan, Radhanath Changkakati, Bholanath Barua, Lakhikanta Barkakati, Kaliprasad Chaliha, Sivaprasaed Barua and Chandranath Sarma who had not been to Calcutta for education but they kept track of the important personalities, ideas and institutions of Bengal and benefitted from them. A creative section proved the linguistic distinctiveness of Assamese, introduced new genres of literature, established journalism as a respectable profession and broadened the mental horizon of the people; a few of them took to tea plantation and trade and by all these they completed the identity crystallization of the Assamese.

It was achieved in two phases, the first phase began in 1873 with the restoration of Assamese to its proper status and ended after 30 years, in 1903 when the first political party of the province, the Assam Association was formed. Such state level unity was heretofore unknown. The second phase started in 1903 and ended in 1921. The association had limited objective and had no plan to broaden its social base. The elitist bias did not fit in with the desperate need of the hour. With the image of a messianic Gandhi looming large in the distant horizon, the call for unity of the people could no longer be ignored and the only popular forum for such unity then was the Indian National Congress.

While talking about the unity we must not ignore some fissures in the social structure. At no point of time did the entire Brahmaputra valley come under the undisputed rule of any monarch. Even during the heydays of the Ahom rule, the river Manah was the extreme western boundary of their territory. Similarly, the Koch kingdom from the west confined to central Assam even at the highnoon of its glory. The valley became a geographically defined unit only during the British rule. Though the territorial continuity came under occassional stress, it survived.

The absence of uniform administrative and social system covering the entire valley before the coming of the English had its effects on the people, their outlook, expression and sensibility. Under the veneer of an unbreakable Assamese society there were, at the same time, some unbridgeable differences. We hope, some day, the complete story would be unravelled by cultural anthropology.

A sense of superiority permeated the sensibility of the Assamese elite of Upper Assam. Haliram Dhekial Phukan wrote that they looked down upon the people of Lower Assam and called them *dhekeri*.[37] Dhekeri was, in fact, a pergunnah under the Koch kingdom. It was their dialect which separated them from the rest. It seems absurd, but nontheless true that Raja Prabhat Chandra Barua of Gauripur, the founder president of the Assam Association was not sure of his linguistic affiliation. Much to the chagrin of the Assamese literary circles, he hosted, in the summer of 1910, the conference of the Uttar Banga Sahitya Sanmelan at Gauripur.[38].

It was even debated whether the Kamrupi (dialect) and Assamese are two different languages or one. The *Banhi*, a leading Assamese journal of the time editorially asserted that there are not two languages, Assamese or Kamrupi, it is one and the same.[39] Harinarayan Dutta Barua (1885–1958) pleaded that the people of Upper Assam should stop calling the people of Kamrup as Dhekeri; he also asked the people of Lower Assam to objure the terms 'Ahom Bamun', 'Ahom Kalita', etc.[40]

Taranath Chakraborty (1880–1953) published a journal *Assam Bandhav* in 1910. His main purpose was to popularize the words and sentence pattern of Kamrup and Goalpara. But he did not succeed.[41] In a paper presented to the first session of the Asam Sahitya Sabha, Ratnakanta Barkakati (1897–1963) cried down the parochial attitude towards language. He noted that such controversy would hamper the interest of Assamese literature in its growing state.[42] In 1917 Kaliram Medhi expressed the view that too much reliance on the grammar written by Hemchandra Barua created some knotty problems. Many words used by the people of Kamrup and Goalpara were not included in the *Hemkosh* believed to be the standard dictionary of the language.[43] Two years later, Kaliram Medhi as the president of the Barpeta session of the Assam Sahitya Sabha put forth a well considered view and favoured the continuance of the *Hemkosh* pattern. Banikanta Kakati, whose philological research later established the originality of Assamese on a scientific basis, analysed the phenomenon from the historical point of view. He noted 'under the influence of the Missonaries, a set of native writers grew up and books and periodicals in the language of eastern Assam were multiplied'.[44] Banikanta unfolded the actualization of one process but perhaps, historically speaking, a different evolutionary possibility also existed. Lakshminath Bezbaroa looked askance at Taranath Chakraborty from the very beginning and severely criticized him. The tension increased further when the fate of the district Goalpara became precarious; it hung in the balance for many years.[45] Led by Prabhat Chandra Barua, some zamindars of Goalpara demanded amalgamataion of Goalpara with Bengal. Their demand was backed by the Indian Association of Calcutta. Pramathnath Chakraborty (1883–1967), a graduate from the Patna National College successfully led an anti-amalgamation campaign.[46] An all-embracing and stable Assamese culture could not grow in such a situation. We have already stated that the influence of the *satra* institutions which brought about cultural unity and community strength was waning fast. Old values were no answer to the new challenges.

Goalpara conjured up an image of the 'other' in popular mind. Sandwiched by Kamrup in the east and Bengal in the west, the dialects and popular culture underlined the otherness to a greater degree.[47] The nationalist movement plugged the vents with remarkable success. Social unity of Assam is not the outcome of any evolutionary process, it is the reflex of administrative or political unity. Therefore it is fragile.

We find a historical parallel of this situation in France. Fernand Braudel observes that 'though at the highest level there has been a single French civilization, side by side there have been at least two civilizations at loggerheads, each with a linguistic realm', the northern civilization of *langue d'oil* and southern civilization of *langue d'oc*. 'As a rule', Braudel remarks, 'What happened in the north did not happen in the same way in the south and vice versa.' Let us, in an extremely limited sense, read 'east' in place of north and 'west' in place of south and we have the answer for Assam. Braudel concludes, 'There always has been and always will be "another" France in the south.'[48] The otherness in Assam cannot assume such absolute form because a souless Anglicism has threatened the base of both the structures. None can survive in isolation. For their common weal they must complement each other.

The Assamese elites devoted the second half of the nineteenth century (1853–1903) to the reconciliation with the British. Reconciliation called for circumspection, flexibility and a good deal of self-assurance. As they acquired a distinct social identity, they needed an agenda for work and soon they chalked out one. In 1903 they entered a more organized and assertive phase. The association politics nowhere challenged the imperium of the Raj in India. The Assam Association was no exception. Yet the government officers kept themselves aloof from the activities of the organization. Because it was patently a political forum.

The middle class for the first time developed political ambition and learnt the art of politics. The leaders of the Assam Association were never out of tune with the Indian National Congress. After 1915, the association developed what may be truly called a party machinery.

Earlier, it demanded the withdrawal of the partition of Bengal but did not organize any anti-partition movement.[49]

The first student organization of the valley Asam Chatra Sanmilan came into existence in 1916. L.N. Bezbaroa was chosen president of the inaugural session. His presidential address had a lasting impact. By showing the example of the Chinese students he tried to awaken the Caliban. Service, reform, excellence, patriotism, discipline, noble humanistic values were merged comfortably by Bezbaroa in his typically conservative creative exhortation.[50] The Chatra Sanmilan played a significant role in the national movement.[51]

The Asam Sahitya Sabha was established in 1917. It was the sanctum sanctorum of nationalism in Assam.[52] The Ahom Sabha also contributed to the growth of political conciousness among the Ahoms. By giving it the status of an associate organization, the Assam Association stole away the support of large chunks of Ahom population for the Assam Association politics. Nationalism in Assam, like Janus, was double-faced, one looked for sustenance and strength in an exclusive cultural consciousness and the other looked for its greater assimilation with the all-India personality.

The Assam Association phase came to an end in 1920 when it merged with the Indian National Congress. Until then, the inner strength and self-assurance of the middle class were intact and they breathed new hopes of social progress. Assam secured a major province status through its efforts.[53]

It is necessary to appreciate the devotion and enthusiasm of a handful of men who answered the call of duty. They succeeded in giving a new direction to the society. H.G. Wells tried to interpret the success of such group in these words:

> I am building my expectation of a new phase in human affairs upon the belief that there is a profoundly serious minority in the mass of our generally indifferent species. I cannot understand the existence of any of the great religions, I cannot explain any fine and grave constructive process in history, unless there is such a serious minority amidst our confusions. They are the Salt of the Earth. these people capable of devotion and of living lives for remote and mighty ends.[54]

From this Arnold Toynbee developed the idea of 'creative minorities' in human society. The creative personalities are fewer in number 'than the total membership of the societies in which they succeed in producing such dynamic social effects'. Toynbee further tells that the creator 'always finds himself overwhelmingly outnumbered by the inert uncreative mass of his kin and kind, even when he has the good fortune to enjoy the companionship of a few kindred spirits'[55]

The uncreative majority cannot impair the genius of the creative minority. Toynbee's formulation offers solution to the dilemma the Assamese society presented itself. On the one hand we find a large mass of the people, illiterate, superstitious and addicted to opium with no flame in their heart to live for a cause of their own, while on the other hand we see a section at the top of the social pyramid looking for a place in the moon. It has been the general refrain of nearly all the early writers of Assam to suggest that the people of Assam were the unerring children of Morpheus and that they had made Assam a veritable land of nod. The success of the creative minority has to be seen and appreciated in this background.

The secret of their success lay in English education. Its influence was not limited to the formal study and acquiring of a university degree, its impact was felt in the physical environment created by Western education. Some *satras* internalized the spirit of the age which benefitted their children beyond measure.

Toynbee writes that the gait of social progress is not a walk but a run and at some moments both feet (the creative minority and the uncreative majority) are off the ground. From the womb of the creative minority, 'a new creative minority' is born and it ushers in 'a new movement of Withdrawal-and-Return in response to a new challenge'.[56] The old creative minority lingers on. But the interplay of the two groups in the brief time-frame we have chosen for our study cannot be examined. Within the first two decades of the twentieth century however, the voice of a new creative minority was heard.

As in the other provinces, a large number of people belonging to the socially backward castes, tribes and ethnic communities were left behind in the run. This was not entirely due to the fault or negligence of those who won the race. It was the result of the government policy of favouring the rich and the advanced section. Charles E. Trevelyan wanted to justify in these words '...while the means at their disposal were extremely limited, there were millions of all classes to be educated. It was absolutely necessary to make a selection, and they therefore selected the upper and middle classes as the first object of their attention....'[57] There was much pushing and shoving for the limited opportunities.

The intellectual splendour of some personalities gave the middle class a rare self-assurance. The pre-colonial Assamese society had no noteworthy intellectual tradition. The creative influence of the Vaisnavite or bhakti movement of the sixteenth century was over long before. We do not find continuity of any creative social thought. There was no noteworthy intellectual output of the period. A few *satra* institutions of Upper Assam kept up a tradition of preservation, study and interpretation of religious books. The striking personality of the *satra* culture was Dattadev Goswami of the Auniati *satra*. He set up a printing press in the *satra* in 1838 and brought out a newspaper which ran uninterruptedly for twelve years. A forward looking man, he kept himself abreast of the political developments in the country and admired the articulate Bengali Press.[58]

Study of Sanskrit had a stable tradition in the district of Kamrup. Dhireswar Acharyya (1851–1919) was a great scholar of the traditional type.[59] Jaykrishna Bhattacharyya, Kahapani Bhattacharyya of the Sundaridiya *satra* were scholars of repute.[60] Lakhikanta Vedantabagich of Barpeta competed with Dhireswar Acharyya for scholarly recognition.[61] About 1878 Dhireswar Acharyya, with the help of Gunabhiram Barua and Padmahash Goswami, both Brahmos, invited Pandita Rama Bai, the eminent Sanskritist of Maharastra for a scholarly discourse. Rama Bai came to Nagaon, sat with her fraternity and left a lore.[62]

Students of modern Indian history are familiar with the great recovery theory of Sardar K.M. Panikkar. We find his exposition of the recovery much useful, particularly in the field of learning.[63]

The 'recovery' was pronounced in the pursuit of classical India. The establishment of the Asiatic Society of Bengal in 1784 was a landmark. Sir William Jones, Charles Wilkins, Lord James Burnett Monoboddo, Colebrooke and Halhed introduced the great treasures of Sanskrit literature to Europe. Notwithstanding the disparagement of James Mill in his *History of British India* (1817) and of Macaulay in his Minute on education in India (1835), there was no lack of enthusiasm for study of Sanskrit. H.H. Wilson, Monier Monier-Williams and Friedrich Max Mueller in Oxford were some of the great names of the nineteenth century associated with Sanskrit learning.[64] Panikkar argues, 'it was through the translations published by European scholars in English that the new middle classes began to know of the higher things in their own thought'.[65] Max Mueller himself thought that 'the discovery of that real India, of that new intellectual hemisphere, is...a far greater discovery than that of Vasco da Gama's'.[66]

Raja Radhakanta Deb (1783–1867), Anundoram Borooah (1850–89) and Pandita Rama Bai (1858–1922) belonged to the first group of Indians who made their mark as Sanskritists and were known to Max

Mueller. Of them, only Rama Bai met Max Mueller and ate salt with him in Oxford.[67] Radhakanta Deb and Anundoram did not have any such opportunity, but they used to keep up correspondence with the great scholar. Besides being a barrister, Anundoram was the fifth Indian to enter the Indian Civil Service in 1872.

Anundoram was the first and finest representative of the 'great recovery' in Assam. After his untimely death in 1889, Lambodar Bora (1860–92) another writer planned a biography of Anundoram Borooah. Though Lambodar could not complete his work, he could identify the ecumenical salt in Anundoram. He presaged that so long as there is love for good things in the world, Sanskrit language and literature would continue to occupy the high altar. He believed that Sanskrit is the high menhir of the Hindus.[68] Lambodar further suggested that Anundoram was the true friend of India.

> He was the shining example of the synthesis of the old and the new... Among the lazy and uninspiring Assamese Anundoram was the incarnation of a burning zeal, perserverence and free thinking....[69]

In his study of Sanskrit, it seems, Anundoram embodied the spirit of the Orientalists. Though men of learning like Rammohun Roy and Bholanath Chandra expressed doubt about the usefulness of Sanskrit, Orientalism kept its flag flying and it lifted the spirit of all those who placed a high premium on Sanskrit. It is pointless to gloss over the recent attack on Orientalism by Edward W. Said. His recherché construction of Orientalism as the mirror image of Chengiz Khan, as destroyer and enslaver, as 'a western style for dominating, restructuring and having authority over the Orient' had few instant takers. He does not spare even Karl Marx and brands him as Romantic Orientalist.[70] It is common knowledge that Orientalism redeemed India from the deep despair of subjection. The nationalist leaders of India were conscious about it. Debunking Orientalism became an all sweetness and light fashion, it would soon become passe. Edward Said is pontifical, yet not in love with the subject he is writing about.

Born out of a limited experience of alien administration, largely developed as an hinterland of Bengal economy, the development of Assam had a sheltered existence. The new middle class always turned to Calcutta for ideas and inspiration. The development of Bengali middle class provided the Assamese counterpart a finished model. This historical phenomenon had its impact. The lack of deep-seated reformation in Hindu religion anywhere in the country had its own influence. 'Service' as an institution and a philosophy of life emphasizing the role of middle class did not in Assam, as elsewhere in India with a qualified exception of Bengal, take firm roots in middle class psychology and its world-view.

It is no wonder that Swami Vivekananda (1863–1902) the most imposing personality on the Indian scene at the close of the century following his matchless success in the Parliament of Religions held in Chicago in 1893, had no followers in Assam.[71] His rationalism, his widely known sympathy for 'man in bondage', his commitment for the regeneration of the motherland through service and his emphasis on universalism of religion sustainable through unity and tolerance of all were unable to strike a single sympathetic chord in Assam. There was no literature on Vivekananda until recently.

The middle class world-view oscillated between a vague sense of humanism and a self-centred personal and class interest. In the absence of any tradition of social thinking it became, in course of time shallow, myopic and often self-destructive. The national movement drew out the best in them when they rose above narrow limitations to great heights of universalism.

It is necessary to refer to the limited impact of the Bengal Renaissance on Assam.[72] The spirit of the new age was represented in Assam by a handful of elite, from Jajnaram Phukan to Anundoram Borooah whose importance in the social history of Assam has already been discussed. The middle class as a whole did not enter into the spirit of the Bengal Renaissance. Its limitations were apparent in the field of science, art and music. Its inability to develop a social philosophy created in the long run social disunity.

Sibnarayan Roy suggests that the principal and permanent achievement of the Bengal Renaissance was the development of Bengali language and literature.[73] The observation holds good in respect of Assamese language and literature also. The effulgence of Assamese literature in the late nineteenth century was the lasting impact of the new awakening.

One particular aspect of this effulgence calls for our attention. Assamese literature of this time included a library on great men and women, their lives, ideas and achievements. Evidently, the role of the heroes in history was grafted in the receptive mind by the indepth study of Thomas Carlyle and a host of other liberal philosophers. Carlyle declared, 'Universal history is at bottom the history of the great men who have worked here'. This central idea of his work, *Heroes and Hero Worship* (1841) became popular in other countries.[74] All inspiration to extol individualism in the social milieu of the Assamese came directly or indirectly from that source. Conscious attempts were made to study individuals and heroes of history transcending linguistic, territorial and national boundaries.

In the period of our study Queen Victoria, liberal politicians like Gladstone of England, Gokhale of India, thinkers and nationalist men of action like Socrates, Benjamin Franklin, John Stuart Mill, Rammohun Roy, Jamsetji Tata, Jagmohan Basu, the Japanese hero Nogi, religious reformer Akbar, humanist and philanthropists like Iswarchandra Vidyasagar, Granville Sharp, John Pounds, Florence Nightingale, Haji Muhammed Mohsin, men of letters like Rabindranath Tagore, Pearycharan Sarkar, W.C. Banerjee, D.L. Roy, R.C. Dutt, Ranganath Shastri, Satishchandra Bandopadhyay, Harinath De, Zibun Nisa and Ramanujan found pride of place in that library. The writers also turned to their own history for inspiration. Along with the cultural heroes like Sankardeva, Madhavdeva and Damodardeva, the lives of Anandaram Dhekial Phukan, Anundoram Borooah, Tularam Senapati, Momai Tamuli Barbarua, and Jaymati Kuwari aroused their interest and found place of honour.[75] The cult of hero worship became a literary fashion. It often betrayed a tendency towards narcissism.

The role of women in society became a subject of debate in our period. The idea of women's education was first introduced in Assam by the Christian missionaries. But the common men generally disfavoured the idea. Nobody came forward to marry a girl with some education. As men of social standing refused to send their daughters to school the missionaries picked up even the streetwalkers for initiation to learning.[76] Some families had the practice of giving the lesson of the alphabet and numeration to the female children at home.[77]

Anandaram Dhekial Phukan was the popularizer of women education in Assam. He was a member of the Bethune Society which popularized women education in Bengal. Women-related issues were later taken up by Hemchandra Barua and Gunabhiram Barua.[78] But a section of the elite remained confused for some more years to come. The Brahmo movement had a positive role in the field of women education. The early educated women of Assam had Brahmo connections.[79]

The Assamese middle class was naturally well-informed about the debate in Bengal on issues like early marriage, widow remarriage, polygamy, etc., which kept the social life in Calcutta in a state of flux. They could have been good issues for debate in Assam as well. But the elites seemed to have left those matters to individual conscience.

Infrequent occurance of such incidents perhaps, gave chance for such remarkable equanimity. Questions of age, consent and dowry were discussed in literary journals. Early marriage did come in for a good deal of criticism in the early decades of the twentieth century.

Marriage was invariably settled by the guardians of the groom and the bride. A word from the girl's father was final on the matter.[80] Miles Bronson, the American missionary, recorded his observation of a marriage in Assam. For the bride, it was, in sense, a route to uncertainity. Bronson noted:

> She knows little of him and he of her. The husband buys his wife as he does a beast of burden and regards her in the pretty much the same light. If the wife be of high birth she is little else than her husband's prisoner.[81]

Bronson's remark seems to exaggerate the uneven position between the bride and the groom. Nevertheless, every social convention was changing and man-woman relationship also changed with it. Consent of the prospective bride and the groom became indispensable in good time. With it appeared the 'newly acquired sin' of dowry demand by educated men.[82] But dowry did not grow into a system in the Assamese society. In 1909 Benudhar Rajkhowa, then a powerful writer, tried to popularize the role-model of virtuous housewife in a book titled *Lakhimi Tirota*. It was in the form of a dialogue between Muruli and Pakhila, the husband and the wife. The dialogue covered subjects like virtue, beauty, taste for music, love for the art of cooking, needle-work and weaving, right conduct, love for the domestic servants and the poor, loyalty and patriotism. It also gave hints how to bring up children, serve guests and patients and how to be a thrifty housekeeper. Though in his scheme the woman had to play a submissive role, Benudhar visualized woman of a new type with a creative and constructive role in the family and the society as well.

Bolinarayan Bora, Lambodar Bora and Ratneswar Mahanta were more or less of the view that the main purpose of education was earning money and that was a male domain. Like Bankim Chandra Chattopadhyaya, Bolinarayan was a little apprehensive of the *navina*—the new woman. Bolinarayan favoured female education within the precincts of the family. These views were not outlandish by the standard of their time and they did not meet with any criticism or opposition. Essentially, Bolinarayan was for a gradual changeover.[83] Some people riveted their angry eyes on superficial issues like the use of sari by Assamese women.[84]

As the women were to queen it over the kitchen they were expected to develop their culinary skill. Traditional sayings were the infallible guide for many, but the educated housewives needed more. The first guide on culinary art made its appearance in 1913. Authored by Prajnyasundari Devi, the book was an instant success.[85] Though a few women made their appearance in literature, they made themselves heard only during the freedom movement. Pandora's daughters were still in the womb of time.[86]

ROLE OF TEA

Importance of tea in the socio-economic life of Assam has yet to be studied thoroughly. An indepth study would have revealed the social, economic and political consequences of tea cultivation from the early British days till the present day. We have the story of tea in general, accounts of some tea companies, some tea planters' families and study of some aspects of tea industry. They together help us to form some broad ideas.[87]

We may begin with the history of Assam written by Gunabhiram Barua. Published in the year 1884, his *Assam Buranji* still provides a dependable picture of the socio-economic life of the people, besides their political history. Gunabhiram observed that luxuriant growth of tea had made large tracts of fallow jungle lands more useful. Large investments had been made on tea cultivation and people were benefited by that. Like many Europeans, some people from this land started tea gardens and made their fortune. Gunabhiram further said that tea had become a major product of Assam.[88]

Next came the *Asamar Buranji* by Padmanath Gohain Barua in 1899. Padmanath also realized the growing importance of tea in the province and devoted one chapter to tea. There he stated, 'tea cultivation has opened up new vistas of livelihood for the Assamese people'. At the time of his writing, he stated that the number of people variously connected with tea cultivation would constitute one fourth of the population of Assam. He pointed out that tea provided a good chance for the development of road communication and introduction of steamer service and railways. He summed up by saying that tea improved the lot of the people and their land.[89] To what extent it was so is doubtful as improvement of the living condition of the people was never the object of the planters. They made huge capital investment, assiduously ensured the growth and maintenance of the gardens, took care to maintain the supply of labour and carried on their work without any interference. Their guiding philosophy was private investment for private gain.

Development of tea cultivation in Assam was entirely due to the efforts of some British entrepreneurs under a government of their own race. In the pre-Mutiny years, Maniram Dewan was the only Indian who developed two gardens at Chenglu and Chenimora. After he was hanged for his alleged conspiracy against the government in the wake of the Mutiny, his gardens were confiscated. In a recent work Maniram has been shown as 'tea's first martyr'.[90] Such hyperbole could make good fiction but bad history. No historian has as yet unearthed any evidence to the effect that Maniram was a victim of conspiracy of British tea planters. He suffered the steely vendetta of a highbrow British officer. The opinion of the historian Surendranath Sen still holds good:

> Major Halroyd, Deputy Commissioner of Jorhat, was on bad terms with Maniram and the evidence on which he was convicted was insufficient, if not unsatisfactory, particularly as Halroyd acted as both prosecutor and judge.[91]

The government in their anxiety to bring more and more land under cultivation encouraged British farmers to take up as much land as they needed. The terms of land grants were extremely liberal. The precedent was set by the King Purandar in 1836. 'On mere request', H.K. Barpujari writes, 'the Raja granted to the Assam Company an extensive area near Gabharu hills for cultivation of tea in anticipation that in near future his subjects would be able to reap the benefit of this new enterprise.'[92] Without such easy terms of land grants, there can be little doubt, investment in the tea sector would have remained shy. The wisdom in that policy had not been questioned by the nationalist leaders before independence nor that policy has been abandoned by them after independence. The hard economic reality does not leave any room for airy idealism.

Organization of capital and labour for tea plantation was no easy task. Yet, the success of British planters must have drawn the attention of some persons and a still fewer of them set off on a race into uncertainity. Not all who joined the race, no matter what their colour was, had won the day. Like any other field of trade there were ups and downs, and larger the investment by individuals or companies, stronger was their recuperative power and louder was their voice in the matters that concerned them. Labour interests received a raw deal in the initial hiccup but as time went by the planters had to learn to nourish their skill and consent in a better way. Tea labour was yet to occupy a space as a single ethnic personality.

Among the Assamese there was no rush for taking up wasteland from the government and those who took to growing tea came one by one. Whatever might have been the size, the participation itself was a significant event. With their participation, they entered upon international trade and their destiny got inseparably linked up with it for ever. From crass amateurs they became past masters of trade.

The Assamese took their first lesson in modern trade with tea as their merchandise. Tea, petroleum and coal industries provided the infrastructure of present day Assam.

The native interest was confined to tea alone. Without tea industry a stable middle class would not have come into existence in Upper Assam. Through tea they secured business links in Calcutta and London.[93] Time was on their side. The arrival of the tea planter in Assam was the arrival of the capitalist. Tea produced the richest Assamese and it seemed as though without tea no Assamese shall be all-time rich at the best of times. Tea is the only force of 'embourgeoisement' in the economy of Assam.

We may bring into discussion some of the leading tea growers of the early phase. Roseswar Barua, a Brahmin, set the example of resolute entrepreneurship at Jorhat. He started with one garden called Lahdoigarh Tea Estate and when he died he left nine gardens for his nine sons. Roseswar Barua was the richest Assamese of his time.[94] Roseswar was followed by Hemadhar Barua, who, after retirement from government service started the Letekujan Tea Estate. The first consignment of tea from Hemadhar's garden was made in 1870.[95]

Hemadhar's son, being the first graduate of Upper Assam came to be known as 'B.A. Jagannath'. Jagannath declined the offer of a post of Deputy Magistrate and settled down to trade.[96] Besides being a successful tea planter he was a man of high public spirit. Jagannath played a leading role in the formation of the Jorhat Sarvojanik Sabha in 1884.[97] The sabha was moderate in outlook and was therefore in complete agreement with the views of the Indian National Congress. Though the organization was based in Jorhat, it took up the cause of the province as a whole. With it began the age of organized public opinion in Assam. Jagannath Barua was the animating spirit behind this and without his interest, energy and resource, the Jorhat Sarvojanik Sabha was inconceivable.[98]

His importance as a public figure was soon recognized. He was invited to the coronation ceremony of King Edward VII of Britain which he attended. After his return he extended his support to the formation of the Assam Association in 1903.[99]

After Jagannath's death, the leadership of the Sarvojanik Sabha, passed on to Debicharan Barua who was also a planter. Earlier, Debicharan attended the second session of the Indian National Congress in Calcutta in 1886. 'A true representative of the new age, Debicharan Barua had firm faith in representative government' and he made his voice felt there.[100] Debicharan was the only Assamese elected to the first Legislative Assembly of India in 1921.[101]

Jagannath Barua consistently endeavoured to draw more and more people into business. Radhakanta Handique, Col. Sibram Bora, Chandrakanta Gogoi and Chandradhar Barua took to tea cultivation mainly through his effort.[102] Of them Radhakanta and Chandradhar became successful tea planters. They are remembered today not for the large fortune they made but for their philanthropic zeal. Almost every successful tea planter of our period was associated with some form of philanthropic service. Radhakanta Handique for instance, donated funds towards construction of the Chandrakanta Handique Bhavan, the central office of the Asam Sahitya Sabha in memory of his son who died young. He also financed the project of *Chandrakanta Abhidhan*, an uptodate dictionary of Assamese language. The Narayani Handique Bhavan where the Department of Historical and Antiquarian Studies of the Government of Assam had been housed and the R.K. Handique Girls' College, the first girls college of the province owed their existence to the tea planter Radhakanta.[103]

Chandradhar Barua, son-in-law of Jagannath gave up law practice and opened tea gardens. He also inherited the gardens of his father-in-law. Chandradhar roped in Raja Prabhat Chandra Barua of Gauripur and Lakheswar Barthakur, a trained agriculturist and opened a garden at Tinisukia.[104] He was a literary figure of some repute and presided over the second session of the Asam Sahitya Sabha in 1918. He patronized sports, art, music, and theatre movement.[105] The first non-government college of the province named after Jagannath Barua was established at Jorhat with the donation of land and building of the planter.[106]

We have no doubt that from the very beginning people looked upon tea cultivation as the most lucrative and prestigious occupation. Dinanath Bezbaroa, Annadaram Dhekial Phukan, Haribilash Agarwala, Manik Chandra Barua, Kaliprasad Chaliha, Gangagobinda Phukan, Chandrakamal Bezbaroa, Budhindranath Bhattacharya, Ghanashyam Barua, Radhanath Phukan, etc., who had successful career in other fields planned to end up with tea gardens.[107] Tea institutionalized hope in the past, it will continue to do so in future. Tea knows no break.

Two other tea planters, Bisturam Barua and Malbhog Barua deserve our attention. Bisturam Barua had little formal education and he began his life as a mauzadar. An ambitious man as he was, imagination and hard work paid them well in life. The Williamson Magor & Co., a British firm saw him through the difficult times more than once.[108] On his death, the periodical *Asamiya* commented: 'To have become the owner of seven gardens by his own strength is no mean achievement.'[109] Bisturam's son Sivaprasad (1880–1937) established himself as the richest Indian tea planter of his time. This family is also known for many acts of philanthropy. The Bisturam Barua Hall at Jorhat and the Bisturam Hospital were raised with the donations of Sivaprasad.[110]

Malbhog Barua became a planter by sheer will and effort. His son Prasannakumar Barua (1884–1958) carried on his father's business in a more favourable situation. Prasannakumar had social commitment and firm nationalist views. He associated himself with the Assam Association and later, with the Indian National Congress.[111]

We have given above a brief account of some early tea planters of the province. They had their stories of success or occasional failure. They had no control over the market conditions which determined their business interests. In the wake of a crisis in the tea industry in 1860s the words *chah era de* (say goodbye to tea) crept into Assamese vocabulary as an expression of despair. Like the South Sea Bubble it was a flying phase. When the business soon looked up more and more people opened gardens. Some tried and tested planters emerged out of the crisis.

We find the coffee planters of Coorg in a similar situation.[112] Coffee played a pivotal role in the growth of middle class in Coorg. The British took over Coorg from the Haleri ruler in 1834. Though some Mopillas grew coffee in the locality its commercial value was not known. Until then coffee was not a popular beverage. The British explored the prospect and found the environment highly promising. Land-grants were made, as in Assam, at the most liberal rates. British speculators flocked in, even from Ceylon and Burma; close at their heels came forward the Kodavas, whom the British called 'the Coorgs', and all of them took to coffee plantation. The Kodavas took advantage of their privileged land tenure system and raised plantation in their *bane* (upland) holdings. It was not a runaway success either. But patience and hard work answered their expectations well. The *bane* holdings which lay unused became covetable assets. By that time coffee became a single common indulgence in every household in the south. The Kodavas not only developed their commercial instinct but also learnt from the British the sure way to success in a transitional environment. They excelled in it. Thanks to the coffee connection, the Kodavas are today a virile people with a strong, stable and ambitious middle class.

The excellent study by K.M. Lokesh reveals that the prosperity brought in by coffee plantation broke up the *okka*, the joint family system and further released the energy of the Kodavas. Some of the wealthiest Kodavas of the early twentieth century were invariably the planters. Without coffee, creation of wealth and capital would have remained an impossibility for many of them. No other field of farming held out a better prospect.

Along with the tea planters we must take into account the large number of supervisory and clerical staff employed in the gardens both by the British and native planters. The 'babus' as they were called, were the indispensable part of the organization. Their exposure to a world of industry, labour, capital, competition, order, punctuality and discipline brought about a metamorphosis in them, they set before them some idealism of life. They acquired new social and economic values. They seldom missed a step in the ladder.

Tea industry offered the Assamese middle class a channel for professional self-expression. It kept on swelling the ranks of the middle class, some of them were employed in the clerical establishments, a few were involved in the growing, trading and sales of tea. Together they were both employers and employed and their labour and talent combined to produce the cheerful aroma of a morning cup of tea in every household. Despite some structural shortcomings the fragrance of the renewed Assamese culture continued to have a strong tea consciousness.

The tea industry was the main economic force behind urbanization in Upper Assam. In the absence of such a force the unbanization process in the Lower Assam districts was slow. For want of precise description, if we use the classification of towns by Felipe R. Martin,[113] Guwahati may be said to have developed, as the names of the old parts of the city like Paltan Bazar, Chandmari and Fancy Bazar suggest, as a 'military town'. Growing importance of the river station and predominance of itinerant traders gradually changed its complexion into a commercial town. The district headquarters towns of Dhubri and Guwahati could not stand comparison to the resourceful towns of Dibrugarh and Jorhat. Nor Barpeta could be compared with Sibsagar as sub-divisional towns. Between them were the towns of Tezpur on the north bank of the Brahmaputra and Nagaon at some remove in the south. As district headquarters, the towns were struggling to acquire a personality of their own. The planters and soldiers raised the colour and spirit of the Tezpur town with the polo field and Chandmari. Nagaon was growing into an agricultural town. The important townships of the Ahom age, Biswanath, Jagi, Raha, Kaliabar, Marangi, etc., lost their importance and became almost ghost towns. Mangaldoi, the former adminsitrative capital of the Darrang Raja, the river port town of Goalpara and the north Lakhimpur town hardly received any impetus for development. As the main social force behind urbanization the middle class developed residential areas of their own in every town. Traders and professional men like lawyers and doctors coming from Bengal constituted a major chunk of urban population.

W.J. Fox in his study of the middle classes of Britain noticed a 'universal unfixedness of positions' in them, 'where every man was rising or falling or hoping that he should rise or fearing that he would sink'.[114] Social historians have taken hint from Fox's epigrammatic phrase. This 'unfixedness' of security perhaps, makes them restive and conscious as a class. They always try to reap the benefit of ideas and institutions to the exclusion of others.

In a colonial situation, the rising middle class could not be hegemonistic in absolute terms. The imperial bureaucracy would not let them forget their contour. In Assam the variation of income within the middle class was too apparent, but compared to the much larger number of people below them, they had enough financial security and social prestige. Those below them had no immediate chance to gain upon their ground. The eclecticism of the Assamese middle class has to be understood from this position. Otherwise, the Jorhat Sarvojanik Sabha, an elite organization, had no business to organize protest against enhancement of revenue in 1892. Some Ryot Sabhas organized and led by men of diverse professional interests raised their voice in defence of the peasantry.[115] We have already shown that the elite were never out of sympathy with the cultivators. The cultivators in turn never doubted their sincerity. The peasantry and others from heterogeneous minor professions began to look upon the middle class as the natural leaders of society. In the formative stage, the middle class gained leadership through work, they did not work to gain leadership. Gradually commercialization of agriculture and growing availability of education for the children of the cultivators engineered upward peasant mobility, the middle class, far from putting obstruction against the trend, helped the process as noblesse oblige. The middle class brought about a change in the living taste which was later copied by men of lower order.

Tea interest looked askance at the growth of nationalism in Assam. The British planters looked upon the nationalist movement with suspicion from the very beginning. But the middle class leadership put its best foot forward and made the non-cooperation movement in Assam a big success.

A large number of students left Cotton College in January 1921 and threw themselves up in the partnership of the leaders. They spared no effort and no sweat. The student community was the primum-mobile of the movement in Assam and Chandranath Sarma, a young lawyer, was the sole potential indoctrinator. Chandranath kept in touch with leaders like Mahatma Gandhi, Chittaranjan Das and Bipinchandra Pal. Bright and articulate, he won his spurs as a leader.

The middle class welcomed the radicalization of Assam politics and learnt for the first time the art of mass mobilization for a movement of a new type. The leaders tried their wings for a future role. Within the next few decades the middle class completely shifted, to use Peter N. Stearn's terms, from the 'power-seeking' to the 'power-defending' position.

NOTES

1. Mention may be made of (1) B. Dutta Roy (ed.), *The Emergence and Role of Middle Class in North-East India*, Delhi, 1983, (2) Manorama Sharma, *Social and Economic Change in Assam*, Delhi, 1990, (3) Prafulla Mahanta, *Asamiya Madhyabitta Srenir Itihas*, Guwahati, 1991, (4) Anil Roychoudhury, *Namoni Asomor Madhyashrenee*, Guwahati, 1998, (5) Hiren Gohain's article on the Assamese middle class in *Sahitya Aru Chetana*, Guwahati, 1976 and (6) B.B. Misra, *The Indian Middle Classes*, Delhi, 1983.
2. S.N. Mukherjee, 'The Bhadraloks of Bengal' in D. Gupta (ed.), *Social Stratification*, Delhi, 1991, pp. 176–82.
3. S.S. Sohal, 'The Middle Classes in the Punjab' (unpublished thesis), G.N.D. University, Amritsar, 1987; also 'The Emergence of the Middle Class' etc., in Indu Banga (ed.), *Five Punjabi Centuries*, Delhi, 1997, pp. 455–70.
4. M. Sharma, op. cit., p. 122.
5. For a complete account of the land system see A.J.M. Mills' *Report on the Province of Assam*, Guwahati, 1984, pp. 3–19.
6. K.C. Bardaloi (ed.), *Sadaraminar Atmajivani*, Guwahati, 1991, p. 180.
7. Sharma, op. cit., p. 120.
8. See A.J.M. Mills' *Report on the Province of Assam*, op. cit., pp. 607 and 609.
9. The play was published in 1897, Gohain, *Works*, Guwahati, 1971, pp. 249–80.
10. See S.N. Sarma, *The Neo-Vaishnavite Movement and the Satra Institutions of Assam*, Guwahati, 1977, Appendix V, pp. 215–27.

11. Sarma, op. cit., p. 191.
12. Sarma, op. cit., pp. 191–3.
13. Sharma, op. cit., p. 133.
14. Biographical accounts of all these persons are easily available in Assamese. See the next note.
15. For our information on their lives and work we have relied mainly on the following books. But views and interpretation of the available facts are my own. D. Neog, *New light on History of Asamiya literature*, Guwahati, 1962; M. Neog, *Maheswar Neog Rachanawali*, Guwahati, 1986, pp. 681–774; P. Gohain Barua, *Jivani Sangrah*, Guwahati, 1969; G. Barua, *Anandaram Dhekial Phukanar Jivan Charitra*, Guwahati, 1971.
16. D. Neog, op. cit., pp. 361–2. S. Barman, *Asamiya Jivani Abhidhan*, Guwahati, 1992, p. 104.
17. H.D. Phukan, *Assam Buranji*, Guwahati, 1962 (edited by J.M. Bhattacharjee), pp. 1–6.
18. G. Barua, op. cit., pp. 17–20.
19. L.N. Bezbaroa, *Works*, Guwahati, 1988, Vol. I, pp. 137–41.
20. *Sadaraminar Atmajivani*, op. cit., pp. 1–283.
21. B. Roy, *Unis Sataker Banglai Bigyan Sadhana*, Calcutta, 1987, p. 217.
22. A.D. Phukan, *Asamiya Lorar Mitra*, Part III, pp. 82–3. I am thankful to J.N. Bhuyan who lent me his copy of the first edition, Calcutta, 1849 of the book. Cf. S.N. Banerjee's statement: To England we look for inspiration and guidance.... From England must come the crowning mandate which will enfranchise our people. England is our political guide.... Quoted in A.R. Desai, *Social Background of Indian Nationalism*, Bombay, 1982, p. 321.
23. See J.N. Bhuyan (ed.), Introduction, *Asamiya Lorar Mitra*, Guwahati, 1992, Part II, p. 30.
24. D. Neog, op. cit., pp. 341–6, and 364–7.
25. L.N. Bezbaroa in *Banhi*, 1831 *Saka* (1909–10). See *Works*, Vol. II, p. 1759.
26. M. Neog, *Rachanawali*, op. cit., pp. 702–3.
27. B.K. Barua, *History of Assamese Literature*, Delhi, 1978, p. 108.
28. J. Goswami, *Hemchandra Barua*, Delhi, 1987, pp. 11- 47.
29. Gohain Barua, *Jivani Sangrah*, op. cit., p. 56.
30. J.N. Bhuyan (ed.), *Ratneswar Mahanta Rachanawali*, Guwahati, 1977, p. 285, pp. 301–4.
31. See, N. Saikia's Introduction, *Sangeet Sadhana*, Jorhat, 1986, pp. 7–19.
32. Lakhiram Barua, *Sangeet-Kosh*, Jorhat, 1986 (1st published 1909), it was a collection of 422 modern songs composed by Barua himself and others.
33. M. Neog, op. cit., p. 760; also B.K. Barua, op. cit., p. 168.
34. Benudhar Sharma, *Hemchandra Goswami*, Jorhat, 1972, pp. 29–58 and 80–90, Nanda Talukdar, *Kanaklal Barua-Rachanawali*, Guwahati, 1973, pp. 12–30, and 119–46. Also see the Introduction by M. Neog, pp. 7–20.
35. I have examined a variety of sources for information on this point to make it as exhaustive as possible. In addition to the books noted in note 15 above, I have consulted some other works. Some of the persons noted above wrote autobiographies.

I owe particular debt to Ajalitara Neog, Akshay Kumar Misra, Atulchandra Hazarika, Benudhar Rajkhowa, Benudhar Sharma, Chandraprasad Saikia, Hariprasad Neog, Jatindranath Goswami, Jogendranarayan Bhuyan, Nanda Talukdar, Omeo Kumar Das, Praphulladatta Goswami, Sivanath Barman, Suryyakumar Bhuyan and Upendra Barkataki.

36. K.B. Neuschel, *Word of Honor*, New York, 1989, p. 203.
37. H.D. Phukan, *Buranji*, op. cit., p. 105.
38. *Banhi*, Vol. I, No. 9, 1832 *Saka* (1910).
39. Ibid., Vol. II, No. 2, 1832 *Saka* (1910).
40. Ibid., Vol. IV, 1834 *Saka* (1913)
41. I have seen copies of the journal in the possession of Dr Praphulladatta Goswami, I was also benefited by my discussion with Dr Goswami.
42. See, J.N. Bhuyan (ed.), *Ratnakanta Barkakatir Gadyasambhar*, Guwahati, 1977, pp. 23–30.
43. *Assam Bandhav*, Guwahati, Vol. VII, No. 10, 1917.
44. Banikanta Kakati, *Assamese, Its Formation and Development*, Guwahati, 1941, See Introduction, p. 15.
45. *Banhi*, vol. III, No. 8, 1834 *Saka* (1912). See Bezbaroa, *Works*, Vol. II, pp. 1795–7.
46. See the address of L.N. Bezbaroa to the 9th session of the Asam Sahitya Sabha at Dhubri, 1926, Bezbaroa, *Works*, Vol. II, pp. 1872–81.
47. B.N. Datta (ed.), *Gowalpariya Lokagit Sangrah*, Jorhat, 1974, see the instructive preface.
48. Fernand Braudel, *The Identity of France*, London, 1989, Vol. I, pp. 85–6.
49. C.P. Saikia (ed.), *Karmavir Nabin Chandra Bardaloi Smritigrantha*, Guwahati, 1975, p. 14.
50. See Atul Chandra Hazarika (ed.), *Bhasanmala*, Guwahati, 1960, pp. 1–27.
51. R. Kalita, *Bharatar Swadhinata Andolanat Asamiya Chatrar Bhumika*, Nalbari, 1986, pp. 30–7.
52. P. Gohain Barua, *Mor Sowarani*, Guwahati, 1971, pp. 217–18.
53. C.P. Saikia (ed.), op. cit., pp. 11, 41, 136.
54. Quoted in A. Toynbee, *A Study of History*, London, 1962, Vol. 3, p. 239.
55. A. Toynbee, loc. cit.
56. A. Toynbee, op. cit., p. 375.
57. B.B. Misra, *The Indian Middle Classes*, op. cit., p. 151.
58. T.N. Sarma, *Auniati Satrar Buranji*, Majali, 1975, pp. 244-86.
59. K.C. Bhattacharyya, *Dhireswar Acharyya*, Guwahati, 1960.
60. B. Barua, *Sundarit Sri Sri Madhavdev Madhav Maral Atiram Barua Aru Anyanya*, Guwahati, 1988, pp. 54–5.
61. K.C. Bhattacharyya, op. cit., pp. 100–1.
62. Ibid., p. 38.
63. K.M. Panikkar, *A Survey of India*, Bombay, 1962, see Ch. XXI, pp. 209–24.
64. Nirad C. Chaudhuri, *Scholar Extraordinary*, Bombay, 1980, pp. 126, 132–33.
65. Panikkar, op. cit., p. 217.
66. Nirad C. Chaudhuri, op. cit., p. 136.

67. Nirad C. Chaudhuri, op. cit., pp. 300–1.
68. N. Talukdar (ed.), *Lambodar Bora: Works*, Guwahati, 1983, pp. 40–1.
69. Ibid., p. 42 (translation mine).
70. E.W. Said, *Orientalism*, New York, 1994, pp. 3, 153–4.
Note: Born in 1935 to Palestinian refugee parents, Edward W. Said is Parr Professor of English at Columbia University. He is also a profound music critic. A zealot of the PLO, he was a theoritician of the Palestine National Council from 1977 to 1991. He looks upon the Oslo Peace Accord of 1993 as a surrender of the PLO and victory for Israel. Often his views are coloured by his aggressive political philosophy.
71. Swami Vivekananda visited Assam about 1901. We find reference of his visit to Assam in K.C. Bhattacharyya, op. cit., p. 57.
72. A useful reading on the subject is an essay by A. Guha, 'The Impact of Bengal Renaissance on Assam', *IESHR*, 1972.
73. See Sibnarayan Roy, 'Banglar Renaissance', in *Shroter Birudhe*, Calcutta, pp. 99–127. A vast literature exists on the subject, though historians and thinkers are divided in their opinions whether an event called the Bengal Renaissance ever did take place. To me it appears that 'Bengal Renaissance' is the convenient term to particularize the epoch-making events of the nineteenth century Bengal.
74. William K. Wimsatt, *Literary Criticism*, Calcutta, 1964, pp. 427–9.
75. Both biographies and biographical sketches have been included for the discussion. Gunabhiram Barua wrote on Anandaram Dhekial Phukan (1880), Ratneswar Mahanta on Tularam Senapati and Jaymati (1891), Padmanath Gohain Barua on Queen Victoria (*Maharani*) (1901), Upendra Nath Barua wrote on Socrates, Benjamin Franklin, Gladstone, Momai Tamuli Barbarua, P. Sarkar, J.M. Basu and Anundoram (1909), Kaliram Das on R.C. Dutt (1910), Harinath De, and W.C. Banerjee (1911), Nagendranath Phukan on R. Sastri (1911), S.K. Bhuyan on D.L. Roy (1913), Gokhale (1914), Rabindranath and Anundoram (1920), L.N. Bezbaroa on Sankardeva and Madhavdeva (1914), K.K. Handique on Nogi, Zibun Nisa and S.C. Bandopadhyay (1913), Narayan Chandra Goswami on J. Tata (1913), Singhadatta Dev Adhikari on Nightingale, H.M. Mohsin, J. Paunds and G. Sharp (1914), Chandranath Sarma on Vidyasagar (1917), and on J.S. Mill; Anonymous (*Jonaki*, 1889).
76. H.K. Barpujari, *Asamar Nava-Jagaran: Ana-Asamiyar Bhumika*, Jorhat, 1984, p. 8.
77. Ibid., p. 9.
78. See P. Sinha, *Nineteenth Century Bengal: Aspects of Social History*, Calcutta, 1965, Appendix B, p. 151; also, H.K. Barpujari, op. cit., p. 9.
79. Mention may be made of Swarnalata, daughter of Gunabhiram Barua, Sarala, daughter of Lakhikanta Barkakati and Lakhiprova Bora, the first woman doctor of Assam. See J. Barua, *Works*, Jorhat, 1981, pp. 138, 263. S. Barman, *Jivani Abhidhan*, op. cit., pp. 271–2.
80. Anon. in *Jonaki*, Vol. I, No. 6, 1811 *Saka* (1889).
81. H.K. Barpujari, *The American Missionaries and North-East India*, Guwahati, 1986, p. 177.

82. Editorial, *Banhi*, Vol. IV, No. 8, 1835 *Saka* (1913); also see L.N. Bezbaroa, *Works*, Vol. I, p. 5.
83. R. Saikia, article on Bolinarayan Bora's *Mau*, in C.P. Saikia (ed.), *Asamar Batari-kakat-Alochanir Dersa Basaria Itihash*, Guwahati, 1998, pp. 173–90.
84. K. Talukdar in *Banhi*, Vol. I, No. XII, 1832 *Saka* (1910). Also, editorial, *Usha*, Vol. I, No. VII, 1828 *Saka* (1907).
85. Prajnasundari Devi is well-known for her three-volume work *Amis O Niramis Ahar*, in Bengali, Calcutta, 1995.
86. I have borrowed the idea from A. Riencourt. He introduces Simone de Beauvoir, the French author and a disciple of Jean Paul Sartre as one of Pandora's daughters for whom there is no eternal feminine only a historical one evolved through male dominance in society. The 'masculine overemphasis' is their rallying point. For a stimulating discussion, see Riencourt's 'Pandora's Daughters', Part V, Ch. 5, pp. 403–18, in *Women and Power in History*, Delhi, 1989.
87. Besides H.K. Barpujari (1980), A. Guha (1977), I have in mind A.K. Dutta (1990 and 1992), P. Griffith (1967), H.A. Antrobus (1948 and 1957), D. Ganguli (1972).
88. G. Barua, *Assam Buranji*, Guwahati, 1972, p. 188.
89. P. Gohain Barua, *Asamar Buranji*, Guwahati, 1976, p. 180.
90. A.K. Dutta, *Cha Garam—The Tea story*, Guwahati, 1992, pp. 62–3.
91. S.N. Sen, *Eighteen Fifty-seven*, Delhi, 1977, p. 408.
92. H.K. Barpujari, *Assam in the Days of the Company*, Guwahati, 1980, p. 117.
93. Almost all the Assamese tea planters had close links with Calcutta, some of them owned personal houses there. From Calcutta they secured links with London.
94. P. Gohain Barua, *Assam Buranji*, op. cit., p. 181.
95. J. Goswami, *Jagannath Barua*, Jorhat, 1976, p. 7.
96. Ibid., p. 12.
97. Ibid., p. 38.
98. See H.K. Barpujari (ed.), *Political History of Assam*, Guwahati, 1977, Vol. I, pp. 159–62.
99. J. Goswami, op. cit., pp. 45–6.
100. H.K. Barpujari (ed.), *Political History of Assam*, op. cit., p. 166.
101. A. Guha, *Plenter Raj to Swaraj*, Delhi, 1977, p. 122.
102. J. Goswami, op. cit., p. 122.
103. My information is based on the biography of Radhakanta Handique by Nakul Chandra Bhuyan (1961). See, *Rachana Samagra*, Guwahati, 1996.
104. D. Sarma, *Sahityaratna Chandradhar Barua*, Jorhat, 1975, p. 10.
105. Ibid., pp. 25–30.
106. Ibid.
107. All the known biographical accounts bear clear testimony of their plantation scheme or their successful careers in them.
108. A.K. Dutta, *The Khongiya Barooahs of Thengal*, Guwahati, 1990, pp. 49–51.
109. Ibid., p. 54.
110. Ibid, p. 87.

111. Guha, op. cit., pp. 115–19 and 342.
112. My information on this point is entirely based on K.M. Lokesh, 'Coffee Plantation in Coorg during the Colonial Regime' (unpublished thesis). Kuvempu University, Shimoga, Karnataka, 1993.
113. F.R. Martin's study of the typology of the towns has been approvingly discussed by F. Braudel. See, his *The Mediterranean*, London, 1981, Vol. I, p. 323.
114. See Norman Gash, *Aristocracy and the People*: *Britain* (*1815–1865*), London, 1963, pp. 24–5.
115. A. Guha, *Plenter Raj to Swaraj*, Delhi, 1977, pp. 61–4 and 181–2.

CHAPTER 6

Middle Class Sensibility: Ideas and Issues

THE UNEVEN social identity of the middle class and its dilemmatic positions were reflected in the issues that influenced the resurgence of Assamese life under the British rule. The middle class sensibility took shape slowly but during the period of seventy years of the present study it matured significantly. The attitudes and approaches of the new middle class were largely expressed through contemporary social and cultural issues and some proto-political social eruptions. We shall scan the ambit of some social issues to locate the crystals of Assamese middle class sensibility.

ANATOMY OF THE LANGUAGE DISPUTE

In 1836, Bengali was made the official language and medium of instruction in the schools of Assam by the government at Fort William. The decision was no better than it should have been. But there was no immediate reaction against the government's decision. An incisive critique of the government policy first came out in 1855 from 'A Native'. The 'native' was none other than Anandaram Dhekial Phukan. In a booklet he elaborated his views expressed two years earlier in his memorandum submitted to A.J. Moffatt Mills. The wrong was righted in 1873. But the matter did not end there. A silent suspicion whispered and after some years prejudice spoke loudly of malice and machination. It sparked off a long debate. Of many similar remarks, we bring in just two: (i) Dimbeswar Neog (1962): '...Bengali usurped the place at the instigation of the Bengali clerks who came to Assam for their living', (ii) Birinchi Kumar Barua (1964): 'Under the influence of these men, recruited mostly from Bengal, the British administrators made Bengali the language of the court and the medium of instruction in the schools of Assam. It was in 1836 that Assamese was thrown out of the law-courts and schools and Bengali was installed in its place.'[1]

No other issue had convulsed the Assamese society for so long a period as this. It was a theme of great eloquence right down to 1973, the centenary year of the 'rehabilitation of Assamese language'. Though the debate is not informed by good logic and evidence, it has so far defied a finality. It was dogmatically preached by the Assamese literati in general that the government of the day took that decision at the prompting of the Bengali clerks. Prominent among those who strongly held this view were Lakshminath Bezbaroa and Padmanath Gohain Barua. What perhaps started as a lurking suspicion transformed itself into a belief and the belief became an opinion and like every opinion it had instant takers. But was there really any foe of the Assamese language in the garb of a Bengali clerk worthy of his steel? The question has been answered differently by different scholars. We shall not go into the details of the debate as that will take us beyond the scope of our study. The simmering discontent was distincly visible in 1853 and until half a century from then, the discontent remained dormant but alive. Within the next twenty years the discontent metamorphosed into a tension. The tension was aggravated by provocation from the other side of the fence. Polarized opinions have cut so deep into the heart of believers of one opinion against the other that they present a perfect case of *argumentum ad hominem*, where one takes advantage of the situation of a particular opponent. We shall confine ourselves to the first part of the story.

The century old clerk-conspiracy theory was a by-product of the *Jonaki* zeal. The *Jonaki* was a journal published in 1889 from Calcutta by an enthusiastic literary group known as the Assamese Language Improvement Society. In spirit it compares favourably with the Welsh *eisteddfod*, revived in 1819. The conspiracy theory started gaining ground from the year 1917 when the Asam Sahitya Sabha came into existence. Two prominent figures of Assamese language and literature put their personal stamp of approbation on the clerk-conspiracy theory and made it the question of the hour. To begin with, addressing the first session of the Asam Sahitya Sabha, its president Padmanath Gohain Barua, said that there was no lack of effort on the part of the British Government to keep Assamese literature alive and vibrant but 'suddenly' a group of selfish Bengalis living in Assam stood on the way, they 'bluffed' the British officers and through them put Bengali on the saddle.[2]

The other stirring address was made by Lakshminath Bezbaroa in 1924. He observed in his inimitable way that with the coming of the

English the days of Trahiram (terror personified) were over. But another Trahiram Daroga, a Col. Blimp appeared on the scene. The Bengali clerks who were part and parcel of the British administration took advantage of their position, he said. They poured advice on the ears of their masters to put away Assamese and introduce Bengali. The rulers were taken in by their plea and they introduced Bengali in Assam.[3]

The sequel of these assertions were momentous. Attempts to explore the basis of these assertions have now brought to focus all aspects of the issue. The first group squarely blames the Bengali clerks for the decision of the English; the belief of this group seems to be based on the logic of Persius—*ex nihilo nihil fit*, that nothing can be made out of nothing. Another group of researchers is of the view that the British favoured and introduced Bengali of their own for administrative convenience.

Scholars have advanced the cause of historical analysis. But there is still scope to go into the root of the changeover.[4]

The Government of Assam was in fact a government under the Governor-General at Fort William. Researchers are well aware of the fact that for every single administrative decision, the Agent and Commissioner had to obtain prior approval of the government at Fort William. It was next to impossible for him to supersede one language of the court or the school by another on the whispering advice of his subordinates. An 'Agent' could hardly do it with a spiteful stroke of the pen.

Going through the extant records and the output of the tedious debate one cannot avoid the conclusion that the catastrophic mutation originated in Macaulay's Minute set down in February 1835. We shall quote only the relevant portions of the Minute to show that the mishap started there.

> 'We have to educate a people who cannot at present be educated by means of their mother tongue. We must teach them some foreign language.' About English he said, 'The question now before us is simply whether, when it is in our power to teach this language, we shall teach languages in which, by uni-versal confession, there are no books on any subject which deserve to be compared to our own... The languages of western Europe civilised Russia. I cannot doubt that they will do for the Hindoo what they have done for the Tartar.'[5]

Macaulay never minced his words whenever he spoke on any Indian language or literature. He believed that scarcity of good textbooks for schools would gradually disappear. He expressed the resolve of the government 'to raise up a large class of enlightened natives'. Macaulay believed that those enlightened natives would introduce Western models of composition, Western ideas and thoughts into the vernacular 'dialects'. Obviously, whatever existed in the name of languages in India, Macaulay was loathe to recognize. 'This I believe to be the only way in which we can raise up a good vernacular literature in this country', he declared.[6]

Lord William Bentinck accepted the recommendations of Macaulay within a month and declared that 'the great object of the British Government ought to be the promotion of European literature and science among the natives of India'.[7] Oriental learning particularly the study of Sanskrit, Persian and Arabic fell out of favour. The vernacular languages also suffered under Macaulay's scheme. Administrative actions taken without giving any thought to the distribution of linguistic communities messed up the situation, besides making the Indian languages unequal among themselves in the eye of law. All the British rulers of the day who headed the provincial administration did not have the same cynical contempt for the Indian languages as did Macaulay, but going by the account of the historian of Indian literature one cannot gloss over the fact that as rulers the British had neither particular love for one language nor hatred against the other. The missionaries among them of course, had all the ecclesiastic enthusiasm to learn and adopt the tongue of every speech community of India. Their gift of tongues had no parallel.

As rulers, the British cannot avoid the moral responsibility for the linguistic tensions generated by their language policy. 'The tension between the English and the Indian languages was never solved in the nineteenth century. It was reflected in the history of each Indian language and also in the history of the Indo-English,' observes Sisir Kumar Das, the historian of Indian literature.[8] So, an attitude of hostility towards Assamese language alone cannot be alleged.

There is no blinking the fact that though not by design yet by default of the rulers, Assamese was suppressed by Bengali, Oriya was sought to be suppressed by Bengali (1841), Hindi (1895) and Telugu (1890); once Telugu itself was sought to be swallowed by Tamil; Konkani came under the hegemony of Marathi in the north and Kannada in the south.

The Hindi-Urdu tussle also had its root in the government decision. In 1837 the government had put paid to Persian dominance in the N.-W. Provinces and switched over to Urdu as the official language. Elsewhere, 'the Hindu power' took up the case of Hindi as 'a question of religious and cultural self-assertion...'.[9] No shred of evidence has so far been unearthed which could show that the government of the day ever solicited the advice of any Indian community on such policy matter.

There is a brassy notion that a divide and rule strategy was at work to manipulate the position of one language against the other. Though without proof, the assertion sounds nice and saleable. But it holds no water. Whom did the government want to divide in 1836? It had no necessity of dividing the divided—the Assamese and the Bengalis. History and geography had already shaped their language and culture differently. The British were not unaware of the fact that they were different from one another for centuries. A common language for them was out of the question. Had the government policy succeeded at all, there would have been unity, not dissention. There is no ground to believe that the government was interested in the unity of the two communities. When they uttered unity of nationalities they uttered Indian nationalism. On the other hand, if the government was bent upon creating friction and disunity, there was no serious compulsion for them either to give it up in 1873. The government acted thoughtlessly in giving a living language like Assamese the go-by. Their prerogative was twisted by arrogance and misused for immediate advantage. The contretemps were inevitable.

The introduction of Bengali in Assam has to be understood in view of the all-India experience. The development took place in the nineteenth century at different points of time. We have already noticed that the hegemony of one speech community over the other was sought to be established by some individual or group by openly declaring their stand. They made no bones about their intention. For instance, in 1868, Kantichandra Bhattacharyya, a Bengali school teacher 'wrote a pamphlet claiming that Oriya was but a patois of Bengali, and he found support from a group of Bengalis, including the distinguished Indologist Rajendralal Mitra'.[10] To be sure, what Kantichandra did would not come under the definition of a conspiracy. He declaimed against a language which he failed to pick up. It is equally important to recall that the man who quickly reacted against Kantichandra's remark and organized a protest was a Bengali gentleman, Gaurisankar Roy. Roy was then the editor of a journal, *Utkala Dipika.*[11] It is well-known that after a brief debate Kantichandra's claim was disproved. In Assam, no historian has so far been able to mark out a Kantichandra in the 1830s; Kantichandra unheard of was Kantichandra unborn.

We should also examine the objective conditions prevailing in Bengal in 1835. The six pioneering figures, Pyarichand Mitra (1814–83), Debendranath Tagore (1817–1905), Akshay Kumar Datta (1820–86), Iswarchandra Vidyasagar (1820–91), Michael Madhusudan Dutt

(1824–73) and Rajnarayan Basu (1826–1900) who contributed to the making of the Bengali prose had not come of their own until then.[12] Rammohun's prose notwithstanding, it is they who gave linguistic self-assurance to the Bengalis. Who before them could be the champions of Bengali language outside Bengal? It is amusing to believe that a few Bengali clerks had gone into a huddle, kissed the Blarney Stone and brought their alien master to fall in line with them. Yet, that was believed as a gospel. The debate mentioned earlier has reduced it to a myth and presumably it would not last longer. One could no more believe it than one could believe that water would flow uphill. Nor is there any comparable evidence where minions of the British imperial colossus fell victim to the tricks of their crooked assistants. We rather have evidence to the effect that many Bengalis who mastered English or even acquired some smattering of it thought scorn of Bengali language. Bankim Chandra has drawn a beautiful pen-picture of such a Bengali babu in his satirical writing *Banga Sahityer Adar* in the form of a dialogue between a husband and a wife.[13]

Many people did not feel sure, until some more years to come, about the utility of learning Bengali. Arguments were necessary to bring them down to earth. In other words, not all Bengalis were aware of the merit of using their own language. Writing for preface of the *Persian Dictionary* in 1838 Jaygopal Tarkalankar indicated that his aim was to instil among the people a faith in the Bengali language, to reinstate it in its legitimate place. He expressed the hope that the people would be pleased to use their own language for reading, writing and conversation. Ramchandra Vidyabagish pleaded with the students of the Hindu Collegiate School in 1840 not to find fault with the deficiency of the *Gauriya Bhasa* (language of Bengal). As it hailed from Sanskrit, any word which existed in Sanskrit, Ramchandra said, could be freely used in Bengali. He told his students that the pious aim of spreading education among the common man could not be achieved except through their common language.[14]

Swapan Basu, the social historian, writes that the newly educated youths of Bengal were disdainful towards Bengali literature. Even in 1849, teaching of Bengali in Hindu College was all but in name. There was no method of teaching Bengali, no teacher, no textbook and none to look after it. Learning of Bengali was entirely the discretion of the students. The Sanskrit pundits of Bengal too looked down upon it.[15] The Bengalis coming to Assam would not be different from those in Bengal in their attitude towards Bengali.

Many leading lights of Young Bengal were more at ease with English than Bengali. The Christian missionaries emphasized the necessity of learning Assamese in Assam and Bengali in Bengal. The enthusiasm of the Bengalis for studying their language developed gradually. Societies like Gyandayini Sabha and Bangabhasanusilan Sabha (1853) popularized the study of Bengali.[16]

We have other evidence to show that the Bengalis were not inveterate lovers of their own language. Some external stimuli were necessary to make them feel for their language and, at the right moment they came in abundance. The *Sambad Prabhakar*, an influencial weekly, made its appearance in Calcutta on 28 January 1831. The editor Isher Chunder Gooptoo complained that newly educated Bengalis, by their neglect had blocked the development of Bengali language.[17] As the *Sambad Prabhakar* strongly favoured Bengali as the medium of instruction, its allegation must have had some basis. Switching over to Bengali as an official language was neither smooth nor particularly favoured by the officials. In April 1848, the *Prabhakar* approvingly quoted from *Rangpur Vertabaha* wherein it was stated, 'The missionaries of Serampore, the great soul late Raja Rammohun Roy and such other worthy people, after considerable efforts brought in the recognition of Bengali as a language..., it is now our experience to relate.., so many years have passed by, yet the native Bengali gentlemen have not cared to learn Bengali perfectly.'[18] The matter was editorially repeated again in the next year. It was alleged that the contempt of the British towards a native language did not surprise him when he found that even the 'native brothers' were all out for its banishment. They wished that English should be the language of this country. It was regretted that it was impossible to find even twelve books of useful knowledge written in Bengali.[19] In such a situation we are unable to accept Assam as the home for the heroes of Bengali expansionism who were said to have roped in alien and native proselytes.

Even before the coming of the British, Bengali, more than Assamese, was used for diplomatic purpose in the region. Surendranath Sen, the historian, collected a large number of letters from archival sources written in Bengali.[20] The collection included quite a good number of letters from Assam. They were not written by the Ahom or the Koch rulers alone. Letters by prominent men were also included. On the basis of the letters collected and published, the historian observed that though Bengali prose literature had not yet been founded on a firm footing, those were the days of infancy of Bengali prose. The rulers of Bhutan, Cooch Behar, Assam, Manipur and Cachar communicated among themselves and with the British in Bengali.[21] The presence of the Sakta and the Vaishava saints of Bengal in the royal durbars made possible the use of Bengali easy and widespread. That was the reason why even Dr John Peter Wade who visited Assam in 1772, stayed there for one and a half years and authored a useful history of Assam in 1780 wrongly believed that the language of Assam was a dialect of Bengali.[22] Nathan Brown (1807–86), the American missionary who had a flair for linguistics and whose sympathy and support for the cause of Assamese language is gratefully remembered, had at first the same erroneous impression about Assamese. Shortly after his arrival in Assam in 1836, he describes it, in a personal correspondence, as 'a sort of barbarous Bengali'.[23] Evidently, Bengali had acquired a semi-official status before it was formally imposed as a court language. But it was never a language of the common man.

In Sen's collection we find that British officers, priests and traders picked up Bengali by the end of the eighteenth century. Bengali was the only language of the region they were familiar with and they were able to handle it with felicity. Portuguese and French nationals also did not lag behind. S.N. Sen remarked that reading through the collection, nobody would question the fact that Bengali was the *rashtrabhasa* or national language of the north-east.[24] That may or may not be the whole truth, but it is undeniable that the first non-European language that any Englishman of Calcutta was familiar with was Bengali. Given the opportunity to make a choice, it was unlikely that he would disown his first acquaintance.

Sisir Kumar Das suggests that multilingualism was a despair of the British in India. They felt that it told upon their 'administrative and judicial efficiency' and therefore they 'tried to minimize the number of languages by giving official recognition to only a few'.[25] For Bengal, already inclusive of Goalpara district in the Brahmaputra valley and Assam the natural choice for this purpose was Bengali. But the solution lay in the recognition of the many and not in the perpetuity of the few.

Every man of means in those days tried to identify himself with the babu culture of Bengal. Whatever little financial resource he possessed, he forked out some portion of it to show off his affinity with his cultured neighbour. Even Raja Purandar gave similar impression. Jenkins, who had the opportunity to observe him closely, spoke of him with disparagement, as 'a Bengalee by education and habits'.[26] On a different occasion Jenkins wrote about the Rajas Purandar Singha and Chandra Kanta Singha in these words: '... in my acquaintance with both, I never heard any other languages spoken than Hindoostanee and Bengali'.[27] When Bengali was introduced in 1836, Purandar was the king of Upper Assam. Though deprived of sovereignty he was not deprived of the trappings of royalty. How the last Ahom ruler reacted to the abolition of his own language we have no means to ascertain. No man whose opinion mattered had uttered a boo against the government policy. Had Purandar ever raised a voice the posterity would have remembered him on that score alone. Though inconsequential as a class, the handful of influencial Assamese gentlemen seemed to have had no concern for their language. What would have been the immediate results of their opposition to the government policy must not be conjectued now, but the conclusion is unavoidable that their indifference and silence signalled their support for the policy.

The new language policy did not pose any threat to their individual status and power. Between the government and the people they were emotionally closer to the government. They were incapable of realizing the tragic upshot of the policy and would have remained so had not the American missionaries awakened them to the task before them.

Let us take a look at the dramatis personae involved in the controversy. Assam came under the shadow of Bengali in 1836 and remained so until 1873. From 1836 to 1853 there was no perceptible reaction against the introduction of Bengali in Assam. The protest came up, loud and clear, in 1853 when A.J.M. Mills visited Assam. Though the American missionaries led by Miles Bronson (1812–83), Nathan Brown and A.H. Danforth (1817–?) were reluctant from the start to fall in line with the government policy in favour of Bengali, they did not openly inveigh against it. They started the first ever Assamese journal *Orunodoi* and kept up its publication since 1846.[28] But they entered into an open debate only after 1853 when the matter came to the surface. William Robinson and Francis Jenkins came out in defence of the use of Bengali. A reliable account of the entire debate is now available.[29] A notable feature of the controversy is that not a single Bengali ever participated in the debate. Educated Bengalis, who were already exposed to polemic since the days of Raja Rammohun ought to have had no reason to fight shy of a debate where their interests were allegedly involved. Certainly they were not unaware of it, they remained indifferent to it. The so called tribe of clerk conspirators, could not have remained silent. At least the fact of their existence would have been known to persons like Anandaram, Bronson and Brown, etc., who waged the battle against the continuance of Bengali. The captain on either side of a battle could not remain ignorant of his opponent. To argue such ignorance on the part of Anandaram would simply water down the merit of his fight.[30]

Lastly, we must not ignore the fact that the clerk conspiracy theory was punctured by an admission of Jenkins himself. 'I was the principally concerned in adopting the Bengali, as the language to be used in the school', he said.[31] Jenkins believed that the adoption of Bengali was 'expedient under every circumstance of policy, for the gradual amalgamation of the people of Assam with our subjects in Bengal...'.[32] About the position of Bengali in the court he explained, it was merely a continuative fact. Every recruit to the court took to Bengali as easily as a duck takes to water. The first or second batch of recruits to the British bureaucracy had no reason to grouse against that 'continuative' fact. The recruits came from some select Brahmin and other high caste families who were well placed during the previous regimes. They left Assam in the wake of the Burmese invasion and took shelter in the district of Rangpur under British protection.[33] Jenkins noted that the people of Upper Assam had very little connection with Bengal, 'but it so happened that all the gentry nearly had been exiles in Bengal, and had there acquired a very competent knowledge of the language of that province'. When they found that knowledge of Bengali gave them enough surety of a job under the new regime, its adoption had been 'made an object of earnest desire to a very large portion of the youth of the better classes of inhabitants'.[34]

This class of people were too willing to seize the opportunity of time. As they fully identified themselves with the winning side, all manner of opportunities came their way and they strengthened their own position. They had no regrets for the loss of position of their own language and had they felt about it, they could have reached out to the government with their feeling of disapproval. 'I do not recollect,' said Jenkins, 'that there was a single proposition made to retain Assamese, or that any difficulty was alleged as to the introduction of Bengali as the language of the courts.'[35] We have no evidence to allege that Jenkins' assertion was coloured by any prejudice. Takers of Bengali clerk-conspiracy theory have ignored this aspect of Assamese clerk-cooperation with the language policy of the government. They blamed uninvented conspirators but overlook the real collaborators. But very soon the British realized the fact that language was very much an *affaire d'honneur* for the nationalities of India.

The importance of language in imperial politics was first realized by the British Government during the Crimean War (1854–6). At the instance of Sir Charles Trevelyan (1807–86), Max Mueller wrote *Languages of the Seat of War* and tried to impress upon them 'the connection between the political role of England in India and a competent knowledge of Oriental language'.[36] Max Mueller's campaign influenced public opinion in London. He always believed that 'the task of governing India would be simplified if the governing race were able, by knowledge of their languages, to enter more readily into the thoughts, lives and aspirations of those they governed'.[37]

The Mutiny of 1857 gave Max Mueller another opportunity to clinch his argument. In December that year he addressed, under a penname Philindus, a letter to *The Times* with a long and self-explanatory heading , 'On the Neglect of the study of the Indian languages considered as a cause of the Indian rebellion'. Among other things he wrote, 'a man need not have been in India to see that in order to govern a people, and to gain the confidence and goodwill of a conquered race, it is necessary to know their language'.[38] He was supported by Sir Charles Trevelyan, Professor Monier Williams and Professor Syed Abdoolah. The practical experience therefore, compelled the rulers not to remain content with the mere 'knowledge' of a language but to grant recognition of it expeditiously wherever possible. The decision of the Government of Bengal to introduce Assamese, Bengali, Hindi, Oriya, etc., in their respective provinces in September 1872 was the product of this experience.[39] Apparently, the Bengali clerks were more sinned against than sinning.

To compare a small thing with a big one, British conquest of Assam had brought into blossom Bengali culture on the soil of Assam as much as the Norman conquest of Britain had brought in French. Geoffrey Chaucer, Langland, John Wyclif, John Mandeville and Gower had done away with the French influence and promised the dawn of a new national life, language and literature. Likewise Anandaram, Hemchandra, Gunabhiram, Lakhminath and Padmanath had done out the Bengali influence on them and placed Assamese on a sure footing.[40]

The controversy strengthened linguistic nationalism in Assam. Eric Hobsbawm has pointed out that linguistic nationalism was not the product of the people who spoke a language but of those who read and write. He remarks that nineteenth century was the period of great authorities of the smaller linguistic groups who had standardized, homogenized and modernized their language.[41] The Nagpur session of the Indian National Congress (1920) recognized twenty-one Provincial Congress Committees on linguistic basis. This reassured the weaker nationalities, the Oriyas, the Assamese, etc., of rightful place of their language. The Congress allayed their fear for good. This was an important factor behind enthusiastic participation of the Assamese in the non-cooperation movement.

RESPONSE TO REFORM MOVEMENTS

The dawn of a new life would be appreciated more fruitfully when one examines the impact of the Brahmo Samaj in Assam. The Brahmo Samaj was founded by Raja Rammohun Roy in 1828. After his death during his tour in England in 1833, the Brahmo Samaj became inactive and almost extinct. It was revived by Maharshi Debendranath Tagore and thus began the phase of Adi Brahmo Samaj (1844–57). It was followed by the brief second phase (1858–66) of the duumvirs Debendranath and Keshubchandra Sen.[42] Following some difference of opinion, Keshubchandra parted company with Debendranath and founded the Brahmo Samaj of India in 1866. The Brahmo movement spread its wings to Assam in this phase. This phase terminated in 1878 when Sivanath Sastri and others left Keshubchandra and organized the Sadharan Brahmo Samaj.[43]

Sivanath Sastri (1847–1919) in his autobiography *Atmacharit*, published in 1918, gave an account of his travel in Assam from end to end. In the month of July 1886 he came to Assam for propagation of the Brahmo religion, and visited the towns of Dhubri, Goalpara, Guwahati, Tezpur, Nagaon, Sibsagar and Dibrugarh.[44] It appears that the news of Sivanath's visit received wide publicity and the Brahmo followers living in the towns made arrangements to receive the Brahmo preacher with due warmth.

Dwarakanath Ganguly (1844–98), also a Brahmo, was then touring Assam, on behalf of the Indian Association to investigate the real state of affairs of the tea garden workers. Dwarakanath joined Sivanath on his way. Sivanath's association with Dwarakanath made the tea garden authorities and the official circles suspicious about the real intention of Sivanath. He convinced them that Dwarakanath being his personal friend, they were moving together each doing his own work.[45]

Sastri's anecdotes of his return journey makes interesting reading, it has not lost its freshness even now. Throughout the journey the missionary zeal of Sivanath Sastri shone out like a beacon. He visited Assam after a few years of the Cooch Behar marriage muddle and when there was a split in the organization and confusion among the members. In view of the growing Hindu Bengali population in the towns of Assam, the Brahmo leaders thought, Assam could provide them the second biggest field for their work, Jajnaram Phukan, the disciple of Rammohun found no opportunity to propagate the new faith in Assam.

The Brahmo movement in Assam was a reflex from the glory of its Bengal phase. Sivanath Sastri, the historian of the Brahmo Samaj, stated that the message of the 'new light' was carried to Assam by Sadhu Aghornath, a missionary of the Brahmo Samaj of India in 1870.[46] But the movement in Assam started off on the right foot with someone else. According to Sivanath Sastri the Brahmo Samaj branches at Goalpara, Guwahati, Nagaon and Tezpur were started in 1870. He borrowed his facts from Miss Collect's *Brahmo Year Book.* The record does not fully conform to the annual report of the Sadharan Brahmo Samaj and other evidence. The Goalpara branch established in 1868 was the oldest Brahmo Samaj.[47] At Dhubri, the district headquarters town, there must have been a branch functioning where Gunabhiram Barua formally joined the Samaj in 1869.[48]

Aghornath found his first batch of sympathetic audience at Nagaon. Sastri writes, 'There were two men who came forward at his call. The first was a youngman named Padmahash Goswami and the second was Babu Gunabhiram Barua. Padmahash was so enthusiastic about the Brahmo ideals that he threw off his Brahmanical thread and went over to the new church. All this happened at Nagaon in June 1870.'[49] By his own admission, Gunabhiram had interest in the work of the Samaj since his Calcutta days though he joined it in 1869. So, his presence next year at the initiation ceremony could be a matter of chance.

By their acceptance of the Brahmo faith, 'the Hindu Protestantism' as Nirad C. Chaudhuri calls it,[50] Gunabhiram and Padmahash shook the native society to its very foundation. As a powerful government officer Gunabhiram had social status and had no fear of social ostracism. But Padmahash on the other hand, was a teacher at the Nagaon Government High School and therefore had less protection. He had to put up with discourtesy and derision of his opponents. Junior to Gunabhiram by not less than twelve years, Padmahash was a man of positive spirit. He suffered indignities, but suffered them proudly.

The Brahmo religion was sought to be popularized in Assam by literary efforts also. The pioneer was Jadunath Chakravarty who edited and published a Bengali weekly called *Assam Mihir* from Chidananda Press, Guwahati in 1872. Shortly afterwards, English was introduced into it and it became a bilingual paper.[51]

The press was owned by Chidananda Chaudhury who was a Bengali enthusiast and therefore, patronized the publication of the English-Bengali weekly. He was the first youth from Sundaridia, a place of historic importance near Barpeṭa, who went to Calcutta for English education. Those were the heydays of the Brahmo movement, but whether he was formally initiated to Brahmoism cannot be ascertained. On his return from Calcutta, he had to undergo a purification rite for his coming into contact with a whole range of unknown people in the city. Later, he formally became a disciple of his ancestral shrine at Sundaridia.[52] Rajnarayan Basu, in his memoir *Atmacharit* wrote that Jadunath Chakravarty was an ardent follower of Keshubchandra Sen. It was likely that the circulation of the paper was confined to the followers of the Brahmo faith only and it had but a short life.[53] The *Assam Mihir* was followed by an Assamese journal, *Assam Darpan* (1874–5) edited by Lakshmikanta Barkakati another Brahmo of Tezpur. Padmahash Goswami brought out *Gyanodoi* (1875–6) officially described as a periodical 'devoted exclusively to scientific and literary subject'.[54] The devout Brahmo Padmahash got to the bottom of the Brahmo ideology and wanted to instill into the popular mind the urge for 'emancipation'. Perhaps he took lessons from the fate of *Assam Mihir* and *Assam Darpan* that no newspaper or journal could thrive as a Brahmo organ. He took recourse to the less provocative method of spreading the ideas. Padmahash authored two tracts, namely, *Features of Brahmo Dharma* and *What is called Brahmo*, in Assamese for the spread of his faith.[55]

With his sure-footed talents Gunabhiram could have sailed safe but he was in no mood to flatter the conservative opinion. His first wife Brajasundari died in 1867. After three years he married Bishnupriya, a Brahmin widow. The marriage was registered in 1872 after the Native Marriage Act (Act III of 1872) came into force,[56] his Brahmo faith apart, Gunabhiram was deeply impressed by the widow remarriage movement of Iswarchandra Vidyasagar. It is gratifying to recall that while studying in Calcutta Gunabhiram made good use of his time. Calcutta was a city of contending ideas and Anandaram Dhekial Phukan introduced that polemical world to Gunabhiram. He nearly stopped swoting for his examination and resolved to go with the rebellious tide while the going was good. Gunabhiram, a boy of 22, was present in the historic widow remarriage ceremony in Calcutta on 7 December 1856 where Srishchandra Vidyaratna married Kalimati Devi. The marriage was organized by Vidyasagar. The second widow remarriage took place after two days, on 9 December, Gunabhiram was present in that marriage also.[57] That is the way how the great oaks from little acorns grow.

Gunabhiram and Padmahash thus significantly gained in social prominence. They were strengthened by the arrival of resourceful believers like Sarat Chandra Majumdar and Gurunath Datta at Nagaon. Regular Brahmo *anusthans* attracted new converts. The believers were inspired by novel experiences. Some Assamese youngmen joined the Samaj and the well-known among them were Anandaram Goswami, Raghunath Bora and Brajanath Bora. Anandaram Goswami married Ambika Sundari Devi, the daughter of a Christian convert, according to the Brahmo rites. 'Thus', observed Sivanath Sastri, 'Nowgong became a source of new influence in Assam in the seventies. From there Brahmoism spread to other centres.' Next to Nagaon, the Tezpur branch was an active unit of the Samaj. Sastri wrote that the Bengali population provided the main base of the organization. Lakshmikanta Barkakati was the only exception.[58] Towards the end of 1878, the Samaj came under the cloud of the 'marriage controversy' but they faced the crisis with fortitude and unwavering loyality to their old faith. A central Assam Upasana Samaj was organized at Tezpur to keep up the morale of the Brahmo followers in the face of the split in the organization in May 1887.[59] Keshubchandra Sen's *Navabidhan* had no takers in Assam.

Sen's New Dispensation was a blending of what he thought to be the best of Hinduism, Christinity, Islam and Buddhism. His *Nava Samhita* was a philosophical extension of his religious posture.[60] In 1881, an organized effort was made by some eight leading Brahmos of Assam to thwart the march of K.C. Sen's New Dispensation and the Brahmo Samaj of India. They published a manifesto from Tezpur wherein they said: 'We think that the New Dispensaiton is a disguised form of the avatarism promulgated in India from time to time and that the observances introduced in the Brahmo Samaj of India tend to encourage some forms of superstition, which it should be the object of the Brahmo Samaj to root out.' Like Tezpur, the Guwahati, Dhubri and Dibrugarh units too refused to fall in line with Sen.[61]

The Dibrugarh unit of the Sadharan Brahmo Samaj was organized in the early eighties. Lakshminath Das, who was a postmaster there, was the central figure of the Samaj. Later he became a teacher in the Dibrugarh High School. He was a regular subscriber of the *Tattwa Kaumudi*, the organ of the Sadharan Brahmo Samaj brought out by Sivanath Sastri. Lakshminath's simplicity, religiocity and honesty made him a Brahmo model of himself. Many people were influenced by his personal qualities and they came to believe that if initiation into Brahmoism could make such an ideal man then such initiation was welcome.[62] In Guwahati also, the lead was taken by a Lahiri Brahmin family. Almost in every town the Bengali settlers were the activists and propagandists of the Samaj. It failed to win over the Assamese in general.

Padmahash Goswami died in 1879. The annual report of the Samaj noted with grief the passing away of Padmahash and recalled his service in these words: 'He was working singlehanded in Assam, propagating the new faith and had been put to much persecution on that account. He died during this year, when he was below thirty, deeply mourned by all who knew him.' (According to our calculation when Padmahash died, he was on the wrong side of thirty.) Sastri noted that the work of the Brahmo Samaj suffered setbacks after the untimely death of Padmahash and the departure of Gunabhiram to Calcutta on his retirement. The responsibility fell upon Ram Durlabh Mazumdar, a lawyer and a prominent personality of the Nagaon town. Ram Durlabh died in the first decade of this century. With him passed off the last inspiring soul of the Samaj at Nagaon.[63]

Sivanath Sastri observed that the influence of the Brahmo movement on the Assamese was marginal. The Brahmo preachers encountered resistance from the conservative society. Here is an instance of how strongly the older generation reacted against the propagation of Brahmo faith in Assam. We have it from the reminiscence of Lakshminath Bezbaroa, the Sahityarathi, who himself became a Brahmo.[64] Pandit Ramkumar Vidyaratna (1836–1901) was a legend in the Brahmo propaganda movement in Assam, Orissa and Bihar. He had extensively toured the districts of Assam and took upon himself the task of probing the labour conditions in the tea gardens of Assam. His *Coolie Kahini* (1888) is a living document of his sincere work. Once Ramkumar visited Sibsagar, the home town of the Bezbaroas and addressed some propaganda meetings for the Brahmo Samaj. Ramkumar was a powerful speaker and he began to draw more and more audience. The elderly section of the society was incensed by this and under the leadership of Dinanath, Lakshminath's father, some people got united and began to penalize every Assamese Hindu who attended the meetings of Ramkumar. To savour the forbidden fruit Lakshminath's elder brother Srinath attended a meeting of the Sabha and he was beaten black and blue by his father Dinanath.[65] In the face of such total hostility Brahmoism could not strike roots in the town. With all his efforts, Ramkumar found a lone follower in Gopal Chandra Ghosh who was a teacher in the Government High School.

The social ostracism of the Brahmos, though not pronounced, was zealously practised in Assam. Gunabhiram and Lakshminath did not have to suffer indignities as they were outsize figures by the standard of their critics. Families embracing Brahmoism had but limited matrimonial choice. So, the Brahmos introduced inter community marriages and promoted better social understanding between the Assamese and the Bengalis. They produced wholesome effects. The understanding disappeared with the decline of the movement.

The Brahmos propularized female education. Gunabhiram's daughter Swarnalata was the first Assamese girl to study in Bethune School, Calcutta. Her father's Brahmo connections helped Swarnalata begin her life in Calcutta with a promising note. She adopted herself to the spreading circle of the enlightened Brahmo families of the city. Her shining talents brought her meed of praise. Her example inspired other girls to go to Calcutta for education.

It is quite interesting to note that a proposal for Swarnalata's marriage with Rabindranath Tagore was almost finalized. But, on hearing about her father's widow remarriage, Rabindranath's father Maharshi Debendranath backed out. The Tagores made it up, if we may say so, to Swarnalata's brother Jnanadabhiram, a barrister, by giving in marriage Lotika Devi, the great grand-daughter of Debendranath in 1906.[66] By the standard of the age it was an uncommon marriage relation and it serves as an index of social metamorphosis.

Fifteen years earlier, when Debendranath was still alive, his granddaughter Prajnasundari was given in marriage to Lakshminath Bezbaroa. Before his marriage Lakshminath was initiated into Brahmoism by Debendranath himself. Bezbaroa held firmly to his faith.[67] Even those who lived in Assam had to opt for inter community marriage. For example, Gurunath Datta, headmaster of Nagaon Government High School and a leading man of the Samaj gave his daughter in marriage to Brahmananda, son of Lakshmikanta Barkakati of Tezpur who was a Brahmo.[68]

Kamalakanta Bhattacharyya (1855–1936) better known as Maharshi Kamalakanta, was a Brahmo. He is known for some philosophical and patriotic writings. His criticism of some aspects of Hinduism, more particularly the dominance of the Brahmins in society made him unpopular. The eccentric iconoclast had torn off his sacred thread, taken to the plough, converted the *saligram* (an idolized stone) into a paperweight and declared his faith in Brahmoism.[69] The immobility of the society made him impatient and the Brahmo faith made him a rebel. So he could hardly gain the ear of his people. His later life was a tale of misery of every form.[70]

Even Jnanadabhiram Barua had to bear up with humiliating situation. In his memoir *Mor Katha* Jnanadabhiram related his experience with men of his society who did not take kindly to his faith. His refined tastes of life and living made no good impression with them.[71]

But such insult pale into insignifance if we consider the persecution of the early Brahmos in Bengal. There the 'Young Brahmos were severely beaten and driven out of their paternal homes. They were disinherited.' The Brahmo missionary Bijoy Krishna Goswami was tortured by the people of his own village Santipur. They smeared his body with treacle and set wasps on him. Umeshchandra Datta, Principal of City College 'was bodily lifted and thrown into a thorny bush' for his association with the Brahmos. There was also record of poisoning for the 'sin' of attending public worship in a Brahmo Samaj.[72] Martyrs blood, they proved, was the seed of the church. Persecution of a supposed heresy became a holy pastime of the believers since the days of the Inquisition.

The Brahmo Samaj in Assam did not become, unlike Bengal, a popular movement. But by introducing significant asthetic values in the social, cultural and religious life, the Brahmo Samaj, despite restrictive following, exercised a wholesome effect on Assamese life. It helped to reduce the hold of orthodoxy on society and made, for the first time, religious faith an object of doubt and debate. It popularized professional life of the new middle class.

Towards the end of the nineteenth century a handful of educated people were bristling with life in the small sub-divisional town of Barpeta. They were educated in Calcutta and were mostly trained in legal and medical professions. Many of them were followers of the Brahmo movement. As they settled themselves for various professions, they set up an organization, the Barpeta Hitsadhini Sabha for public service. Ambikagiri Raychaudhury recalled that the inaugural session of the Sabha was opened with a *Brahmo sangeet.* Until then modern songs of secular and patriotic spirit were unknown.[73] Research on the subject would reveal if the *Brahmo sangeets* were the forbear of modern Assamese songs.

The general impact of the Brahmo movement went beyond the caste-ridden Assamese society. The Boro Brahma movement may be cited as a case in point. The movement was started by Kalicharan Mech who later called himself Kalicharan Brahma (1860–1938). Kalicharan began his career as a disbeliever of the traditional faith of his own society. He noticed a lack of religious beliefs and embraced different religions at different places. The disintegrating tendency worried him so much that ultimately he searched out an answer in the *Brahma Dharma* of Paramhansa Sibnarayan. In the process he metamorphosed himself, a sceptic became an ardent preacher. He exhorted the people to give up the belief of many deities and preached the philosophy of one God.[74]

More than anybody else, Kalicharan realized the necessity of English education for the Boros. His movement helped the spread of education in the tribal areas of the entire district of Goalpara. He himself founded a school (Brahma Boarding School) at Dhubri, a weaving centre and a carpentry workshop. He discouraged production and consumption of liquor and called upon the people to take to profitable occupations, trade and various crafts. To inspire the people he set up 'Brahma Company' himself. The Boros were slow on the uptake of the advanced ideas of Kalicharan, so his movement had but limited success. Yet it brought dynamism into a stolid society and created an awareness among the people about the changing world around them.[75]

A.R. Desai showed the importance of such 'religio-reform movement' in our country. Its programme included, besides religious reform, creation of new social values and social institutions.[76] Kalicharan's religion too adumbrated a social vision. His followers assumed the title 'Brahma'. The three notable personalities of the resurgent Boro society, Rupnath Brahma, Modaram Brahma and Sitanath Brahma Chaudhury emerged from the residuum of the Brahma movement.

The early Muslim settlers used to live in and around the medieval towns and in matters of language, dress and social manners they had little difference with the Hindu Assamese. Shahabuddin Ahmad Talash, the chronicler, recorded his impression in 1663 in these words.

> As for the Muslims who had been taken prisoner in former times and had chosen to stay here, their descendants act exactly in the manner of the Assamese and have nothing of Islam except the name, their hearts are inclined far more towards mingling with the Assamese than towards association with the Muslims.[77]

Haliram Dhekial Phukan noted that these Muslims were little aware of the orthodox tenents and practices of their religion. They adopted many practices of Hinduism and even worshipped Hindu gods and goddesses. In view of the government orders allowing people to follow their religious faith freely, he surmised that the Muslims of Assam would soon follow those of Bengal.[78]

Md. Enamul Haq finds that even in the 1970s worship of Hindu deities by some Muslims was a commonplace thing in Bengal. He records that Siva 'receives homage from a section of the Muslim masses of Bengal'.

Besides *Ola Bibi*, they worship Lakhmi, Manasa, Sitala, Sasthi and Brahma Daitya.[79]

In the absence of any organized band of followers the effects of the liberal teachings of the itinerant saint Ajan Fakir dimmed in Assam. Interest in him was revived later.[80] Ajan Fakir is yet to be placed historically.

As Heracles, of the Greek myth, in pursuit of the Ceryneian Hind, shot an arrow, pinned its forelegs together without causing bleeding and captured it alive; similarly, the scintillating liberalism of the earlier Muslims was mauled and conquered by the innate conservation of the new settlers without offending them.

The Aligarh movement led by Sir Syed Ahmad Khan (1817–78) did not find any follower in Assam. The Muslims of Assam found no novel content in the Aligarh movement whose prime object was to spread Western education among the Muslims.[81] Their differences with the laterday immigrants from eastern Bengal were too apparent to bc noted. Until several decades to come the class identity differed greatly with the religious identity. In Assam the benefit of Western education was fully shared by them with the Assamese Hindus from the very beginning. The first doctorate from the Brahmaputra valley came from this community. Moidul Islam Bora (1899–1944) of Sibsagar did his Ph.D. from the London University in 1931.[82] M.I. Bora is renowned for his translation of the *Baharistan-i-Ghaibi* from Persian into English.

The genesis of the Pan-Islamic movement in India, according to Ravinder Kumar, lay in the attempt of the liberal Muslim gentry to seek rapport with the poorer sections of Muslims through the assistance of the *ulema*. The movement led by liberal Muslims thus 'rested upon the social distress of the poor, it fanned the ideological hostility of the *ulema* to the British government, it drew upon the intimate link between the *ulema* and the Muslim masses'.[83]

The formation of the province of eastern Bengal and Assam in 1905 gave the Muslims of Bengal for the first time an opportunity to locate some conquerable frontiers. From the 1920s onward their dominant political psychology had been shaped and battened more and more by their interaction with the outside world. Assam could not keep herself away from the influence.

Pan-Islamic thinking had no ready buyers in Assam. Mosleh Uddin Ahmed, a poet, pointed out in 1915 that Hindu–Muslim animosity was against the vital interests of both the communities. He believed that the wrong doer was the Indian historian who had copied the British historians and drawn lines of cleavage. We reproduce below a brief paraphrase of one stanza of his poem *Adbhut Jati* (*Strange Nation*) to show his disdain for Pan-Islamic pretentions.

> Heard that we are the grandchildren of
> some Badshah, though we are living
> here as Assamese. Like a tutored
> parrot we read up Arabic and say
> our prayers sloppily. Urdu, we are
> now told, is our mother tongue,
> how strange, why then we hear
> the Assamese voice from the moment
> of our birth?[84]

Communal ideology ultimately struck the chord of Syed Muhammad Saadullah (1885–1955). His political life entered a decisive phase after 1920 in the wake of the Line System debate. His role is not held in reverence by many. A man of admirable personal qualities, his policies contained a tincture of communalism.[85] Maulana Tayyabullah (1884–1960), a brilliant student of the University of Calcutta was set up as a counterbalance to Saadullah by the Indian National Congress from the early Congress days. But pious thought proved no match for a deep rooted campaign and it was unable to keep the rising tide of Pan-Islamism at bay.[86]

OPIUM: A STICKY SITUATION

One significant issue that confronted the middle class was the addiction of the Assamese to opium. Opium was the worst impediment to profitable economic motivation. It may not be amiss here to examine the complex reactions of the middle class and its fight against the drug.

Opium was an important commercial crop in the nineteenth century India.[87] But it was outside the purview of agriculture in Assam which we have discussed in Chapter 3. Here, its importance as a commercial crop was inconsequencial. A.J. Moffatt Mills made some inquiries in this regard and came to the conclusion that the condition of the province was not favourable for production of opium on a large scale. He feared that the difficulty of procuring labour would operate against the establishment of a factory.[88] The establishment of an opium agency was considered commercially unworkable. Bengal was the source of supply of opium before it was locally produced. The use of opium in the province was not a thing of the distant past. The Assam Congress Opium Enquiry Committee (1925) held the view that it started towards the end of the seventeeth century when Assam came in contact with the Mughal soldiers. But this widely accepted view is rebutted by the fact that the use of opium in Assam was known even during the days of Sankardeva (1449–1568). In one biography, for instance, Sankardeva is said to have 'removed one Surya Sarasvati from the office of the *Bhagavati* for his addiction to opium'. In his account of the *satra* institutions of Assam, Satyendranath Sarma tells us that within the precincts of a *satra* 'addiction to opium eating, smoking and drinking was never tolerated' and though the habit of drinking wine was nowhere reported, the other two vices were found among the devotees. Punishment was instant and heavy and very often the situation called for penalty.[89]

The cultivation of poppy in Assam was started during the reign of Lakshmi Singha in the eighteenth century. There was an erroneous belief that opium cures dysentry. At first its use was restricted, it was a privilege for the members of the nobility. Soon it became a consumers' delight and a thing of common use. Gunabhiram Barua rightly observed that it made its way into Assam as a destroyer of disease but ere long it turned out to be the root of diseases.[90] It was believed that poppy grown in Beltola, near Guwahati, was a quality product and the royal house had the supply of its quota from there. Gradually, its use became widespread, some people grew it with the connivance of the government. Elsewhere in the country the government had total control over its cultivation. Poppy cultivation in Bihar and Benares in the period from 1845–6 to 1885–6 increased by 221 per cent—from 2,96, 282 *bighas* to 9,51, 870 *bighas*.[91]

We have an account of an opium factory at Patna written by the historian George Travelyan. He wrote:

> It is the most romantic of manufactures. Everywhere the drowsy scent of the poppy prevails, and lulls the pleased visitor into a delightful consciousness of oriental languor and boundless profits, and into a sweet oblivion of the principles of competition and Free Trade.[92]

He showed up the snag in the government policy. 'What is the alchemy which can turn silver into gold, which can extract yearly six millions net from the pockets of an alien, often a hostile nation?'[93] he asked. No other source of trade gave as much of profit as opium. The slipshod restrictive measure of the government was not adequate, but even slight laxity on their part might turn the whole nation into 'one vast De Quincey', he warned.[94]

The opium policy of the government was mainly influenced by revenue consideration. By 'exercising a monopoly control over the production and sale of opium' the government never failed to maximize revenue. The Chinese market was also another point of consideration.[95]

In Assam, government or what was more appropriately described as 'excise opium' was introduced in 1852.[96] The sale was regulated by a license system under which the number of retail shops were fixed for each district. The consumption of opium naturally differred from region to region. According to the report of the Opium Commission, the consumption of opium was below average in the Madras Presidency and in the provinces containing the greatest opium producing tracts, viz., Bengal, the N.-W. Provinces and Oudh. It was above average in Assam, Bihar, Bombay, etc.[97]

Reactions against the baneful effects of opium were expressed in Britain for the first time by the Quakers, Evangelicals and others. In 1843, Lord Ashley raised the matter in the House of Commons and challenged the monopoly rights of the East India Company on opium.[98]

In India, the first voice of protest was raised by the missionaries of Bombay and Calcutta. In 1852, the missionaries of Bombay deprecated the government policy of collecting revenue from a 'demoralising and ruinous traffic'. The Calcutta missionaries were more outrageous in their attack. They accused the government of committing 'a breach of faith' and involving itself 'in a guilty and ruinous trade'.[99]

The Assamese elite had been expressing a well-informed reactions against opium right from the beginning. Anandaram Dhekial Phukan first raised the voice of protest against the opium policy of the government. He was fully aware of the harmful effects of opium. In his memorandum of 1853 submitted to A.J.M. Mills, he cited the experience of China. He stated that introduction of excise opium or frequent enhancement of its price would not have a deterrent effect on the consumers. He confidently asserted that 'before the accession of the British power, twenty eight years ago, the use of opium was not half so universal'. He favoured a gradual and calculated suppression of opium and warned, 'the tree will grow so long as the root is not destroyed'.[100]

Maniram Dewan was also aware of the destructive effects of opium. He maintained that 'during the Burmese rule the old penalties against opium-eaters having been removed, the practice became universal' and that every season of fresh opium, in February and March, found new batches of opium eaters. He pointed out that opiumeaters never hesitated 'to sell or give in servitude their wives and families' to get at any amount to obtain opium and that women addicts would even 'sell their domestic utensils without the knowledge of their husbands, and even barter their chastity or forsake the path of virtue to get the drug...'.[101] It was really a cadaverous situation. Like Anandaram, Maniram Dewan also pleaded for a gradual control of opium supply. Both of them appeared to have believed that opium had medicinal properties to heal dysentery. Poppy cultivation in Assam was finally stopped by the government in 1861.[102] But it did not, in any way, reduce the revenue flow to the treasury. There lay the rub. The point of debate in England was whether revenue derived from opium could be strictly called 'a tax on the people of India...'. R.C. Dutt (1848–1909) looked upon opium as 'a paying article' for the cultivators and 'a profitable industry' and therefore, 'no sound economist will' he thought, 'deny that a Government monopoly which excludes the people from' all those benefits, 'is a tax on the people....' He also noted that against opium 'there is no strong feeling in India'.[103] So far as Assam was concerned R.C. Dutt's remark was an understatement.

Hemchandra Barua (1835–96), a leading publicist of contemporary Assam wrote the first manifesto of prohibition in the form of a farce in 1861. True to his virtue of a social thinker Hemchandra wrote *Kaniyar Kirtan* (Opiumeaters' Carol) to spread the message of mischief caused by opium.[104] This manifesto against opium was perhaps, the first of its kind in the annals of the anti-opium agitation of the world.

The government, it must be noted, could not escape the moral responsibility of the drift that set in and their policy influenced the consumption pattern. In 1874, the Government of Assam introduced a system under which any person could open any number of shops he wanted on payment of a fixed license fee. But in view of the growing controversy in India and Britain, they reverted to the old policy of giving license to a limited number of applicants and at the same time kept raising the price of opium under the cover of an inefficacious policy of 'maximum revenue with minimum consumption'.[105] As we find, the number of opium shops were reduced from 5,137 in 1873–4 to 306 in 1919–20, but the consumption level remained almost the same, 1,856 *maunds* in 1873–4 and 1,748 *maunds* in 1919–20. Price of opium per *seer* was Rs. 5 in 1835, it spiralled up to Rs. 32 in 1884 and then to Rs. 65 in 1924. The Opium Enquiry Committee proved to the hilt that contrary to the expectations of the government, revenue and consumption went up together. We reproduce the findings of the committee in Table 6.1.[106]

The fall in demand in the year 1920–1 was due to the active resistance against opium consumption in the wake of the non-cooperation movement in Assam.

It is well-known that Britain was the centre of anti-opium agitation at the international level. At the initiative of some Quaker reformers, evangelicals and representatives of various missionary societies, the Anglo–Oriental Anti-Opium Society was established in 1874 in London. China was their immediate concern. But very soon they noticed the ramifications of opium trade and so broadened the base of their agitation; they took up the case of India as well. The Society submitted a petition to the House of Commons in May 1882 demanding, among other things, reduction of area of poppy cultivation in India and of the government's dependence on opium revenue. Another landmark of anti-opium propaganda was the report of Dr D. Morrison, a presbyterian medical missionary in Rajshahi, Bengal, published in the *Friend of China* (1890), the organ of the Anti-Opium Society.[107] Voluntary organizations such as the Society for the Suppression of the Opium Trade, the Urgency Committee, the Christian Union and the Women's Urgency Committee were also active against opium in India and China.[108]

These propaganda gained the ears of the influential circles of London. The liberal prime minister W.E. Gladstone had three members of the Anti-Opium Society in his cabinet. But economic interest was stronger in the mind of the prime minister than his liberal principles. So, willynilly, Gladstone appointed a Commission of Enquiry to look 'not into how but whether the opium traffic should be suppressed'.[109] The Royal Commission of Opium thus came into existence, but everything was not coming up roses for it. As the Commission was the product of a movement launched mainly in England, it failed to evoke response of the Indian elite. The Indian Press, generally speaking, was also hostile towards it and they even questioned the necessity of such a Commission. The silence of the Indian National Congress on the opium question lent itself

TABLE 6.1

Year	*Opium revenue (Rs.)*	*Opium consumption (maunds)*
1874–5	12,25,141	1874
1885–6	16,75,363	1446
1915–16	30,53,933	1560
1919–20	38,37,125	1747
1920–1	44,12,308	614

to several interpretations. Either the social programme of the Congress was too narrow to include it in their agenda or, on the opium question there was no unanimity of views among the leaders who represented various interests. Or, like the British Indian Association, the Congress might have feared that a fall in opium revenue might lead to increased taxation on the people. Moreover the use of opium, unlike alcohol, was not repugnant to religious sensibility.[110]

The most inveterate opponents of opium in India were the Brahmos. They pointed out the degrading effects of opium, pleaded for its total suppression and refused to concede the government stand to continue with it on grounds of loss of revenue. The position of the Brahmos, it is worthwhile to remember, was strengthened by a majority of the British and American missionaries who appeared before the Royal Commission. The Calcutta Missionary conference had also called for a ban on opium. Among the Brahmos of Assam, Ram Durlabh Mazumdar, a prominent lawyer of Nagaon pleaded with the Commission to stop opium trade on the ground that the lower classes of people had suffered by it. They used to spend, he stated, 10 to 20 per cent of their earning on opium.[111]

The Opium Commission was aware of the efforts of Hemchandra Barua, the lone crusader in the farthest corner of the country. Hemchandra was called to appear before the Commission in Calcutta which he was unable to do for reasons of health. However, he got his *Kaniyar Kirtan* translated into English through Upendranath Barua, one of his ardent supporters, and sent it to H.J. Wilson, a member of the Commission.[112] But the Commission had perhaps, little will of their own and as the Sanskrit saying goes, the mountain gave birth to a mouse. The commission underscored 'the dangers of flying in the face of widespread Indian opposition and claimed that prohibition would be extremely unpopular'[113] and therefore, put their stamp of approval on the existing system. This was a complete non sequitur from what had been going on in Britain and India.

Hemchandra Barua passed away in 1896. After him there was none among the leading lights of the Assamese society to carry on his unfinished war against poppy. Campaign against opium was weakened earlier by the strong dissenting voice of the Jorhat Sarvojanik Sabha. More than the weight of its arguments, it was for the weight of the leaders that the growing consciousness against opium took a bad tumble. The sabha was not called by the Commission to give evidence. In the wake of their inquiry, the Sarvojanik Sabha organized a public meeting at Jorhat, suo moto prepared a memorial to send it to the government for its onward transmission to the Commission. The main arguments of the sabha against the idea of prohibition and suppression of opium were: (i) that opium had useful medicinal properties, such as, it cures dysentary, alleviates pain, prevents malaria and gives longivity, etc., its abolition would result in loss of livelihood of a large number of people, (ii) a fall in excise revenue would lead to an increased taxation of the common men, and (iii) the use of opium was not barred by any religious principle.[114] There should not be any doubt that as against the handful of critics, the defenders of opium were legion.

The Jorhat Sarvojanik Sabha by their self-righteous zeal did only a disservice to the community. Though the president and the secretary of the Sabha were tea planters we do not find any ground to allege that as planters they had any vested interest in doing so. At a time when the harmful effects of opium were established beyond all doubt, such sanctimonious ignorance on the part of the most enlightened section of the native community proved a curse to the people. The sabha's contentions went unchallenged for about a quarter of a century and in spite of two anti-opium conferences in Dibrugarh in 1907 and 1912, the anti-opium campaign and movement were not fruitful. The first conference recommended the formation of an organization called Assam Temperence Association which did not come about. The second conference succeeded in forming a Temperence society, but its impact was not widely felt. Obviously, the consumption pattern was so extensive and invidious that nothing short of a mass awareness compaign and mass resistance could touch upon the heart of the matter. The Government of Assam appointed a committee headed by A.W. Botham to go into the matter. Among its members were Kaliprasad Chaliha and Radhanath Phukan. The committee's final report came in April 1913. The committee gave short shrift to criticisms of government opium policy and made some light-hearted recommendations.[115]

Among the leading members of the community only Padmanath Gohain Barua continued to give vent to his indignation and he never betrayed his consistent opposition to the use of opium under any pretext. Lakshminath Bezbaroa paid no heed to the opium debate which was going on. He never associated himself with the anti-opium campaign in the state. His most intimate friend, Chandrakumar Agarwala was equally silent on the issue for he knew that his father Haribilash Agarwala owned an opium shop. Likewise Madhabchandra Bardaloi, an overzealous government servant who was later made a Rai Bahadur, never found fault with any government policy.[116]

Manikchandra Barua, Bolinarayan Bora, Satyanath Bora and Pandit Hemchandra Goswami, never troubled themselves with the thought of opium. Two other Rai Bahadurs, Phanidhar Chaliha and Ghanashyam Barua, however, spoke out against the abuse of opium in the provincial legislative council. Phanidhar Chaliha having been talked down to by the chairman of the council over a remark resigned his seat in 1919. His friend Ghanashyam Barua exposed the hollowness of the government policy on opium and pressed for some drastic steps, but the government refused to concede anything and stuck their heels in.[117] About that time, the leaders of the Assam Association started bringing round its members and followers to the idea non-cooperation proposed by the Congress. In a meeting of the Assam Association, attended among others, by Ghanashyam Barua and Rai Bahadur Nilambar Dutta, a course of action was finalised. Temperence was at the top of their agenda. Gandhi's visit to Assam in August 1921 strengthened the movement against opium and it became an integral part of the non-cooperation movement in Assam. It had limited success. Its importance lay in the fact that for the first time the All India Congress Committee (AICC) was made aware of the grave problem.[118]

In 1924, when a world conference on opium was held in Geneva, the AICC asked C.F. Andrews 'to undertake an investigation in Assam with the help of the Congress workers'. The Assam Congress Opium Enquiry Committee came into existence following it. The Committee made an indepth study of the opium question and published its report in September 1925. The report said that according to the League of Nations the medical requirements of opium for every 10,000 of the population were 6 *seers* or about 12 pounds, but the rate of consumption in Assam was much higher than that. The committee noted the quantity of consumption district-wise[119] (see Table 6.2).

C.F. Andrews noted, 'both in opium smoking and in opium eating for non-medical purposes, Assam held by far the blackest record in India'. There were two forms of opium consumption in Assam, namely *kanikhowa* or eating and *kanipan khowa* or smoking opium. 'The number of opium smokers has always formed a considerable portion of the indigenous Assamese population.'[120] The enquiry committee, consisting mostly of the leaders of the Congress made use of the opportunity that came their way and brought into focus the disastrous effects of opium in Assam. If there was ever an appropriate time to ban the use of opium completely, it was then.

TABLE 6.2

District	*Population*	*Issue of opium*	*Consumption per 10,000 in seers*
Kamrup	7,62,671	3,472	45,534
Darrang	4,77,935	5,101	1,06,729
Nagaon	3,97,921	6,909	1,73,627
Sibsagar	8,23,197	9,133	1,10,945
Lakhimpur	5,88,295	11,176	1,89,972

The question of opium was raised, discussed and debated in right earnest by the leading members of the community; some pious proclamations were also wrested from the government, but it could not be forced into giving up opium monopoly.

NOTES

1. D. Neog, *New Light on History of Asamiya Literature*, Guwahati, 1962, p. 334 and B.K. Barua, *History of Assamese Literature*, Delhi, 1978, p. 104.
2. P. Gohain Barua, *Rachnawali*, Guwahati, 1971, pp. 884–5.
3. L.N. Bezbaroa, *Works*, Guwahati, 1988, Vol. II, p. 1854.
4. Some aspects of the debate have come to light through the efforts of H.K. Barpujari, *Asamar Nava Jagaran*, Jorhat, 1984, pp. 33–79; F.S. Downs in *Journal of the Gauhati University*, 1981. Also see, S. Barman and P. Choudhury, *Bastavne Bibhram*, Dibrugarh, 1986.
5. Quoted in G.O. Trevelyan, *The Life and Letters of Lord Macaulay*, London, 1978, Vol. I, pp. 370, 373.
6. G.O. Trevelyan, op. cit., p. 380.
7. Ibid., p. 373.
8. S.K. Das, *A History of Indian Literature*, Delhi, 1991, Vol. VIII, p. 137.
9. S.K. Das, op. cit., pp. 125–44.
10. F. Senapati, *Atmacharit*, Delhi, 1977, pp. 78–9; also see S.K. Das, op. cit., p. 138.
11. F. Senapati, op. cit., p. 80.
12. S. Sen, *History of Bengali Literature*, Delhi, 1979, pp. 170–4 and 193–203, on his views on Rammohun, pp. 167–8.
13. B. Chatterjee, *Bankim Rachanabali*, Calcutta, 1988, Vol. II, pp. 44–7.
14. Detinenne, *Gadya Parampara*, Calcutta, 1977, pp. 18–19.
15. S. Basu, *Banglai Navachetanar Itihas*, Calcutta, 1985, pp. 230–1.
16. Ibid., p. 234.
17. B. Ghose, *Samayikpatre Banglar Samajchitra*, Calcutta, 1978, Vol. I, p. 297.
18. Ibid, p. 298.
19. Ibid., pp. 302–3.

20. S.N. Sen (ed.), *Prachin Bangla Patra Sankalan*, Calcutta, 1942.
21. S.N. Sen, op. cit., p. 84.
22. J.P. Wade, *An Account of Assam*; B. Sharma (ed.), Guwahati, 1972, p. ii.
23. H.K. Barpujari, *The American Missionaries and the North-East India*, Guwahati, 1986, p. 122.
24. S.N. Sen, op. cit., p. 84.
25. S.K. Das, op. cit., p. 139.
26. M.S. Barkataki, *British Administration in North-East India*, Delhi, 1985, p. 233.
27. H.K. Barpujari, op. cit., p. 148.
28. D. Neog, *New Light on History of Asamiya Literature*, op. cit., pp. 339–43.
29. H.K. Barpujari, op. cit., pp. 122–50. Also F.S. Downs in the *Journal of the Gauhati University*, op. cit., pp. 122–59.
30. The fact of his being a government servant could not deter him to tell the truth of a conspiracy if he knew it. One must not ignore the fact that Anandaram made carping criticism of the police administration and revenue policy of the government in his memorandum to Mills in 1853.
31. H.K. Barpujari, op. cit., p. 144.
32. Ibid., p. 150.
33. Ibid., p. 148.
34. Ibid., p. 146.
35. Loc. cit.
36. Nirad C. Chaudhuri, *Scholar Extraordinary*, Bombay, 1980, pp. 181–2.
37. Ibid., p. 184.
38. Ibid., p. 183.
39. For details, see C.E. Buckland, *Bengal under the Lieutenant Governors*, Calcutta, 1901, Vol. II, pp. 527–30.
40. Cf. W.J. Long, *English Literature*, New Delhi, 1978, pp. 67–88.
41. E.J. Hobsbawm, *The Age of Empire*, Calcutta, 1992, pp. 147–51.
42. J. Das, 'The Brahmo Samaj', in A.C. Gupta (ed.), *Studies in the Bengal Renaissance*, Calcutta, 1977, pp. 485–9.
43. Ibid., pp. 490–9.
44. S. Sastri, *Atmacharit*, Calcutta, 1983, pp. 202–4.
45. K.L. Chattopadhaya, Introduction, in D. Ganguli's *Slavery in British Dominion*, Calcutta, 1972, p. ix. Also S. Sastri, loc. cit.
46. S. Sastri, *History of the Brahmo Samaj*, Calcutta, 1974, p. 518.
47. W.W. Hunter, *A Statistical Account of Assam*, Delhi, 1982, Vol. II, p. 47.
48. G. Barua, *Anandaram Dhekial Phukanar Jivan Charitra*, Guwahati, 1971, p. 176.
49. S. Sastri, *History of the Brahmo Samaj*, op. cit., pp. 518–19.
50. N.C. Chaudhuri, *Hinduism: A Religion to Live By*, Delhi, 1979, p. 112.
51. J.N. Bhuyan, *Uwalijoa Nathir Para*, Nagaon, 1991, p. 83.
52. B. Barua, *Sundarit SriSri Madhavdev Madhav Maral Atiram Barua Aru Anyanya*, Guwahati, 1988, pp. 14–16.
53. R. Basu, *Atmacharit*, Calcutta, 1985, p. 57.
54. J.N. Bhuyan, op. cit., p. 86.

55. J.N. Bhuyan, ibid.
56. J.N. Bhuyan (ed)., *J. Barua Works*, Jorhat, 1981, pp. 11–12.
57. J.N. Bhuyan, loc. cit., also B. Ghose, *Vidyasagar O Bangali Samaj*, Calcutta, 1984, pp. 265–9.
58. S. Sastri, *History of the Brahmo Samaj*, op. cit., p. 519.
59. Sastri, loc. cit.
60. N. Sinha (ed), *Freedom Movement in Bengal*, Calcutta, 1968, p. 252.
61. S. Sastri, *History of the Brahmo Samaj*, op. cit., p. 520.
62. B. Rajkhowa, *Mor Jivan Dapon*, Guwahati, 1969, p. 20.
63. S. Sastri, *History of the Brahmo Samaj*, op. cit., pp. 289 and 519.
64. M. Neog (ed.), *Lakshminath Bezbaroa: The Sahityarathi of Assam*, Guwahati, 1972, p. 66.
65. L.N. Bezbaroa, *Works*, Guwahati, 1988, Vol. I, p. 38.
66. J.N. Bhuyan (ed.), *J. Barua Works*, op. cit., pp. 159–60.
67. L.N. Bezbaroa, *Works*, op. cit., p. 66.
68. *J. Barua Works*, op. cit., pp. 164 and 179.
69. P. Goswami (ed.), *Kamalakanta Works*, Guwahati, 1982, p. 8.
70. P. Goswami, loc. cit.
71. *J. Barua Works*, op. cit., p. 151.
72. J. Das in *Studies in the Bengal Renaissance*, op. cit., p. 491.
73. A. Raychaudhury, *Mor Jivan Dhumuhar Echati*, Guwahati, 1973, pp. 152–4.
74. R.N. Mosahary, 'Brahma Religion and Social Change Among the Boros', in *Progs. North East India History Association*, 1985.
75. Ibid.
76. A.R. Desai, *Social Background of Indian Nationalism*, Bombay, 1982, pp. 285–6.
77. See S.K. Bhuyan, *Studies in the History of Assam*, Guwahati, 1985, pp. 88–96.
78. H.D. Phukan, *Assam Buranji*, Guwahati, 1962, p. 90.
79. M.E. Haq, *Sufism in Bengal*, Dacca, 1975, pp. 346–55.
80. An account Ajan Fakir's life may be found in S.A. Malik, *Ajan Fakir aru Suria Jikir*, Guwahati, 1988.
81. A.R. Desai, op. cit., pp. 395–6.
82. P. Gohain Barua (ed.), *Jivani Sangrah*, Guwahati, 1969, pp. 152–6.
83. R. Kumar, *Essays in Social History of Modern India*, Calcutta, 1986, p. 25.
84. *Banhi*, Vol. 6, pp. 315–17, 1837 *Saka* (1915).
85. A.C. Bhuyan (ed.), *Political History of Assam*, Vols. II and III, Guwahati, 1978 and 1980, Vol. II, pp. 309–14, 318–21, 347–57; Vol. III, pp. 105, 253–317, 353–71.
86. A.C. Bhuyan, ibid., Vol. II, pp. 147–8, 321–2; Vol. III, pp. 359–87.
87. See, B.B. Chaudhuri, 'Growth of Commercial Agriculture in Bengal', *IESHR*, 1970, Vol. 7, No. 1, pp. 49–56.
88. Mills' *Report*, Guwahati, 1984, p. 21.
89. S.N. Sarma, *The Neo-Vaisnavite Movement and the Satra Institution of Assam*, Guwahati, 1977, pp. 150–1.
90. G. Barua, *Assam Buranji*, Guwahati, 1972, pp. 120–1.
91. B.B. Chaudhuri, op. cit., pp. 49–50.

92. G. Trevelyan, *The Competition Wallah*, Delhi, 1992, p. 38.
93. Ibid.
94. Ibid., p. 41.
95. B.B. Chaudhuri, loc. cit.
96. H.K. Barpujari (ed.), *Political History of Assam*, Guwahati, 1977, Vol. I, p. 89.
97. G.A. Oddie, *Social Protest in India*, Delhi, 1979, p. 223.
98. Ibid.
99. Ibid., p. 224.
100. Mills' *Report*, op. cit., pp. 110–11.
101. Ibid., p. 619.
102. H.K. Barpujari (ed.), *Political History of Assam*, p. 89.
103. R.C. Dutt, *The Economic History of India*, Delhi, 1970, Vol. II, p. 111.
104. J. Goswami, *Hemchandra Barua*, Delhi, 1987, p. 35.
105. *Assam Congress Opium Enquiry Committee Report*, Jorhat, 1925, p. 24.
106. Ibid., p. 29.
107. G.A. Oddie, op. cit., pp. 228n. and 230–2.
108. *The Statesman*, 15 February, 1894.
109. G.A. Oddie, op. cit., p. 237.
110. Ibid., p. 238.
111. A. Guha, *Planter Raj to Swaraj*, Delhi, 1977, p. 56.
112. J. Goswami, op. cit., p. 36.
113. G.A. Oddie, op. cit., p. 230.
114. Cf. A. Guha, op. cit., pp. 348–50.
115. A. Guha, op. cit., pp. 88–9.
116. A Guha, op. cit., p. 56.
117. Ibid., pp. 90–1.
118. The AICC did not extend support for the anti-opium campaign in a body. But Gandhi's encouragement went a long way into mobilizing the congressmen in Assam as ardent anti-opium agitationists. It became a commonplace reference point of every political history.
119. See, 'Introduction' by C.F. Andrews for the *Assam Congress Opium Enquiry Committee Report*, op. cit.,
120. Ibid., p. 38.

CHAPTER 7

Conclusion

In the earlier chapters I have examined the major aspects of the socio-economic life of the people of Assam in the Brahmaputra valley. Anglo–Assamese relations from the beginning to the end passed through several phases. The present study is confined to the Anglo–Assamese connection as the ruling power and the ruled for a period of about seventy years. This period is not singularized by a happy combination of events. There were remarkable moments of peace, orderly change and momentous drive; but there were also odd challenges and crippling strokes. Decline of the old order and the old crafts were not simultaneously succeeded by a new order of things. So, there was a vacuum which was filled in by external squads of men and their wares. The result on the whole was not an unmixed blessing.

The fallout of the disappearance of the old order was nowhere more pronounced than in the lives of the old governing class. The suppression was followed by a calculated policy of appeasement. The government declared pensions for different members of the old ruling family and their officials. These pension benefits were merely an extension of similar facilities granted to the surviving members of the vanquished powers elsewhere in the country.

Along with the British came, as was inevitable, the Bengali middle class—enterprising, intelligent and self-conscious and the Marwari businessmen with keen eye on economic prospects, new opportunities and remarkable adoptability. If the Bengalis found their way, among other places, in administration, plantation and educational system, the Marwaris established a close nexus between the new centres of business, shops, *hats* and agricultural moneylending communities.

Marx analysed that the English social order was the fruit of a compromise between the aristocracy and the bourgeoisie.[1] Every social order thrives on compromise, it founders when the compromise exhausts itself. In Assam the old aristocracy was a spent-up force. The emerging middle class had no necessity of seeking support from them. Whenever a question of compromise arose it compromised with the government. To put it in brief, therefore, the British Government and the rising middle class together served descending orders on the nobility. Their drift was beyond redemption. The alien intervention was the immediate pretext of their disappearance. They were unable to organize themselves in a body and put up a fight as the impoverished families of Maharastra did against the British.[2] Decline of the nobility was followed by the decline of the old crafts. The decline of the crafts was neither sudden nor totally unexpected. The Commercial Treaty (1793) between the Ahom King Gaurinath Singha and the East India Company inflicted the first blow on the traditional crafts of Assam. Even earlier, the *silakuti* or stone-engraving became a vanishing art. The nobility could no longer patronize the crafts. Though they had enough landed property agricultural receipts were insignificant.

In agriculture, the effects of the ryotwari land system became distinctly visible. We have already noticed the imprints of transition in agriculture in spite of demographic reverses caused by recurring epidemics. Natural calamities like flood, fire, earthquake and cattle disease aggravated the situation. Locusts and white ants did not lag behind in their destructive operations. These little unknown agents did not always go unnoticed. Peasants and landlords dreaded survey and settlement operations for different reasons. Revenue assessment had been a continuous source of irritation for the peasantry. Their 'primitive fury' burst out in Lower Assam. The relatively well-off among them, never missed an opportunity to fish in troubled waters. We are yet to explore, what E.P. Thompson calls, the 'moral economy' of the vexed and rebellious peasantry. A good crop of literature on agriculture came up at the right moment but the peasantry could hardly make use of them. The peasants of Assam did not show any exploratory skill.

The people of Assam were not conscious about the floristic grandeur and richness of their province. For them the vast and varied natural resources have always been some inert and undervalued assets.

The Indian teak saved England during her long hostilities with Napoleon.[3] Yet the forest conservation measures of the British in India left much to be desired. Assam was no exception. The forests were thinning out, and the green face of the province became patchy. The floral and faunal disturbances continued unabated.

Before the government could adopt any policy of conservation of forest in Assam, the woodcutters of Bengal made their appearance. First they laid waste the forest of Goalpara, then they advanced towards the east Kamrup, Nagaon and Darrang.

Gustav Mann, an officer of the Forest Department prepared a report on the condition of forest in the Brahmaputra valley during 1868–70. In Goalpara, 'the Bengal woodcutters were carrying out uncontrolled felling and forest were being devastated. Large quantities of partly used trees were left on the ground.' They paid for every recorded tree they felled, just 2 annas to the department, but every tree delivered at fixed points on the Brahmaputra fetched them Rs. 10 to Rs. 15. Bumper profit was the order of the day. Matters were no better in Kamrup where 'valuable forests had been made over to the Lower Assam Tea Company as wasteland'. In Darrang and Nagaon *sal* forest 'had been so heavily worked that only small sized trees stunted in growth and saplings were left, no big trees remained and some of the best *sal* forest had been sold as wasteland. In Sibsagar, the forest was scattered and until then not subjected to any damage. In Lakhimpur, the forest between Saikhowaghat and Dibrugarh catered to the requirement of the Upper Assam Tea Company's Sawmill. The Dehingmukh Sawmill used to the full the forest upto Jaipur. The forest beyond Jaipur remained untouched. These operations were carried out by the contractors without any difficulty.[4]

Their commercial interest did not come in conflict with the local interest, because the local interest had only short-term requirements which the larger network of timber trade could easily fulfill. Every tribal workman was a willing horse of any contractor.

The wanton destruction of forest continued until the Forest Act of 1878 came into force. By that time the British had devastated the forests of Ireland, South Africa and north-eastern America.[5] This was necessary to keep up the energy of their giant colonial system lording over myriad men and women, their tongues and values, land and waters in the eastern and western hemispheres.

Initiated by Lord Dalhousie, the forest policy of the government was the product of a good deal of deliberation in the presidencies. The brighter side of the British character asserted itself. A delightful sense of responsibility dawned on them. They resolved to protect the goose that lays golden eggs. We therefore, find them both as destroyer and preserver of the forest in Assam. They sustained the growth of forest through systematic plantation and studied reliance on natural regeneration. But the gigantic operations for decades on end contributed nothing substantial to the economy of the province. The government derived satisfaction from the fact that the forest revenue always exceeded the cost of forest administration.

The rivers of Assam contributed greatly to the material life of the people. The Brahmputra with its masculine image occupied the central position in the utility system evolved by them. They depended on the rivers for livelihood, pleasure and spiritual succour. The river as a source of electricity and tourism promotion were to gain in importance much later.

Tea, petroleum and coal ushered in a new economy of great promise. Of them petroleum and coal industry remained exclusively under the British. Though tea was also under their control, some enterprising Assamese planters carved out a position of their own. I have discussed the gains derived from tea. But one must not overlook its drawbacks. From the very beginning tea was grown in large tracts of land. Bigness, as it were, was the hallmark of tea cultivation. The government policy was solely responsible for this situation. The minimum acreage was fixed at 100 acres, therefore, no man with small capital could ever dream of such a venture. Some retired government servants with their savings entered the field and a few of them became successful tea planters.

Plantation science and production technology had revolutionized tea industry over the decades and improved the fortune of the planters. But nobody ever seemed to have thought of developing small-scale tea farming, although such farming was possible and economically viable. Owners of small size holdings could not have dictated terms of trade, they could have played a subsidiary role and enhanced their own financial standing. Small-scale tea farming could have changed the entire face of peasant economy in Upper Assam. Tea did not lead to contraction of agriculture. In spite of enough surplus land under the jurisdiction of the tea gardens, cultivation of rice was not encouraged. The entire population of the tea gardens of the province was fed on imported rice. Small-scale tea cultivation could have had no adverse effect on agriculture. More than a hundred years ago *The Statesman* editorially commented:

> Assam has always been, and is still, known as the 'garden of Bengal', but notwithstanding its vast agricultural and mineral resources, it is still a comparative wilderness after more than sixty years of British rule. The reason is not far to seek. It has never been properly governed. It has been simply allowed to grow. Not yielding a large revenue, it has always been, and is still, neglected.... The province is so closely associated, in the popular mind, with the production of tea that we are in danger of forgetting its capacity for yielding other products....[6]

The editorial of *The Statesman* represented the considered view of many that Assam was not getting the attention she deserved. On 16 February 1894 five Assamese gentlemen of Calcutta, Gunabhiram Barua, Jagannath Barua, Kaliprasad Chaliha, Abhaycharan Talukdar and Ramakanta Barkakati presented an address to the newly arrived Viceroy, Earl of Elgin. They urged him:

> to take a special interest in the affairs of Assam, and the same attention may be directed in due course to questions of vital importance to Assam, such as the extension of education, the improvement of internal communications, the development of her natural resources and a larger gradual employment of the children of the soil in the Public Service of the province.[7]

The priorities had been fixed—education, communication, development and employment. The agenda was set before the government for implementation. The demand for employment of the 'children of the soil' was quite innovative. They hinted at the competitive advantage of the Bengalis over the Assamese and therefore pleaded for some protectionist measure. It is no secret that freedom of opportunity was abused even in those days. The protectionist slogan became a rallying point of the depraved middle classes in various parts of the country much later.

The memorialists expressed satisfaction over the construction of the Assam Bengal Railways. They apprised the Viceroy of the importance of tea and implored him to 'facilitate the solution of a great many other important questions, such as the supply of adequate labour force to the tea industry, which has gone far towards making Assam what she is'.

The Assam Association raised the demand for major province status for Assam in 1919. Nothing was known about those memorialists of 1894 who made a similar demand. Under the Indian Councils Act of 1892, four important provinces secured the right of recommendation of a member to the Supreme Legislative Council. They requested the Viceroy to concede a similar privilege to Assam.

Allegations of neglect were made even by the officers of the provincial administration. Sir Henry Cotton who was the Chief Commissioner of Assam from 1896 to 1902, felt it strongly. He did not hesitate to give vent to his feelings when Lord Curzon, the Viceroy, visited Guwahati in 1900. In his reply Curzon remarked,

> It is not fair of you to tax the Government of India with neglect, as a matter of fact, it has always taken a very great interest in the province, but the true secret of the woes of Assam is the same as that which Mr. Disraeli said was the true secret of the woes of Ireland. He said that Ireland lay under weeping skies surrounded by a melancholy ocean.[8]

But Henry Cotton was not taken in by such argument. Within his limited resources, he did improve the rail and river communications.

Henry Cotton could foresee the importance of tea. The general contradiction of labour and capital drew his attention. He believed that within the parameters of colonial rule the interests of labour could be adequately protected. But he failed to improve the service and recruitment conditions of labour. An embittered Cotton laid down office in disgust. The nationalist opinion was behind him but that was of little help. Henry Cotton was, of course, not a partisan champion of labour. The egalitarian in him believed that improved conditions of labour would lead to the development of tea industry and that was his main objective. In his reminiscences he recorded with pride,

> I spent the public funds liberally in the furtherance of tea interests. I devoted by private funds to the same object. I gave every encouragement to planters to take up lands for ordinary cultivation in the neighbourhood of their gardens, and granted them leases on very favourable terms for the cultivation of new staples, such as sisal, hemp, rhea and rubber. I helped them in their endeavours to strike oil and coal and other minerals.[9]

The triumph of tea in Assam was absolute. The *satras* discovered that the most profitable use of their large landholdings could be made only through tea; and accordingly the principal *satras* leased out their land to tea planters. The grandeur of many *satras* of Upper Assam owes a lot to the tea industry.[10] The source of their financial strength was hard cash brought in by tea.

The *satradhikars* picked up the art of capitalist revenue-farming with conspicuous alacrity but their minds could swing back to feudal values any moment. The old mindset was so unyielding that even a forward—looking *satradhikar*, Dattadev Goswami never missed an opportunity to show off his holier than thou attitude towards his fellow countrymen. He refused to take a seat equally with the natives, at the Durbar of Sir Cecil Beadon, Lieutenant Governor of Bengal held at Sibsagar in the summer of 1862. To clarify his stand, Dattadev wrote to the commissioner of Assam that the 'natives were not authorized by the ancient Rajas to accept any respectable seat in my presence but those nobles who were not my own disciples and if they are next in rank to the king alone, were allowed a plantain leaf'. The Commissioner pointed out that the representative of the Queen could not change the arrangements of his court to suit the fancies of individuals. 'The Rajas of Assam,' he reminded, 'had ceased to have any power long before the British Rule Commenced in Assam and all honours that are now enjoyed in British Durbar can only be enjoyed in so far as they are conceded by the British Government which seeks to elevate all of its subjects and desires the object degradation of none.' The *satradhikar* realized his 'fault' and tendered apology.[11]

I have discussed the idea of 'creative minority' in the context of the late nineteenth century Assamese society. I have equally emphasized the social vision of Anandaram Dhekial Phukan.

Though his life flamed out before he was thirty, his achievement established him as a creative force. The available writings of Anandaram have established beyond doubt that he was an ardent believer of the positivist motto '*order and progress*'.

Judged by the weight and the breadth of vision, the memorandum of Anandaram Dhekial Phukan submitted to A.J.M. Mills in 1853 stands comparison to Dr Sun Yat-Sen's (1866–1925) historic Petition to Li Hung-Chang of the Ching Dynasty in 1894. Dr Sun Yat-Sen urged the government to:

> Open schools for training various types of personnel; appoint officials responsible for agricultural administration and the development of irrigation so as to increase farm production; build mines, railways and factories and bring modern machinery into use; institute policies for the protection of trade, and enable the businessmen to make profits so they would exert themselves in enterprises.[12]

At the time of submitting the petitions, Anandaram was 24 and Dr Sun Yat-Sen was 28. Their views were indistinguishable as though the latter was echoing and re-echoing the agenda put forth by the former. But Anandaram's death with nobody to carry forward his agenda and a diffident and uncommunicative society failed him beyond measure.

Eric Hobsbawm remarks that positivism 'combined a passionate belief in science and inevitable modernization with the secular equivalent of religion, non-democratic progress and planned social engineering undertaken from above'. This ideology, Hobsbawm reminds us, had particular appeal to the elite of the 'backward, traditionalist countries'.[13] The Assamese elites, therefore represented a pattern which was not anachronistic.

Anandaram's idea of progress was intellectually sound by the standard of his age. His call for self-reliance was always rewarding, but he was unable to perceive the negative impact of alien rule, particularly its exploitative nature. Though the fullest development of an individual personality was often possible in a colonial situation, no nation can shape its destiny in the way it chooses under foreign domination.

Anandaram was dazzled by the commercial supremacy of England. Many years later Swami Vivekananda talked about that supremacy with disparagement. Vivekananda felt that British rule in India projected the 'Vaisya Supremacy'.[14] Even without denying the positive role played by Vivekananda it may be argued that Anandaram's exhortation was not a voice in the wilderness. No nation can wish away the importance of commerce. Anandaram was capable of creative thinking on basic solutions to backwardness.

After the death of Anandaram in 1859 there was a brief vacuum in the realm of thought. The Hindu Mela Movement founded by Nabagopal Mitra in 1867 failed to evoke any response in Assam. Yet, generally speaking, it was a period of great hope. The middle class set out with limited ambitions and still fewer commitments. If collective fantasy blurred its vision in one place, it was made up by achievements in other field. Throughout the period, one cannot but appreciate the absence of ethnic and religious animosities. The social credibility of the middle class was provided by a social awareness which grew up with some institutions. Expansion of concept of law and regulative society based on judiciary and school system were clearly perceptible.

Loyalty to the Raj was the dominant trend of social thinking. Kandarpeswar Singha who suffered so much in the wake of the Mutiny, later played a role not quite expected of him. Like many others Kandarpeswar was in the enjoyment of a pension. An organization called the Hitkari Sabha was active about that time in Guwahati. Though not much information is available about it, the sabha was an uncritical admirer of British rule. It sympathized with the Englishmen who lost their lives in the Afghan War (1879–80). Kandarpeswar Singha associated himself with the Hitkari Sabha and together with Harakanta Sadar Amin and others raised subscription for the victims of the massacre in Kabul (of Major Cavagnari, the first Resident and his staff) in September 1879. Change came over the passive mutineer of 1857 (and he fully identified himself with the pursuit of 'setting the red line on the Hindu Kush'). He had no sympathy for the valiant Afghans who tried to defend their freedom. Earlier, in 1875 Kandarpeswar went to Calcutta to catch a glimpse of Edward, the Prince of Wales who was on a tour to India.[15] It was no case of, as the saying goes, he that fights and runs away, may live to fight another day. The reason was simple, Kandarpeswar could not live outside the collective consciousness of the society.

That Kandarpeswar was in tune with the spirit of his age can be understood from a remark of Dadabhai Naoroji. In his presidential address to the Indian National Congress in its second annual session held in December 1886 in Calcutta, he declared:

> Let us speak out like men and proclaim that we are loyal to the backbone, that we understand the benefits English rule has conferred upon us.[16]

On the occasion of Queen Victoria's completion of fiftieth year of reign in 1887 there had been a surfeit of such chorus. Libraries, schools and colleges, waterworks and dispensaries named after Victoria in different towns and cities of India survive to this day. In Assam, parades, processions, display of fireworks, illumination, elephant and horse races, various kinds of sports, drama, *bhaona*, *jatra*, *nautches* and *nahabat* and on 17 February 1887 a cricket match in Guwahati were organized to mark the occasion.

Bhabanipriya Baruani, zamindar of Gauripur founded an annual medal for the best successful entrance candidate from Dhubri High School. The zamindar of Chapar opened a charitable dispensary. At Nagaon, the foundation stone of the Victoria Jubilee Hall was laid. The large jubilee playground, since renamed, continued to vivify the memory of the celebration. Though the Bengali babus were the enthusiastic organizers of the festivities in the towns, others did not lag behind. All the three main *satradhikars* of Majuli participated in the jubilee durbar at Sibsagar. A *bhaona* troupe of the Auniati *satra* entertained the durbar. Another leading Gossain, Thanukrishna led the show at Lakhimpur.[17]

In Bengal, nationalism made its appearance as 'Muslim Nationalism' and 'Hindu Nationalism'. According to R.C. Majumdar, 'Throughout the nineteenth century the two types of nationalism developed side by side'.[18] Later they fused into Indian nationalism. But the only nationalism developed in Assam was Indian nationalism. The Assamese journal, *Mau* captured the time spirit and made this unforgettable appeal:

> Oh Assamese brothers, broaden your heart and give room there for all nationalities of India as brothers. Do away with the differences if you can, if you cannot, play them down. Do not raise the banner of disunity, raise only that which unites. Then only Assam will prosper, India will prosper.[19]

The early generation of the Assamese middle class gave of its best and it deserves gratitude of posterity. Its most enlightened section was notable less for reformist rhetoric than for practical abilities.

The personality of the Assamese middle class crystallized in a process of cooperation and confrontation: cooperation with the government for sustaining the rule of law, orderly progress, expansion of education and opportunities; confrontation against the supersession of the Assamese language, denial of appropriate status to the province, oppressive revenue policy and imperialism. The printed word was the catalyst of the new social formation. Memory was placed on the back burner. Printeries conquered the collective Assamese mind for ever.

It is easy to make allegation against its supposed failure on certain counts. The common charge is that it collaborated with the alien rulers. This is the result of viewing history 'with an eye on the present'. If we apply the same yardstick, no Indian before Gandhiji will pass for a patriot. Rammohun Roy, Dadabhai Naoroji, Jyotirao Phooley, M.G. Ranade, Badruddin Tyabji, W.C. Banerjee, D. Wacha, Pherozeshah Mehta, Surendranath Banerjee and Madhusudan Das, who, by common consent, were the pioneers of nationalist thought and action, did not emerge from their founts breathing fire and brimstone against British rule. The question is, whether the Assamese elites lagged behind their contemporaries. They did not. Their weakness lay in the fact that they were imitative, not innovative. Imitators are hardly extraordinary achievers.

Those who constituted the backbone of the middle class trained their hands in public activities from an early age. Anandaram Dhekial Phukan, it has already been said, submitted his historic memorandum when he was 24 years of age; when Jagannath Barua and Manikchandra Barua submitted memorial to Lord Northbrook in 1872, both of them were 21. The founders of the epoch-making journal *Jonaki* (1889) were all youths; Chandrakumar Agarwala was 27, Lakshminath Bezbaroa 25 and Hemchandra Goswami 17. When *Bijuli*, another Assamese journal was published in 1890, the founder editor Padmanath Gohain Barua was 19. All the major contributors to the journals were also in their early or mid-twenties. Behind the setting up of the Assam Association, the Asam Chatra Sanmilan and the Asam Sahitya Sabha was the spirit of the youth. Close scrutiny shows that whenever their spirit slackened the organization drifted downhill. It was mainly through the effort of the young leadership that the Assam Association merged with the Indian National Congress. It was again the students and the youths who spread the message of non-cooperation in Assam.

They do not fail the test of comparison either. When Rammohun sent his famous petition to Lord Amherst in 1823 he was 51. Dadabhai entered public life with the East India Association at the age of 42, Ranade at 45, Tyabji at 43, W.C. Banerjee and Pherozeshah at 41, D. Wacha at

52, Madhusudan Das at 55. Only Jyotirao and Surendranath entered public life before they were 30.

By the end of the nineteenth century the presence of the middle class was felt as a major social phenomenon in Assam. As it was at the top of the social pyramid it played the role of the bourgeoisie in the Western societies, who, to quote H.G. Wells, as a class 'talk, think and dream possessions'.[20] I have shown that the middle class really talked, thought and strengthened the base of a new competitive society. Its dream of possessions is endless.

Assam does not provide ground to test the validity of Max Weber's view that occupations based on all pervasive caste system in Indian society was responsible for perpetual fragmentation of the artisanal, mercantile and service communities and absence of any idea of civil liberty. Interestingly, C.A. Bayly has challenged his view from a firmer ground of the caste-ridden belt itself.[21]

On the question of opium the middle class was divided against itself. But unlike in China, there was no resistance against anti-opium campaigns. The opium-barons of China who grew in political clout had a field day until 1952.[22] Though opium is banned in India, its cultivation still continues in some parts of Madhya Pradesh under a license system. Opium was certainly not the last train in the drug world. Society can lower its guard against this only at its own risk.

The Assamese attitude towards life and nature is marked by non-capitalistic values. But for a very tortuous racial memory it was easy to reach them by jingoism. Occasionally it drove them into fearful paroxysms of frustration and anger. Misfortunes stemming from this source yoked them to some historical debts. The middle class was unable to bear itself well in the face of some later-day adversities. It was no longer possible to skate over the drift and the unprepossessing quality of its leadership. The Assamese society was, therefore, obliged to search for new leadeship and new direction. To what end, only history will tell.

NOTES

1. F. Bedarida, *A Social History of England*, London, 1991, p. 39.
2. R. Kumar, *Essays in the Social History of Modern India*, Calcutta, 1986, p. 19.
3. M. Gadgil and R. Guha, *This Fissured Land: An Ecological History of India*, Delhi, 1992, p. 119.
4. P. Smith et al., *A Short History of the Assam Forest Service*, Shillong, 1946, pp. 2–3.
5. M. Gadgil and R. Guha, op. cit., p. 118.
6. *The Statesman*, 9 May 1893.
7. Ibid., 17 February 1894.
8. Quoted in Henry Cotton, *Indian and Home Memories*, London, 1911, pp. 243–4.
9. P. Goswami, *Journal of Indian History*, Trivandram, 1972, p. 337.
10. See M. Sharma, *Social and Economic Change in Assam*, Delhi, 1990, p. 129.
11. See the petition of the *satradhikar* and the reply from J.C. Haughton to the Deputy Commissioner, Sibsagar in J. Barua (ed.) *Jorhat 200*, Jorhat, 1997, pp. 381–2.
12. Compilation Group, *The Revolution of 1911*, Peking, 1976, pp. 12–13.
13. E.J. Hobsbawm, *The Age of Empire*, Calcutta, 1992, p. 284.
14. See T. Raychaudhury, *Europe Reconsidered*, Delhi, 1988, pp. 219–315.
15. K.C. Bardaloi (ed.), *Harakanta Sadaraminar Atmajivani*, Guwahati, 1991, pp. 203, 216.
16. Quoted in A.R. Desai, *Social Background of Indian Nationalism*, Bombay, 1982, p. 322.
17. Reports published in *The Englishman*, 21, 25, 28 February and 11 March 1887.
18. R.C. Majumdar's essay, 'The National Movement 1833–1905', in N.K. Sinha (ed.), *The History of Bengal (1757–1905)*, Calcutta, 1996, pp. 188–216.
19. *Mau*, 1887, S.N. Sarma (ed.), Guwahati, 1980, pp. 42–43 (translation mine).
20. Quoted in E.J. Hobsbawm, op. cit., p. 165.
21. See C.A. Bayly, *Rulers, Townsmen and Bazaars: North Indian Society in the Age of British Expansion 1770–1870*, New Delhi, 1998, Ch. 4 and Ch. 11; and John Love, 'Max Weber's Orient', in Turner Stephen (ed.), *The Cambridge Companion to Weber*, Cambridge, 2000, pp. 172–99.
22. Carl A. Trocki, *Opium, Empire and the Global Political Economy: A Study of the Asian Opium Trade 1750–1950*, London, 1999, pp. 130-4.

Bibliography

PRIMARY SOURCES

Reports and Official Records

REPORTS

1. *Report on the Administration of Land Revenue in Assam*, for the years 1878–79, Shillong, 1880; 1879–80, Shillong, 1881; and 1880–81, Shillong, 1882.
2. *Report on the Administration of Land Revenue in Assam* for the years 1881–82, 1882–83, 1883–84, 1884–1885, 1885–1886 and 1886–87. Published every following year from Shillong.
3. *Administration Report on the Province of Assam*, 1880–81 and 1897–98.
4. *Provincial Gazetter of Assam*, 1906.
5. *Report on Jute Cultivation in Assam*, by F.J. Monahan, Shillong, 1898.
6. *Report on the Census of Assam for 1881*, Calcutta, 1883.
7. *Report of the Agricultural Department, Assam*, Shillong, 1918 (for the year ending on 30 June 1916).
8. *Report of the Agricultural Department, Assam*, Shillong, 1918 (for the year ending on 30 June 1918).
9. *Report of the Agricultural Department, Assam*, Shillong, 1919 (for the period 1 July 1918 to 31 March 1919).
10. *Progress Report of Forest Administration in Assam* for the years from 1881–82 to 1898–99. Published every following year from Shillong.
11. *Provincial Gazetteer of Assam*, compiled by Authority (1st edn., Shillong, 1906), rpt. Delhi, 1983.
12. *Assam Congress Opium Enquiry Committee Report*, Jorhat, 1925.
13. *Report on Province of Assam* by A.J.M. Mills, 1854, rpt. Guwahati, 1984.
14. *Report on the Census of Assam for 1901*, Vol. I, Delhi, 1984.

OTHER ARCHIVAL RECORDS

Fort William Revenue Proceeding 1853–73, Home Political and Foreign Consultation (NAI), New Delhi. Letters issued to the Government of Bengal (Assam Secretariat Records).

Letters Received from the Government of Bengal (A.S. Records).

MONOGRAPHS, CORRESPONDENCES AND OTHER ACCOUNTS

1. *Monograph on Cotton Fabrics in Assam* by Samman, Shillong, 1897.
2. *Monograph on Ivory Carving in Assam* by J. Donald, Shillong, 1900.
3. *Monograph on Gold and Silver Wares of Assam* by F.C. Henniker, Shillong, 1905.
4. *Monograph on the Silk Cloths of Assam* by B.C. Allen, Shillong, 1899.
5. *Monograph on Wood Carving in Assam* by A. Majid, Shillong, 1903.
6. *Monograph on Dyes and Dyeing in Assam* (author and year of publication not known). Bound with the monograph on Ivory Carving (NAI, New Delhi).
7. *Monograph on the Iron and Steelwork* (author not mentioned), Shillong, 1907.
8. *A Survey of the Resources and Industries of Eastern Bengal and Assam, 1907–08* by G.N. Gupta, Shillong, 1908.
9. *Fort William—India House Correspondence* (Public), Vol. I (1748–1756), edited by K.K. Datta, NAI, Delhi, 1958.
10. *Fort William—India House Correspondence*, Vol. III (1760–1763), edited by R.R. Sethi, NAI, Delhi, 1968.
11. *Fort William—India House Correspondence*, Vol. IV (1764–1766), edited by C.S. Srinivasachari, NAI, Delhi, 1962.
12. *Fort William—India House Correspondence*, Vol. VI (1770–1772), edited by B. Prasad, NAI, Delhi, 1960.
13. *Fort William—India House Correspondence*, Vol. IX (1782–1785), edited by B.A. Saletore, NAI, Delhi, 1959.
14. *Fort William—India House Correspondence*, Vol. XIII (1796–1800), edited by P.C. Gupta, NAI, Delhi, 1959.
15. *A Statistical Account of Assam* by W.W. Hunter, Vols. I & II (1st published in 1879), Delhi, 1982.
16. *The Imperial Gazetteer of India* by W.W. Hunter, Vol. IV, London, 1881.
17. *A Descriptive Account of Assam* by W. Robinson (1st published in 1841), rpt. Delhi, 1975.
18. *Report on the Eastern Frontier of British India* by R.B. Pemberton, Guwahati, 1966.

ARTICLES (ENGLISH)

1. 'The Assam Burma Route to China' by Dilip K. Chakraborti and Nayanjot Lahiri, in *Man and Environment*, Vol. X, June 1986.
2. 'The Impact of Bengal Renaissance on Assam by A. Guha, in *IESHR*, September 1972.
3. 'Missionaries and the Language Controversy in Assam' by Fredrick S. Downs in the *Journal of the University of Gauhati*, Vols. XXVII–XXIX, No. 1, 1977–78.
4. 'Growth of Commercial Agriculture in Bengal (1859–1885)' by B.B. Chaudhuri, *IESHR*, Vol. 7, Nos. 1 & 2, 1970.
5. ·'Cotton Improvement Programme in Dharwar in Mid nineteenth Century' by K.L. Tuteja, in *Progs. of the Indian History Congress*, 51st Session, 1990, pp. 399–405.
6. 'Sir Henry Cotton (1845–1915)' by P. Goswami, in *Journal of Indian History*, Trivandrum, Vol. I, Part II, August 1972, pp. 333–42.
7. 'Imperialism, Botany and Statistics in Early Nineteenth Century India: The Surveys of Francis Buchanan (1762–1829)' by Marika Vicziany, in *Modern Asian Studies* 20, 4 (1986), pp. 625–60.
8. 'The Example of the English Middle Class' by Eric Hobsbawm in *Bourgeois Society in Nineteenth Century Europe*, edited by J. Kocka and Allen Mitchell, Oxford, 1993, pp. 127-50.
9. 'Brahma Religion and Social Change Among the Boros' by R.N. Mosahary, in *Progs. of North East India History Association*, 6th Session, 1985, pp. 347-52.

NEWSPAPERS, JOURNALS, ETC.

ENGLISH

The Englishman (Calcutta).
The Statesman (Calcutta).
The North East Times (Guwahati).
The Journal of the Asiatic Society of Bengal.

ASSAMESE
Ajir Asam (Guwahati).

JOURNALS

ASSAMESE

Jonaki, Chetana.
Banhi Awahan, Assam Bandhav.

BENGALI

Akademi Patrika, No. 3, Pachim Bangla Akademi, 1990.

OTHERS

B. Rajkhowa, *Mor Jivan Dapon*, Guwahati, 1969.
M. Neog (ed.), *Orunodoi* (1846–1854), Collected volume, Guwahati, 1983.
N. Saikia (ed.), *Assam Bandhu* (1885–1886), Collected volume, Guwahati, 1984.
S.N. Sarma (ed.), *Mau* (1886–1887), Collected volume, Guwahati, 1980.
K.C. Bordoloi (ed.), *Harakanta Sadaraminar Atmajivani*, Guwahati, 1991.
G. Barua, *Anandaram Dhekial Phukanar Jivan Charitra*, Guwhati, rpt. 1971.
J. Barua, *Jorhat* 200, Jorhat, 1997.
P. Chaliha, *Purani Asamar Karikari Silpa*, Guwahati, 1998.

SECONDARY SOURCES

ASSAMESE

Adhikari, S.D., *Sadhu Charit*, Shillong, 1321 B.S. (1914).
Barbarua, H., *Ahomar Din*, Guwahati, 1981.
Barman, S. and P. Chaudhury, *Bastav ne Bibhram*, Dibrugarh, 1986.
Barman, S., *Asamiya Jibani Abhidhan*, Guwahati, 1992.
Barpujari, H.K., *Asamar Nava Jagaran: Ana Asamiyar Bhumika*, Jorhat, 1984.
Barthakur, P., *Swadhinata Ranar Samsparsat*, Dibrugarh, 1968.
Barua, A., *Biswa Bandita Chah Silpa*, Jorhat, 1991.
Barua, B., *Sundarit SriSri Madhavdev Madhav Maral Atiram Barua Aru Anyanya*, Guwahati, 1988.
Barua, B.K., *Asamar Loksanskriti*, Guwahati, 1961.
Barua, G., *Assam Buranji*, Guwahati, rpt. 1972.
Barua, L., *Sangeet Kosh*, 2nd edn., Jorhat, 1986.
———, *Sangeet Sadhana*, 2nd edn., Jorhat, 1986.
Barua, P. Gohain (ed.), *Jivani Sangrah*, 1st rev. edn., Guwahati, 1969.
Barua, P. Gohain, *Mor Sowarani*, Guwahati, 1971.
———, *Gohain Barua Rachanawali* (Works), Guwahati, 1971 (edited by M. Neog).
———, *Asmar Buranji*, Guwahati, 1976.
Bezbaroa, L.N., *Bezbaroa Granthawali* (Works), Vols. I & II, 2nd edn., Guwahati, 1988 (edited by A.C. Hazarika).
Bhattacharyya, K.C., *Dhireswaracharyya*, 2nd edn., Guwahati, 1960.
Bhuyan, J.N. (ed.), *Ratnakanta Barkakatir Gadya Sambhar*, Guwahati, 1977.
———, *Ratneswar Mahanta Rachnawali*, Guwahati, 1977.
———, *Jnanadabhiram Barua Rachanawali* (Works), Jorhat, 1981.
———, *Asamiya Lorar Mitra*, Part II, 2nd edn., Guwahati, 1992.
Bhuyan, J.N. (ed.), *Uwalijoa Nathir Para*, Nagaon, 1991.
———, *Sadagar Bholanath Borooah*, Diphu, 1993.

Bhuyan, N.C., *Nakul Chandra Bhuyan Rachana Samagra*, edited by J. Goswami, Guwahati, 1996.
Chaudhury, A.C., *Koch Rajbonshi Jatir Itihas Aru Sanskriti*, 2nd edn., Bangaigaon, 1993.
Datta, B.N. (ed.), *Gowalpara Lokagit Sangraha*, Jorhat, 1974.
Gogoi, L., *Asamiya Lok Sahityar Ruprekha*, Golaghat, 1968.
Gogoi, L. and H.P. Neog (eds.), *Asamiya Sanskriti*, Jorhat, 1966.
Gohain, H., *Sahitya Aru Chetana*, Guwahati, 1976.
Goswami, P. (ed.), *Kamalakanta Bhattacharyyar Rachanawali* (Works), Guwahati, 1982.
Goswami, J., *Jagannath Barua*, Jorhat, 1976.
Guha, A., *Jamidarkalin Goalpara Jilar Arthasamajik Awastha: Eti Aitihasik Dristipat*, Dhubri, 1984.
Hazarika, A.C. (ed.), *Bhasanmala*, Guwahati, 1960.
Kalita, N., *Bardowar Silpavastu*, Nagaon, 1985.
Kalita, R., *Bharatar Swadhinata Sangramat Asamiya Chatrar Bhumika*, Nalbari, 1986.
Mahanta, P., *Asamiya Madhyabitta Srenir Itihas*, Guwahati, 1991.
Malik, S.A., *Ajan Fakir Aru Suria Jikir*, 2nd edn., Guwahati, 1988.
Neog, M., *Maheswar Neog Rachanawali*, Guwahati, 1986.
Phukan, A.D., *Asamiya Lorar Mitra*, Part III, Calcutta, 1849.
Rajkhowa, B., *Asmiya Khandavakya Kosa*, rpt., Guwahati, 1980.
Raychaudhury, A., *Mor Jivan Dhumuhar Echati*, Guwahati, 1973.
Roychoudhury, A. *Namoni Asomor Madhyashrenee*, Guwahati, 1998
Saikia, C.P. (ed.), *Asamar Batari-Kakat-Alochanir Dersa Basaria Itihash*, Guwahati, March 1998.
———, *Karmavir Nabinchandra Bardaloi Smriti Grantha*, Guwahati, 1975.
Sarma, T.N., *Auniati Satrar Buranji*, Majuli, 1975.
Sharma, B., *Asamiya Sahityar Paramcharya Pandit Hem Chandra Goswami*, Jorhat, 1972.
———, *Tokora Banhor Kuta*, Guwahati, 1987.
Sharma, D., *Sahityaratna Chandradhar Barua*, Jorhat, 1975.
Talukdar, N. (ed.), *Kanaklal Barua Rachnawali* (Works), Guwahati, 1973.
———, *Lambodar Bora Rachanawali* (Works), Guwahati, 1983.

BENGALI

Basu, R., *Atmacharit*, 6th edn., Calcutta, 1985.
Basu, S., *Banglai Nabachetanar Itihas*, 2nd edn., Calcutta, 1985.
Bhattacharya, S., *Aupanibesik Bharater Arthaniti*, Calcutta, 1396 B.S. (1989), rpt. Calcutta, 1987.
Chatterjee, B., *Bankim Rachanabali*, Vol. II, Sahitya Samsad, 10th edn., Calcutta 1395 B.S. (1988).
Chattopadhyay, S.C., *Sarat Rachanabali*, Vol. II, Tulikalam, Calcutta, 1989.

Dan, S.C., *Bardhaman Parikrama*, Calcutta, 1992.
Detinenne, F., *Gadya Parampara*, Calcutta, 1977.
Devi, P., *Amis O Niramis Ahar*, rpt., Calcutta, 1995.
Ghose, B. (ed.), *Samayikpatre Banglar Samajchitra*, Vol. I, Calcutta, 1978.
Ghose, B., *Vidyasagar O Bengali Samaj*, Calcutta, 1984.
Mukhopadhyay, S.K., *Banglar Arthik Itihas (19th century)*, Calcutta, 1987.
Phukan, H.D., *Assam Buranji*, Guwahati, 1869 B.S. (1962), edited by J.M. Bhattacharjee.
Roy, A., *Banglar Renaissance*, 2nd edn., Calcutta, 1388 B.S. (1981).
Roy, B., *Unis Sataker Banglai Bigyan Sadhana*, Calcutta, 1987.
Roy, S., *Shroter Birudhe*, Calcutta, 1984.
Sastri, S., *Atmacharit*, 2nd edn., Calcutta, 1983.
Sen, R., *Atmakahani ba Swarachita Jibankatha*, Santipur, Sutragarh, 1339 B.S. (1932).
Sen, S.N. (ed.), *Prachin Bangla Patra Sankalan*, Calcutta, 1942.
Senapati, F.M., *Atmacharit* (Bengali translation), Delhi, 1977.

ENGLISH

Ali, M.H., *Observations on the Mussulmauns of India*, rpt., Delhi, 1975 (edited by W. Crooke).
Antrobus, H.A., *A History of the Assam Company (1839–1953)*, Edinburg, 1957.
———, *A History of the Jorehaut Tea Co. Ltd. (1859–1946)*, London, 1948.
Bagchi, A.K., *Private Investment in India (1900–1930)*, rpt., Delhi, 1980.
Banga, I. (ed.), *Five Punjabi Centuries*, Delhi, 1997.
Barkataki, M.S., *British Administration in North East India (1826–1874)*, Delhi, 1985.
Barkataki, P. (ed.), *Silent Revolution*, Guwahati, 1991.
Barman, S., *Zamindari System in Assam During British Rule*, Guwahati, 1994.
Barooah, N.K., *David Scott in North East India*, Delhi, 1970.
Barpujari, H.K. (ed.), *Political History of Assam*, Vol. I, Guwahati, 1977.
Barpujari, H.K., *Assam in the Days of the Company (1826–1856)*, 2nd edn., Guwahati, 1980.
———, *The American Missionaries and the North East India*, Guwahati, 1986.
Barua, B.K., *History of Assamese Literature*, 2nd edn., Delhi, 1978.
Baruah, S.L., *A Comprehensive History of Assam*, Delhi, 1985.
Bayly, C.A., *Rulers, Townsmen and Bazaars*, Indian Edition, New Delhi, 1998.
Becker, C., *History of Catholic Mission in North East India*, Shillong, 1980.
Bedarida, F., *A Social History of England (1851–1990)*, 2nd Routledge edn., 1991 (English translation by A.S. Forster).
Bhattacharjee, J.B., *Cachar under British Rule in North East India*, Delhi, 1977.
Bhattacharya, S. (ed.), *Essays in Modern Indian Economic History*, Delhi, 1987.
Bhuyan, A.C. et al. (eds.), *Political History of Assam*, Vols. II and III, Guwahati, 1978 and 1980.
Bhuyan, S.K., *Anglo-Assamese Relations (1771–1826)*, 2nd edn., Guwahati, 1974.

———, *Studies in the History of Assam*, 2nd edn., Guwahati, 1985.

Birdwood, G.C.M., *The Industrial Arts of India* (1st edn. 1880), rpt., London, 1971.

Braudel, F., *The Mediterranean and the Mediterranean World in the Age of Philip II*, Vols. I and II, English translation by Sian Reynolds, 4th edn., London, 1981.

———, *The Identity of France*, Vol.1 (1986), English translation by Sian Reynolds, 1st Fontana Press edn., London, 1989.

Buckland, C.E., *Bengal under the Lieutenant Governors*, Vol. II, Calcutta, 1901.

Butler, John, *Travels in Assam* (1st edn. 1855), rpt., Delhi, 1978.

Canning, J. (ed.), *100 Great Books*, Delhi, 1987.

Chaudhuri, N.C., *Clive of India*, Bombay, 1977.

———, *An Autobiography of an Unknown Indian*, Bombay, 1979.

———, *Hinduism: A Religion to Live by*, Delhi, 1979.

———, *Scholar Extraordinary: The Life of Professor Friedrich Max Muller*, Bombay, 1980.

Chaudhury, M.K. (ed.), *Trends in Socio Economic Change in India (1871–1961)*, Simla, 1967.

Choudhury, P.C. (ed.), *Hastividyarnava*, Guwahati, 1976.

Compilation Group, *The Revolution of 1911*, Peking, 1st edn., 1976.

Cotton, H., *Indian and Home Memories*, London, 1911.

Das, S.K., *A History of Indian Literature, Vol. VIII (1800–1900)*, Delhi, 1991.

Dasgupta, K.K., *Wood-Carvings of Eastern India*, Calcutta, 1990.

Desai, A.R., *Social Background of Indian Nationalism*, rpt. Bombay, 1982.

Dutt, K.N., *Landmarks of the Freedom Struggle in Assam*, rpt. Guwahati, 1969.

Dutt, R.C., *The Economic History India*, Vol. II, 2nd paperback edn., Delhi, 1970.

———, *The Peasantry of Bengal*, rpt., Calcutta, 1980.

Dutta, A.K., *The Khongiya Barooahs of Thengal*, Guwahati, 1990.

———, *Cha Garam—The Tea Story*, Guwahati, 1992.

Dutta Roy, B., *The Emergence and Role of Middle Class in North East India*, Delhi, 1983.

Fletcher, A., and J. Stevenson, *Order and Disorder in Early Modern England*, London, 1985.

Fonseca, A.J. (ed.), *Challenge of Poverty in India*, Bombay, 1969.

Gadgil, D.R., *The Industrial Evolution of India*, 5th edn., Delhi, 1982.

Gadgil, M. and R. Guha, *This Fissured land: An Ecological History of India*, Delhi, 1992.

Gait, E.A. *A History of Assam*, 3rd edn., Guwahati, 1967.

Ganguli, D., *Slavery in British Dominion*, Calcutta, 1972.

Gash, N., *Aristocracy and the People: Britain (1815–1865)*, London, 1963.

Gawthrop, W.R. *The Story of the Assam Railways and Trading Company Limited, 1881–1951*, London, 1951.

Ghose, L.N., *The Modern History of the Indian Chiefs, Rajas, Zamindars*, Part II, Calcutta. 1881.

Goswami, I., *A Saga of South Kamrup*, Delhi, 1993.
Goswami, J., *Hemchandra Barua*, New Delhi, 1987.
Goswami, P., *Bihu Songs of Assam*, Guwahati, 1957.
Goswami, P.C., *Economic Development of Assam*, Bombay, 1963.
Griffiths, P., *The History of Indian Tea Industry*, London, 1967.
Guha, A., *Planter Raj to Swaraj*, Delhi, 1977.
Gupta, A.C. et al. (eds.), *Studies in the Bengal Renaissance* (rev. and enlarged edn.), Calcutta, 1977.
Gupta, D. (ed.), *Social Stratification*, Delhi, 1991.
Haq, M.E., *A History of Sufism in Bengal*, Dacca, 1975.
Hill, A.F., *Economic Botany*, Indian edn., Delhi, 1983.
Hobhouse, H., *Seeds of Change*, London, 1999.
Hobsbawm, E.J., *The Age of Empire 1875—1914*, 1st Indian paperback edn., Calcutta, 1992.
Kakati, B., *Assamese: Its Formation and Development*, Guwahati, 1941.
Kalita, N. (ed.), *A Descriptive Catalogue of Manuscripts*, Nagaon, 1990.
Kumar, D., *The Cambridge Economic History of India*, Vol. II, Delhi, 1984.
Kumar, R., *Essays in the Social History of Modern India*, 1st paperback edn., Calcutta, 1986.
Long, W.J., *A History of English Literature*, New Delhi, 1978
Ludden, D., *Peasant History in South India*, 2nd edn., Delhi, 1993.
Marx, Karl, *Capital*, Vols. I, II and III (date of publication not mentioned), Moscow.
M'Cosh, J., *Topography of Assam* (1st edn. 1837), rpt., Delhi, 1986.
Medhi, S.B., *Transport System and Economic Development in Assam*, Guwahati, 1978.
Mehtab, H.K., *History of Orissa*, Vol. II, Cuttack, 1960.
Misra, B.B., *The Indian Middle Classes*, 2nd paperback edn., Delhi, 1983.
Neog, D., *New Light on History of Asamiya Literature*, Guwahati, 1962.
Neog, M. (ed.), *Lakshminath Bezbaroa: The Sahityarathi of Assam*, Gawahati, 1972.
Neuschel; K.B., *Word of Honor*, New York, 1989.
Oddie, G.A., *Social Protest in India*, Delhi, 1979.
Panikkar, K.M., *A Survey of Indian History*, 3rd edn., rpt. Bombay, 1962.
Premchand, *Godan* (English translation by J. Ratan and P. Lal), Bombay, 1984.
Randhawa, M.S., *A History of Agriculture in India*, Vols. II & III, Delhi, 1982.
Ravindra, T.K. (ed.), *Journal of Indian History*, Vol. L., Part II, Trivandram, August 1972 (Indian Independence Silver Jubilee Number).
Raychoudhury, T., *Europe Reconsidered*, Delhi, 1988.
Raychoudhury, T. and I. Habib, *The Cambridge Economic History of India*, Vol. I, Delhi, 1984.
Reincourt, A., *Women and Power in History*, 1st Indian edn., Delhi, 1989.
Renford, R.K., *The Non-official British in India to 1920*, Delhi, 1987.
Roy, T., *Traditional Industry in the Economy of Colonial India*, Cambridge, 1999.

Roy, T., *The Economic History of India 1857–1947*, New Delhi, 2000.
Said, Edward W., *Orientalism*, New York, 1985 (paperback), 1994.
Sarma, S.N., *The Neo-Vaisnavite Movement and the Satra Institution of Assam*, Guwahati, 1977.
Sastri, S., *History of the Brahmo Samaj*, combined edition, Calcutta, 1974.
Scott, J.C., *Weapons of the Weak*, 1st Indian edn., Delhi, 1990.
Sen, S., *History of Bengali Literature*, 3rd edn., Delhi, 1979.
Sen, S.N., *Eighteen Fifty-seven*, Delhi, 1977.
Sharma, M., *Social and Economic Change in Assam: Middle Class Hegemony*, Delhi, 1990.
Sharma, M.M., *Inscriptions of Ancient Assam*, Guwahati, 1978.
Singh, V.B., *Economic History of India (1857–1956)*, rpt., Delhi, 1981.
Sinha, N. (ed.), *Freedom Movement in Bengal (1818–1904)*, Calcutta, 1968.
Sinha, N.K., *The Economic History of Bengal*, Vol. II, Calcutta, 1968.
Sinha, N.K. (ed.), *The History of Bengal, 1757–1905*, Calcutta, 2nd edn., 1996.
Sinha, P., *Nineteenth Century Bengal: Aspects of Social History*, Calcutta, 1965.
Smith, P. and A. Purkayastha, *A Short History of the Assam Forest Service (1850–1945)*, Shillong, 1946.
Stephen, T., *The Cambridge Companion to Weber*, Cambridge, 2000.
Tchitcherov, A.I., *India: Changing Economic Structure in the Sixteenth-Eighteenth Centuries: Outline History of Crafts and Trade*, 3rd revd. edn., New Delhi, 1998.
Toynbee, A.J., *A. Study of History*, Vol. III, 1st paperback edn., London, 1962.
Trevelyan, G., *The Competetion Wallah* (2nd edn. 1866), rept., Delhi, 1992.
Trevelyan, G.O., *The Life and Letters of Lord Macaulay*, paperback edn., London, 1978.
Trocki, C.A., *Opium, Empire and the Global Economy: A Study of the Asian Opium Trade 1750–1950*, London, 1999.
Vidyarthi, L.P., *Art and Culture in North East India*, Delhi, 1986.
Visvanath, S.N., *A Hundred Years of Oil, Delhi*, 1990.
Wade, J.P., *An Account of Assam*, edited by B. Sharma, Guwahati, 1972.
Warner and Marten, *The Groundwork of British History*, London, 1932.
Wimsatt, William K., *Literary Criticism*, 1st Indian edn., Calcutta, 1964.

UNPUBLISHED THESES

1. 'British Rule in Assam (1845–1858)' by Bhupendranarayan Chaudhury, Ph.D. thesis in the University of London, June 1956.
2. 'Anandaram Dhekial Phukan and Early Nineteenth Century Renaissance of Assam' by Nanda Talukdar, Ph.D. thesis in the Gauhati University, 1982.
3. 'The Middle Classes in the Punjab (1849–1947)' by Sukhdev Singh Sohal, Ph.D. thesis in the Guru Nanak Dev University, Amritsar, 1987.
4. 'Coffee Plantations in Coorg during the Colonial Regime (1834–1948): A Socio-Economic Study' by K.M. Lokesh, Ph.D. thesis in the Kuvempu University, Shimoga, Karnataka, 1993.

Index